November 2–7, 2014
Salt Lake City, Utah, USA

I0053561

**Association for Computing Machinery**

*Advancing Computing as a Science & Profession*

# SIGUCCS'14

Proceedings of the 2014 ACM
## SIGUCCS Annual Conference

*Sponsored by:*
*ACM SIGUCCS*

*In cooperation with:*
*BOMGAR, JAMF Software, Apogee Electronics, HDI, LANDesk, CCI, Instructure, LabStats, and Ruckus Wireless*

**Association for**
**Computing Machinery**

*Advancing Computing as a Science & Profession*

**The Association for Computing Machinery**
**2 Penn Plaza, Suite 701**
**New York, New York 10121-0701**

**Notice to Past Authors of ACM-Published Articles**

**ISBN:** 978-1-4503-2780-0 (Digital)

**ISBN:** 978-1-4503-3384-9 (Print)

Additional copies may be ordered prepaid from:

**ACM Order Department**
PO Box 30777
New York, NY 10087-0777, USA

Phone: 1-800-342-6626 (USA and Canada)
+1-212-626-0500 (Global)
Fax: +1-212-944-1318
E-mail: acmhelp@acm.org
Hours of Operation: 8:30 am – 4:30 pm ET

Printed in the USA

# 2014 SIGUCCS Chair Welcome

Welcome to Salt Lake and the SIGUCCS opportunity!

Whether this is your first time or, like me, your plus 10th time attending SIGUCCS, it is my great pleasure, on behalf of the program committee, to welcome you here.

The 2014 conference theme is BYOD – build your own destiny. To do so, you must be willing to embrace change. We recognize that change represents great opportunity. But those of us who serve in IT support also know that we must "sell" change to our clients. This conference will provide you with plenty of opportunity to grow your skills, prepare for change, and the inspiration to improve your pitch to make that sale. There's nothing more energizing than being here, among peers who are all striving forward.

Building your destiny is all about forward-thinking and there is a lot of momentum built into this program so hold on for an amazing ride! If you are new this year, know that you are surrounded by colleagues who share many of your professional struggles. SIGUCCS is known as a place to share ideas, create new experiences, collaborate and encourage each other. We pride ourselves on being a welcoming group of higher education professionals. We are looking forward to meeting you so please, don't be shy, jump right in!

I must say that it has been an honor to work with the SIGUCCS 2014 team. These volunteers have served from across the country to organize this conference around strong, relevant content and outstanding motivational speakers. I would like to personally thank each and every one of our volunteers for their hard work, guidance, creativity, team spirt and good humor over the last 18 months! We wouldn't be here without their collective efforts. Thank you.

We are proud of the conference we have organized. By the time you leave, we hope you'll have extended your network and expanded your contacts, picked up new ideas to implement right away, and perhaps gained some insights that challenge you to rethink your thinking. We hope you also agree that SIGUCCS is the place to be for innovative IT support. We hope this conference plays a role in building your IT destiny. Here's to your great conference experience in Salt Lake!

**Rene Thatcher**
*St. Lawrence University*

# Service and Support Chairs' Welcome

The SIGUCCS 2014 planning committee would like to thank you for choosing to attend SIGUCCS 2014!

As program chairs, we were blessed to work with a large committee of dedicated professionals who worked hard to bring you a solid conference experience. That committee includes the track chairs and readers who helped shape the programming of the conference. We could not have pulled together a program of this caliber without their efforts.

In planning this conference, it gave the committee an opportunity to reflect on the opportunities and challenges facing our industry. Technology changes every day and higher education often finds itself reacting instead of proactively seeking ways to stay ahead of the curve. Regardless of you role in Higher Education, this conference will provide resources to grow your leadership skills in a forward-thinking way. This week will provide valuable professional development experiences for those of you who want to learn more about the tools others are using to navigate technological changes while simultaneously preparing for tomorrow's challenges. The future of our industry belongs to those who are adaptable and excited about what technology will bring us in the years ahead. How we equip ourselves and our colleagues will determine our institution's destiny.

This week will offer you a variety of opportunities. You will listen and engage with the best thought leaders in the industry, discuss ideas in stimulating breakout sessions, and take advantage of several opportunities to collaborate and network with peers from across the country and beyond. SIGUCCS will give you everything you need to grow, lead and adapt. We encourage you to look at the schedule and make a plan for what you want to attend so that you don't miss anything!

We also hope you will take the opportunity to provide solid feedback about your experience to help us continue to shape this conference into a meaningful experience.

If you approach this week fully engaged, we promise you will leave ready to inspire. Be selfish and disconnect from everything outside of this conference as much as you can!

This is just the beginning of your opportunity to BUILD YOUR OWN DESTINY!

**Kelly McLaughlin**
*Hobart and William Smith Colleges*

**Brett Williams**
*University of Wyoming*

# Table of Contents

## Session 5

## Poster Session

## Author Index

# 2014 SIGUCCS Organization

**Chair:** Rene Thatcher *(St. Lawrence University)*

**Management Symposium Program Chair:** Cindy Dooling *(Pima Community College)*

**Services & Support Program Co-Chairs:** Kelly McLaughlin *(Hobart and William Smith Colleges)*
Brett Williams *(University of Wyoming)*

**Treasurer:** Mike Cooper *(West Virginia University)*

**Conference Coordinator:** Nicole Adner *(St. Lawrence University)*

**Incoming and Outgoing Board Liaison:** Melissa Bauer *(Baldwin Wallace University)*
Parrish Nnambi *(University of California San Diego)*

**Publications:** Jacquelynn Hongosh *(Oberlin College)*

**Communication Awards:** Trevor Murphy *(Williams College)*

**Webmaster:** Heidi Wasem

**Session Chair Coordinator:** Kelly Andolina *(Union College)*

**Publicity/Marketing/Social Networking Chair:** Laurie Fox *(SUNY Geneseo)*

**Evaluations Chair:** Parrish Nnambi *(University of California San Diego)*

**Vendor Chairs:** Scott Saluga *(Oberlin College)*
Terry Ruger *(Ithaca College)*
Bobby Siegfried *(Lehigh University)*

**Program Committee:** Miranda Carney-Morris *(Lewis & Clark College)*
Eddie Vidal *(University of Miami)*
Allan Chen *(Menlo College)*
Mark Fitzgerald *(Boise State University)*
Leila Shahbender *(Princeton University)*
Lori McCracken *(Penn State University)*
Brian Allen *(Hennepin Technical College)*
Andy Schuler *(Pima Community College)*
Olivia Ward *(St. Joseph's University)*
Lauren Adams *(St. Joseph's University)*

**Additional reviewers:**

| | |
|---|---|
| Tim Akers | Jamie Richardson |
| Kristen Dietiker | Mary Schantz |
| Melissa Doernte | John Tyndall |
| Patrick Doyle | Elizabeth Wagner |
| Debbie Fisher | Ashley Weese |
| Momi Ford | Chris Wisemen |
| Karl Owens | Susan Wood |

# SIGUCCS 2014 Sponsor & Supporters

Sponsor:

Platinum Supporters:

Gold Supporters:

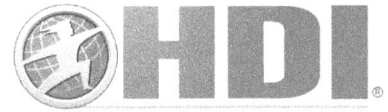

Silver Supporters:

Ultra Supporters:

# Lessons from Farming for IT

Christopher King
NC State University
Campus Box 7109
Raleigh, NC 27695
(919) 515-5431
chking@ncsu.edu

Dana Peiffer
University of Northern Iowa
1227 West 27th Street
Cedar Falls, IA 50614
(319) 273-7137
dana.peiffer@uni.edu

Nik Varrone
SUNY Geneseo
1 College Circle
Geneseo, NY 14454
(585) 245-5577
varrone@geneseo.edu

## ABSTRACT

Your average "person on the street" would probably put IT and farming at opposite ends of most spectrums. People tend to associate "IT" with bright screens in dark rooms with a lot of glass and steel, while "farming" generates images of sunshine, green fields with an obligatory cow, and country folk in overalls and gingham. In reality, those differences are what make life interesting for those of us who choose to live in both worlds. As IT solutions "go green", and farm equipment becomes guided by satellites, there are lessons to be learned and applied from each field (no pun intended) that can help the other. This paper and presentation will include discussion by farmers in higher education IT from New York to North Carolina to Iowa (whose hardware needs go from motherboards and mice to hay bailers and hotwire) and will focus on how lessons from farming really can improve IT at your institution.

## Categories and Subject Descriptors

K.7.0 The Computing Profession, General

## General Terms

Management, Performance, Reliability, Human Factors, Theory

## Keywords

Bellwether; Death; DISC; Haymaking; Seasons; Gift Horse; dressage; limits

## 1. INTRODUCTION

The average person would not imagine that there are commonalities between Information Technology (IT) and farming. But if you ask a farmer who works off the farm in IT and it's almost certain they would say otherwise. Farming, like IT, is a broad field and both the IT worker and the farmer are required to have a wide variety of knowledge in many areas in order to succeed.

*SIGUCCS'14*, November 2–7, 2014, Salt Lake City, UT, USA.
Copyright is held by the owner/author(s). Publication rights licensed to ACM.
ACM 978-1-4503-2780-0/14/11…$15.00.
http://dx.doi.org/10.1145/2661172.2661175

## 1.1 Chris King
### 1.1.1 Chris the IT Guy

Chris started in computing at a young age, getting a TRS-80 Color Computer 2 in the early 80's. When he started writing programs too large to be loaded into RAM, the thrill was gone, and he walked away from computing for years. In college, his roommate was the sole student worker in the campus help desk and when they needed a second body to man the phones and the door, Chris got recruited. He went for the paycheck, not the technology, but the environment made it easy to rekindle his old love. That was 1993 and now, over 20 years later; Chris still works at NC State University in an office 30 feet from the door he was hired to watch as a student. Now, however, he acts as an Assistant Director in Technology Support Services, overseeing Help Desk Services.

### 1.1.2 Chris the Farmer

Chris comically refers to himself as a "farmer-in-law" or, more commonly, a "horse widower". He met his wife Heather in Mu Beta Psi, a coed music fraternity at NC State University, and it was their love of music that started things off. Over the years, however, it was her love of horses that guided much of what they did, despite Chris having never touched a horse or a bale of hay in his life. Heather started her own riding and training business soon after they were engaged, and as any "in-law" will tell you, that means hauling groom buckets at horse shows, sleeping in the barn for foal watches, learning that "mending fences" is not a euphemism, and the meaning of terms like "twitch" and "sheath cleaning". They currently live on a farm just east of Raleigh, North Carolina where Heather still teaches people and horses, and occasionally her farmhands like Chris and their son Dylan.

## 1.2 Dana Peiffer
### 1.2.1 Dana the IT Guy

23 years ago Dana was repairing Audio Visual equipment for a large school district of 22 schools and felt at that time that he would never have a need for a computer. Very shortly after that he was asked to assist with the computer repair part of the AV department. As AV equipment evolved it quickly became obvious that computers indeed were involving the majority of his job. Today Dana is the Manager of the Computer Consulting Center at the University of Northern Iowa. The Consulting Center employs 3 full time staff and 11 student employees.

## 1.2.2 Dana the Farmer

Having grown up on a farm in Northeast Iowa Dana never enjoyed the simple life. Summers involved baseball, fishing, camping, bicycling, and with no technology to assist (there may have been an AM Transistor radio). The farm raised hogs (farrow to finish) and cattle and crops of corn and beans on 1000 acres so long days were quite common. Dana now lives on a small acreage not far from the University and has 4 horses, 20 chickens (for eggs), 2 dogs, bales his own hay, gardens, and all 3 of his tractors would be considered antique. He refers to himself as a Digital Immigrant (or Ignorant if you catch him at the right time). He truly appreciates how technology has made life easier, quicker, more productive, and fun for many people though he considers himself lucky that this technology was not available when he was young. Had it been he might not have the same fond memories of his childhood and a simpler time.

## 1.3 Nik Varrone
### 1.3.1 Nik the IT Guy

Nik Varrone Started with Desktop support before he knew it was a career option. When he had finished his high school Pascal assignment he would walk around the classroom assisting others with their homework. His first real IT job was in college at Temple University where he worked as a consultant in a computer lab until he became the manager of the Engineering College's Computer lab. Nik eventually left Temple to complete a bachelor's degree in Horticulture before returning to IT working as a Mac Genius for Apple Retail. This was the perfect training ground for his current role as a Desktop Support Technician and Desktop Management enthusiast for SUNY Geneseo.

### 1.3.2 Nik the Farmer

As a young man Nik was exposed to gardening though his grandparents. As a Boy Scout he was taken out of the urban environment and into a more natural setting. He often found himself doing horticulturally oriented service projects; though he never considered a life in agriculture. Young love would change that. After a trip to upstate New York, Nik decided he would have a future in farming. He completed a bachelor's degree in horticulture from Temple University where he took many food crops courses. Nik and his wife eventually purchased a 19-acre farm in Hemlock New York. His farm is diversified and organic. They raise sheep, goats, geese, ducks, and chickens. They also grow a variety of vegetables using horse power.

## 2. DEATH
### 2.1 Death in Farming

Death is ever present on the farm. Bad weather, disease, predators, and even just old age all will come for both plants and animals. If a farmer does not have the fortitude to deal with death then they will not be farmers for long. This is not to say that farmers are completely hardened against death. There are many cases on the farm where death, either expected or unexpected, causes a great deal of grief and hardship. Farmers who raise animals know the hardship of a dead calf or lamb but accept death as a part of the process of farming and have come to accept it.

### 2.2 Death in IT

Death is present in IT as well, though it's not commonly perceived that way. IT professionals are like grizzled "salt of the earth" farmers who have accepted that death comes to all technology. For example, IT pros at SUNY Geneseo watched Oracle Calendar going out and Google Calendar coming in and were excited for that transition while the users dreaded it. The end user is like the food consumer and is rarely ready for their technology to die. All too often IT organizations ask the customer to speed through the process of grief that the IT pro went through in an instant. This is unreasonable and cause distance between the IT organization and the people it's there to support. When the customer's concern is considered a process of grief it should be more understandable to IT professionals why the customer is not ready to accept a new product. Many is the IT professional who has listened to customers griping about how unnecessary a new product is and how inferior that customer feels the new product is as compared to the older one. Of course, often this isn't true and the new technology or product chosen by the IT department is far superior to the old model. It's up to IT professionals to guide customers through the process of grief. In the Kübler-Ross model of Grief the 5 stages of grief are denial, anger, bargaining, depression and acceptance. Each of these 5 stages are observable in IT consumers facing the end of a technology, service, or piece of hardware. Being aware of these stages and how to guide the user through their process of grief will allow the organization to smooth the process of introducing these technologies, raise their overall acceptance rate, and hopefully the opinion of the IT department within the organization.

## 3. MAKING HAY
### 3.1 Making Hay in Farming

Making Hay is all about timing. A farmer is constantly watching the weather during hay season and always worrying if it's going to rain on the hay that's been cut down and turned a few days. If a farmer bales wet hay it may be inedible or worse yet, burn down the barn. If the hay is too mature or dry there won't be enough nutrients in it for animals to thrive on in the winter. Cutting and stacking hay is laborious so a farmer has to coordinate a great number of people to be ready to show up and work hard at almost a moment's notice. For many farmers making hay is the most stressful part of the year and they can rest easy when the barn filled to the brim with beautiful stacked and properly dried bales.

### 3.2 Making Hay in IT

IT also has its timing and labor issues to consider. When should you upgrade product X? How do you manage your big transitions? How do you coordinate changes for different divisions? Like the farmer listening intently to the National Oceanic and Atmospheric Administration ( NOAA ) weather radio the decision maker in IT must have sources that they go to to keep up with what's going on. Blogs, magazines, and professional organizations are all great sources of information about what's happening in IT. But, just as every source of weather isn't entirely accurate neither is every blog, magazine, and professional organization. Keep your options for information open and don't hesitate to remove old ones if necessary.

Communication from the IT is also crucial. It never hurts to expand the many ways to communicate with the departments that we support. Social networks, emails, phone calls and even in-person visits can all make a big difference in increasing support from customers. Stacking hay with too few is no fun and can cost money just as making a major transition to a new service is in IT.

# 4. SEASONS

Just as seasons change so do the technology needs of the students. Crops and livestock are susceptible to weather, disease, and pests. Computing is susceptible to viruses, malware, pop-ups, and of course frequent updates. Best practices along with along with training need to be made available to users at all times to ensure safe computing. As students mature we see them putting best practices in place more often.

## 4.1 Spring=Freshman

Crops are new and need more attention/Freshman are new and require extra attention to acclimate to their new settings. Just like new crops we try to keep an extra close eye on our new students and make sure that the technology available to them is current, working, and easy to access and understand as they acclimate to their new life.

## 4.2 Summer=Sophomores

Crops are in the ground and don't require as much attention/Sophomores are acclimated to college life but still need some guidance. After 1 year under their belts Sophomores are comfortable with their life at campus. A continued Coaching role is now taken to reinforce best practice use in technology. Many of our student employees in the Helpdesk come to us as Sophomores allowing us to better understand their needs and ever changing use of technology.

## 4.3 Fall=Juniors

Time to prepare for harvest and look forward to a good crop/Juniors are looking at one more year of college and making sure that earlier preparation will be enough for a successful graduation. After two years Juniors are well accustomed to all technology available to them at our University and our role starts switching to a support role as they look towards their Senior year. At our helpdesk we quite often rely on our students (particularly Juniors and Seniors) to assist us in understanding new technology, particularly that of the portable variety. Who better to ask that those who live by it!

## 4.4 Winter=Seniors

Crops are in and now it's time to market the crop/Seniors are wrapping up their education and preparing to market their skills. As Seniors the students concentrate on Finals, grades, jobs, and anything else they can worry about. It is now more important than ever to offer support to keep them focused. We remind them that the always upgraded technology provided at the University is there to help them succeed as sometimes they forget due to self imposed stress. At the helpdesk we employ our Seniors to mentor the new student employees as this gives them a sense of ownership and reassures them that they really do have the tools to succeed and graduate.

# 5. LIVESTOCK
## 5.1 Best Choices for Healthy Livestock

What you want from your livestock determines what you buy. If you want fresh eggs you don't purchase old hens. You research the best breed for egg production and purchase chicks, knowing that production won't begin until 5 months of age, and also realize that the best production will usually be the first 3 years meaning that you may need to consider a rotation plan for continued good

egg production. The same should apply for any animal on the farm making sure to first determine the desired end result and figuring out the best first step.

## 5.2 Best Choices for Productive Computing

As in Farming, when purchasing any piece of technology you first need to determine what your needs or goals are and then determine the best way to achieve those goals or meet those needs. If your technology needs require you to be mobile in your job then a portable device is to be considered. The features and functions of that device are based on what you will be doing. For instance if you will be doing a lot of typing you probably won't be looking for something without a keyboard. Also, Cloud computing plays a large role in your purchasing decision. If you are a person who does a significant part of your job in the Cloud then the emphasis on Processor speed, memory, and storage might not be as important. These 3 factors can have a significant effect on the purchase price of the computer.

# 6. LIMITS AND INJURY
## 6.1 Limits in Farming

Most farmers and anyone who has ever worked on a farm are familiar with aches and pains. Farming is a physical occupation and there are things that simply need to get done so the farmer will push their body on a regular basis. Being too tired or working too hard will find a farmer in the hospital and laid up for too long. Nik experienced this early in the spring of 2014 when he would up in the hospital with an inguinal hernia. Nik has a small frame and even though he has a farm has to be careful what he tries to lift. The challenges in farming are eternal and there are plenty of heavy things to lift that can hurt you.

## 6.2 Limits in IT

Fortunately for the IT professional there are very few things that can cause a hernia or otherwise injure one in the day to day. However, it is also easy to get pushed to one's limits and quickly find yourself overwhelmed in IT. You have to be careful about what you agree to. At the SIGUCCS Conference in 2013 Scott Saluga noted it is important to know your limitations and learn how to say no now and then. This can be difficult for people who are either High S or High I DISC personality types. Nik considers himself a High I personality type and is usually eager to take on a new challenge. This would result in a frazzled Nik who was not as useful to his organization. To ameliorate this he began to check with his supervisor before agreeing to a new responsibility. Since that time his efficiency has improved and he no longer feels overly stressed by work.

Taking on too many responsibilities is not the only way to get in trouble in IT. Taking on a project that requires specialized knowledge can be dangerous for anyone without that knowledge. It's important that IT workers grow in their roles but they must also remember that the organization has goals that must also be maintained. Nik provides a good example with his work in Desktop Management. Nik has long worked with Desktop computers that have a very different scope and impact when compared to his growing work in Desktop Management. In Desktop Support there's a great deal of flexibility with attempting to apply solutions to existing problems. Problems in Desktop Management affects a much wider audience and requires careful planning and work to ensure that an entire campus is not adversely affected by a careless error. An error in late 2013 adversely affected all of his computers bound to a Profile Manager that didn't get resolved until early 2014. While Nik now knows how better to introduce new technologies it would have been better for his organization if he had practiced greater care with a bad software update.

# 7. SHEEP, THE BELLWETHER, AND PEOPLE

Sheep are short sighted, selfish, and easily spooked. This should sound familiar to anyone who has worked in IT or just worked with people in general. Even still, sheep are animals that mankind has kept for a long time and without them, just like IT consumers, the work of an IT department is nothing. Perhaps the bellwether is the key to this perplexing problem. The bellwether is the sheep that other sheep will follow. In the Middle Ages a ram would be castrated, making them a wether, and a bell would be hung on their neck. The ewes would follow this wether so a shepherd need only keep their ear out for the sound of the bell to know where their flock was moving to. Those who work with the end user are familiar with the "Pro users" who have a deeper understanding of the technology. Just as a good sheep is not necessarily a proper bellwether that other sheep will follow, being a pro user alone is not sufficient to function as a bellwether in technology. A technological bellwether should have the intersecting skills of influence and technical prowess. Some power users are less likely to be able to assist with influence and be more likely to focus on their own devices. Those customers are still beneficial for beta or trial testing. Identifying those users in the field that will help us to beta test and move forward with influencing how users will adapt to new technology is always a worthwhile endeavor. Keep an ear out for the bellwethers in your institutions.

# 8. ALWAYS LOOK A GIFT HORSE IN THE MOUTH

For those folks not aware of the origins of the phrase, "old-school" farmers and horse traders would check a horse's teeth and gums to determine age, relative health, and other qualitative aspects of the animal. "Don't look a gift horse in the mouth" implies that the quality of "it's free" outweighs the concern of "it might be of an inferior quality" because, hey, it was free. People, especially those in positions of entitlement, place an almost inversely-appropriate level of value on things that are given to them for free. As a consequence, they don't look gift horses in the mouth -- instead, they go out and look for the shiniest saddle and bridle, and tell the grooms to get those horses ready to win the Rolex or run the Preakness. What they don't realize is that the initial cost of the horse is just a fraction of the overall cost of the animal, both for its own survival and development as well as for the barn as a whole. Poor-quality horses can have destructive habits, personality issues, health concerns, or skills in a different area than yours, and those are expensive to correct or mitigate, and those costs can cascade quickly.

The same applies to technology. Just because Brand X wants to give your institution fifty laptops or licenses for software does not mean that you should immediately say yes. Those laptops will need software, security, training, and infrastructure that you might not have, and that will cost thousands of dollars to implement and maintain. That free software needs to run somewhere, and if your current hardware or data center cannot handle the requirements,

then money gets funneled into that "free" project as well. Whenever people come up to me and ask about our Google migration a few years ago, they tend to lead off the conversation with "Google is free." No, it isn't -- the service and infrastructure is free, but the hard work necessary to move to it and then maintain it means an investment that many don't consider beforehand.

A better farmer's phrase for this topic is one that my wife's farrier often uses: "It costs the same to feed a pretty horse as it does to feed an ugly one." If you are going to get a horse, do it right from the beginning, and make sure that the initial investment is worth the expenditures later down the road. Talk to subject matter experts, gather your own needs beforehand, and make sure that the horse you pick is the right one for you. Five years from now, that sleek black coat won't matter as much as a horse that doesn't kick holes in your brand-new trailer or who gets tired because she was 15 when you got her -- for free.

# 10. ALWAYS SET LIMITS THAT YOU CAN LIVE WITH

My mother's family is from Wisconsin so, naturally, at some point there was a dairy farm. She once told me about a cow pasture that my great-grandfather fenced in for his dairy cows. When the pasture became too small, he moved the fence line to expand the grazing area. What he noticed, however, was that the cows never grazed beyond the original boundaries of the pasture. You could see very clearly the gap between the old fence line and the new fence, and despite the grass tempting them, none of the cows ever violated those earlier limits. The reverse was also true -- the cows that remained in the opposite pasture, now smaller because of the shifting fence, frequently tried (and occasionally succeeded) to go through the fence for the grass that they still assumed was theirs.

Do not assume that this behavior is limited to dairy cows. While you may focus your time and attention on the vocal minority when it comes to technology, many people just want to know their limits so that they can work within them. Users may have specific needs that require shifting over time, whether it involves additional disk space, bandwidth, or training, but for the most part if you tell them that their students have 10Gb of network storage available, they will use that to determine the complexity of their assignments and expectations. On the other hoof, once you've given it is almost impossible to take away. If the decision is made to reduce network storage to 5Gb, there will be wailing and gnashing of teeth from people who rightly complain about spending time conforming to a limitation that is then becoming more limited. Even if the reduction is because 50Gb is available on another system, that change is seen as a limit on the original, and that can cause stress and anger -- and believe me, a faculty member bursting through a fence is far scarier than any cow. Strategically set your system and behavioral limits based on needs at the time and expectations in the foreseeable future., and your pastures will be much calmer.

# 11. SAVE IT FOR THE RING

My wife teaches dressage (among other things) to both horses and students. Eloquently summed up as "horse ballet"(6), dressage involves the horse and rider executing a predetermined series of maneuvers from memory. Dressage tests are separated by levels of training and experience, and the maneuvers range from "circle left 15 meters" at the lower levels to "working half-pirouette left approximately 3m in diameter" and more. It is a competition that involves countless months of preparation and hard work for the horse and rider individually and as a team. Stories abound about that moment when the team "clicks", and the test is completed for the first time. After that, the spit and polish are applied so that the show results will be perfect, resulting in more weeks of work and effort. But, in the end, years of training and tears are summed up in six minutes from the judge's salute to the final halt. The judge only sees that hard work in the result, and no points are awarded for those little "clicks" throughout training that turned two animals into a cohesive unit.

Keep that in mind during your next big project. Your users won't care about the hours of team building necessary beforehand, or the technological hurdles that were climbed, bulldozed, or flown over, or the budgetary battles won or lost. Your users will expect a result, and they expect to see that result exactly as promised. A good judge can see how a maneuver was done and expound on the work involved, but that judge is an informed observer. your users, for the most part, are not. They want an authentication method or identity management system or email client that does what they want it to do, and you are the wizard who can snap their fingers and produce that. If you are going to put forth the huge amount of effort, make it worth the result. A horse and rider who can do Prix St. George won't see the same amazement when they perform the Beginner Novice test. By the same token, the journeyman rider and new horse trying for a test above their station will only appear lacking, even if their effort and will were Herculean. Do as much as you can do well, and be satisfied.

On a small tangent, coaches and managers live for those "clickable moments", because it allows them to reward progress and effort that the judge will never see. The best leaders in both cases tell their students and workers beforehand and after the show that what matters for personal development is the journey,

not the ribbons. Their satisfaction will never be quantified with awards, but it will mark their skill and career development for their entire lives.

## 12. CONCLUSION
While farming and IT are wildly different pursuits, the lessons from one can apply to others. It's likely that this is true for other occupations but agriculture lends a special wisdom due to it's ancient nature. So, perhaps the next time an IT professional is having a particularly difficult time with a problem at their institution they should sit down and explain it to a farmer.

## 13. ACKNOWLEDGEMENTS
The IT Farmers would all like to thank their institutions for allowing them to participate in the conference, their families, and the land.

## 14. REFERENCES
1. Wikipedia, "Kübler-Ross Model" http://en.wikipedia.org/wiki/K%C3%BCbler-Ross_model

2. Wikipedia, "Bellweather" http://en.wikipedia.org/wiki/Bellwether

3. Scott J. Saluga: Minimal computing: minimizing technology to maximize work/life balance. SIGUCCS 2013: 209-212

4. discus, "Understanding DiSC, The Four Factors: S for Steadiness" - http://www.discusonline.com/udisc/s_steadiness.html

5. discus, "Understanding DiSC, The Four Factors: I for Influence" http://www.discusonline.com/udisc/i_influence.html

6. Oliver, John, and Andy Zaltzman. "Bugle 203 - No Medals for Syria." Audio blog post. *Bugle 203 - No Medals for Syria.* TheBuglePodcast.com, 3 Aug. 2012. Web.

# A Large-scale PC Environment for Research and Education Based on NetBoot Thin Clients

Masaru Okumura
Fukuoka University
8-19-1, Nanakuma,Fukuoka
Fukuoka, Japan
okkun@fukuoka-u.ac.jp

Sho Fujimura
Fukuoka University
8-19-1,Nanakuma,Fukuoka
Fukuoka, Japan
fujimura@fukuoka-u.ac.jp

## ABSTRACT

Fukuoka University provides more than 1,000 PCs in 20 PC rooms for education and research. In our setup, it is important to keep all PCs clean and in uniform condition within the short break time between classes to reduce maintenance costs. In order to achieve these goals, over the past 9 years, we have implemented NetBoot thin clients and have been appropriately adjusting the setup. In the current system, the clients boot image is stored in high-speed storage on SSD and is transferred via the high-speed campus network. This system, enables centralization of all necessary hardware resources for NetBoot in a single location and optimizes hardware resources and management methods. As a result, when all PCs are booted at once, we can control the PCs boot time to within 90 seconds. In this paper, we will describe the system configuration, the management methods of disk image files, performance evaluation and operation experiences.

## Categories and Subject Descriptors

C.2.4 [**Client/Server**]: Thin Clients and Disk Image Delivery Servers; C.5.5 [**Servers**]: Computer System Implementaion Servres

## General Terms

Design,Performance

## Keywords

NetBoot;Thin Client;Windows;Disk Image

## 1. INTRODUCTION

Fukuoka University is located in Fukuoka-city, Fukuoka Prefecture, Japan. This is a private university with undergraduate and graduate courses. In undergraduate studies there are 31 departments, and 9 faculties. We also have a graduate school with 33 specialties, and 10 graduate courses. There are approximately 21,000 students. In addition, there

are 2 hospitals, 2 high schools, and 1 junior high school affiliated with the university. Also there are many divisions in this school, one of them being the information technology center. Here, there are 30 clerical staffs and 3 associate professors working as a team.

Fukuoka University commenced operation of the FUTURE (Fukuoka University Telecommunication Utilities for Research and Education) system in 1994. This ICT education and research system caters to the needs of students and the 1,400 academic and administrative staff via LAN and high speed network to PC rooms providing a diverse and multifunctional platform. In September 2005 the third generation FUTURE3 became operational, replaced by the fourth generation FUTURE4 in September 2010. This version is currently in use. The system update was not incremental but total, at a scale unsurpassed in any other university in Western Japan. The architecture of a system of this scale required 12 months to complete.

## 2. WHY WE REQUIRE NETBOOT THIN CLIENTS?

The FUTURE4 system employs a NetBoot thin client, as did its predecessor FUTURE3. Reasons for the use of NetBoot thin-client over these two generations of systems range from maintenance, cost reduction and stability issues with the previous generation FUTURE2 as well as providing a more user friendly system. The second generation FUTURE2 education and research system consisted of 800 PCs (local boot). The client PC disk image was updated biannually when new software or security patches were installed, and after operation checking and drafting a disk image updating manual staff would then go to each classroom and conduct updates as per manual instruction.

Due to there being 30 different types of disk images the drafting of the manual was time consuming and the creation of the disk image for transmission and testing required about a week. In addition, the distribution system meant the disk image could only be installed on to 20 to 30 PCs in each classroom at a time, resulting in a 2 week timeframe required to complete the task on all 800 PCs, making it a total of 3 weeks for the task. This also led to high labor costs. There were as many as 30 types of disk images which led to maintenance and operational difficulties. In some cases there were classrooms where only certain rows had the updated software, and the classrooms which did have the updates were constantly used and had no vacancies. It was an extremely inconvenient setup.

These circumstances led us to reduce the number of disk images (from 30 to 5) which in turn reduced the bloated time required for updates, and introduced thin client in FUTURE3 for a more user friendly lower maintenance system. When moving from FUTURE3 to FUTURE4 we continued to use the NetBoot thin client, with greater expectations of its user friendliness, running stability and easy maintenance.

However, in FUTURE3 we sometimes encountered mysterious errors when copying the disk image from the server. In FUTURE3 the disk image copy between servers included OS function such as a network drive(SMB). We abandoned this method, instead using storage function (snapshot) in FUTURE4 which resulted in practically no disk image copy errors, resolving issues which were present in FUTURE3[1].

The current FUTURE4 system boots on Microsoft Windows 7 Enterprise 32bit, and we are currently testing a NetBoot with Windows 8.1. However it is still in the testing phase.

# 3. THE CONFIGURATION OF THE SYSTEM

## 3.1 Design Policy

The server of NetBoot system and the network load increases when all PCs power on simultaneously in a classroom. The boot-time required for one client PC is less than the boot-time of several PCs at the same time. In FUTURE3, much time was required for boot-time of PCs in classrooms. This resulted in us not having enough lecture time. Therefore, in the design of FUTURE4, we shortened the PC's boot-time to have ample time for lectures.

In order to resolve the problems of FUTURE3, we decided design policies as following,

1. All necessary hardware resources for NetBoot are centralized in one location, where is server room of FUTURE4.

2. In network design, we provide enough network bandwidth between the PC clients and servers.

3. On duplication of the disk image, we employ a new method. We describe the details of design policies in 3.2 and 3.3.

## 3.2 Machine Specifications

The client PC which we adopted in FUTURE4 works as a thin client the NetBoot method, the specifications are as follows,

- Model: Dell Optiplex 780

- CPU: Intel Core2Quad(Q9550) 2.83GHz

- Memory: 4GB

- HDD: 1TB (The thin client system uses storage area as temporary area when files are changed in drive C.)

- Network: 1000BASE-T

- OS: Microsoft Windows 7 Enterprise 32bit Edition

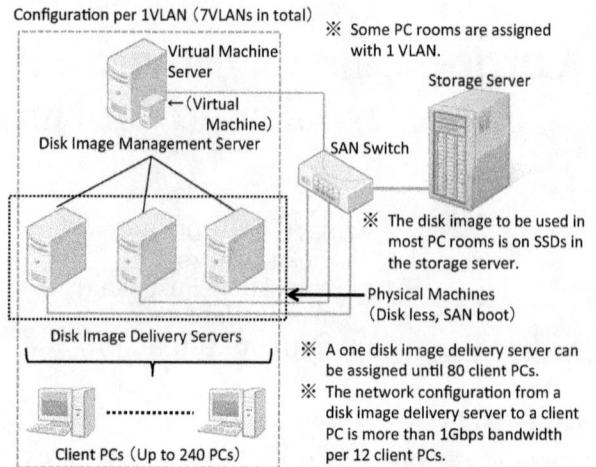

**Figure 1: System Structure**

As server group manages thin clients, it must comprise of the following: disk image delivery servers for client PCs, disk image management servers (virtual machine) for the delivery servers. The specifications and configuration of the disk image delivery server are as follows,

- Model: HP BL460c (Blade Server)

- CPU: Intel Xeon L5520 2.26GHz x2

- Memory: 8GB

- HDD: None (Fiber Channel, SAN boot)

- Network: 10Gbps

- OS: Microsoft Windows Server 2008 Standard Edition 64bit Edition

The configuration system is shown in figure 1. As you can see, there is one disk image management server and three disk image delivery servers per 1 VLAN. So, there are 7 VLANs in this configuration. Moreover, the disk image delivery server has an automatic load distribution function. It automatically assigns a client PC to server depending on the load of the server.

In the design of the NetBoot system, we can predetermine the boot-time of the client PCs including the maker's client PC specifications. One disk image delivery server can be assigned to a maximum of 80 client PCs. Also, the network configuration from a disk image delivery server to a client PC is more than the bandwidth 1Gbps per 12 client PCs.

All servers for NetBoot are centralized in one location and servers are connected to storage system with SAN, and to PC clients via high speed campus network. The storage server provides SAN storage area for disk image delivery server and NAS for users in FUTURE4.

On the other hand, all PC clients are equipped with HDD, but the client PC does not use it as disk cache area for NetBoot. The results of our investigation show that if the NetBoot system has enough bandwidth for transferring the disk image, we could not archive to decrease boot-time by using HDD as disk cache area. So, we decided that all client PCs just use it as temporary storage for writing files when files are replaced in drive C.

## 3.3 Duplication of disk image

The disk image is scheduled to be duplicated automatically once a week so that security updates can be performed, new software can be installed, or unnecessary software can be deleted, and virus pattern files can be updated regularly to shorten the boot-time. When duplicating disk images, we created a system which automatically performs the update of the disk image for all disk image delivery servers once a week. We made this structure for simplification and certainty of the work when we perform the disk images for update or patch application of a pattern files for virus check software, OS and installed software (To be updated in the latest pattern at the boot-time of client PC automatically, but to shorten boot-time make the updates smaller in volume). In the previous FUTURE3 system, we had the structure which duplicated the latest disk image to the second unit from the first unit server that it is stored as duplicate method of the disk image (Figure 2).

We performed the restart of the duplication manually at night because duplication sometimes fails. In addition, we were carrying out the automatic duplication of the disk image at night, but two consecutive nights were required to complete the process (from 11:00 p.m. to 7:00 a.m. the next morning). We reconsidered the duplication method of the disk image in FUTURE4, and were able to ensure the duplication of the disk images. We also could reduce that time. The disk images were duplicated with the function of the OS on between servers in FUTURE3. But in FUTURE4, they are on a storage server and they are duplicated with the function (snapshot) of the storage system (Figure 3).

The disk image duplication failure issue was resolved in the new system. All processes of the duplication of the disk image can be completed in approximately four hours. Therefore, we were able to perform stable system operation by this function.

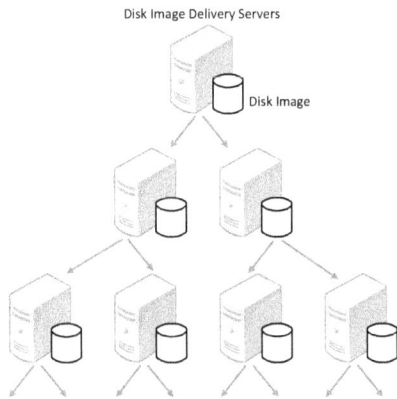

Figure 2: Duplication in FUTURE3

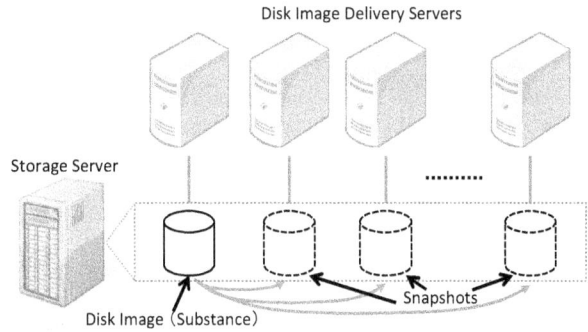

## 4. MEASUREMENT

In our situation, it is important to reduce the boot-time of the PCs so that it does not encroach on lecture time. We measured all simultaneous boot-times to confirm the effect of the design. In this section, we report the boot-time and network traffic. In this paper, boot-time means the time from switching on the PC to login screen display. When we test 10 PCs, boot-time is calculated as the time from when

Figure 3: Dupliaction in FUTURE4

10 PCs are switched on simultaneously to when the login screen is displayed on all 10 PCs.

## 4.1 Boot-time

According to our past experience, we employed a system configuration to make boot-time as short as possible. Blade servers, which boot from SAN are used as disk image delivery servers which the load depended on most. All disk image files are stored in dedicated storage server connected disk image delivery servers with FC (Fiber Channel). Especially, the most frequently used disk image files - one for Student PC and the other for the teacher's PC, are located on the SSD volume in the storage system. The enclosure of blade servers connected to main network switch at 10Gbps. On the other hand, all PC clients in classroom are connected to L2 network switch via 1000BASE-T and L2 network switch was uplinked via a 10Gbps link to the main network switch.

Table 1 shows the boot-time of Windows 7. The second row of Table 1 shows the boot-time of "Windows 7 disk image type1" simultaneously in a 94 PC client classroom. "Windows disk image type1" is used for classes, and it includes Windows 7+ SP1 (32bit) and commercial applications, such as Microsoft Office and free applications. It also includes antivirus software for security. The total size of "Windows 7 disk image type1"was 60GB. Maximum boot-time of "Windows 7 disk image type1" was about 110 seconds in the 94 PC client classroom.

The third row of Table 1 shows the boot-time of "Windows 7 disk image type2" simultaneously in the 94 PC client classroom. The difference between type1 and type2 is the addition of starting of antivirus software. "Windows 7 disk image type2" includes antivirus software, but its start-up timing is after the login procedure. According to our past experience, we found that antivirus software generates a lot of network traffic at its start-up. In order to reduce network traffic, we tuned the start-up timing to be delayed until after the login procedure. As a result, maximum boot-time of "Windows 7 disk image type2" was within 90 seconds (Average 73 seconds) in the 94 PC client classroom. After login procedure, the desktop screen displays within 20 seconds (Average 14 seconds). As a result, we had improved boot-time. Currently, we provide "Windows 7 disk image type2" to users of FUTURE4.

For reference, we show the boot-time not including any applications, as "Windows 7 only", too. The fourth row of table 1 shows the boot-time of "Windows 7 only" disk image. "Windows 7 only" disk image size was 10.7GB.

**Table 1: Boot-time of Windows7 disk image**

| PC | Windows 7 disk image type1 | Windows 7 disk type2 | Windows 7 only |
|----|----------------------------|----------------------|-----------------|
| 10 | 62 sec | 65 sec | 57 sec |
| 30 | 71 sec | 76 sec | 52 sec |
| 50 | 92 sec | 89 sec | 54 sec |
| 70 | 104 sec | 88 sec | 58 sec |
| 94 | 106 sec | 89 sec | 64 sec |

## 4.2 Network Traffic

Along with the measurement of the boot-time, we also measured network traffic.

Figure 4 shows the network traffic of "Windows 7 disk image type1" at boot, which includes two measurements (Left side is First measurement, Right side is Second one). Each has two traffic peaks. The reason for this is the delayed start of the antivirus software. We intentionally delay the start of antivirus software to avoid competition for bandwidth. First peak is the traffic for OS booting, and second one is the traffic of antivirus software.

Figure 5 shows the network traffic of "Windows 7 disk image type2" at boot, which includes two measurements (Left side is First measurement, Right side is Second one). Compared with figure 4, network traffic in each has only one peak. The antivirus software traffic did not appear on the network. The effect of the tuning is clearly displayed in figure 5.

In FUTURE4, as shown in figure 4 and figure 5, we confirmed that the maximum bandwidth was 3.5Gbps. In system design, we allocate more than 1Gbps per 12 PCs on network bandwidth, thus avoiding a network bandwidth bottleneck.

## 5. TRIAL FOR WINDOWS8

In 2014 we provide a Windows 7 environment instead of Windows8 due to the fact that our NetBoot system does not officially support Windows8. However, we would like to provide the Windows8 environment for tablet PCs and new

OS to students. Therefore, we are preparing the disk image of Windows 8 as a trial version.

We measured the boot-time of Windows 8 simultaneously in the 94 PC classroom. Windows 8 provides fast startup mode. Table 2 shows the boot-time of Windows 8 with fast startup ON and with fast startup OFF. The disk image of Windows8 does not include any application software. As a result, we could not confirm a difference in boot-time with fast startup mode.

Figure 6 shows the network traffic of Windows 8 with fast startup ON and figure 7 shows the network traffic of Windows 8 with fast startup OFF. Both of figures include four measurements at 94 PC clients simultaneously. As you can see, the peak bandwidth was 2.5Gbps, lower compared with Windows 7.

**Table 2: Boot-time of Windows8 disk image**

| PC | Windows 8 Fast Startup ON | Windows 8 Fast Startup OFF |
|----|---------------------------|----------------------------|
| 10 | 71 sec | 69 sec |
| 30 | 66 sec | 66 sec |
| 50 | 84 sec | 77 sec |
| 70 | 89 sec | 92 sec |
| 94 | 93 sec | 93 sec |

## 6. CONCLUSION

In this paper, we provided an overview and operation experience of a large-scale PC environment based on NetBoot thin clients. According to our experience over the past 9 years, we found the boot-time depends on system architecture and the tuning method of disk images. As a result, we could resolve some operational issues in FUTURE4.

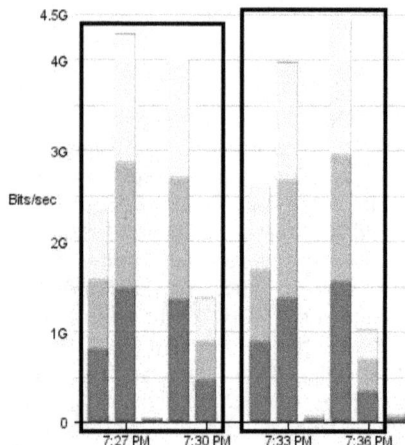

Figure 4: Network Traffic of Windows 7 disk image type1

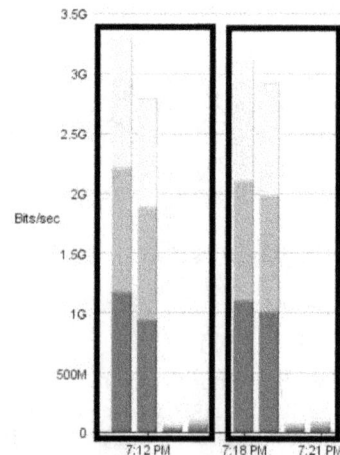

Figure 5: Network Traffic of Windows 7 disk image type2

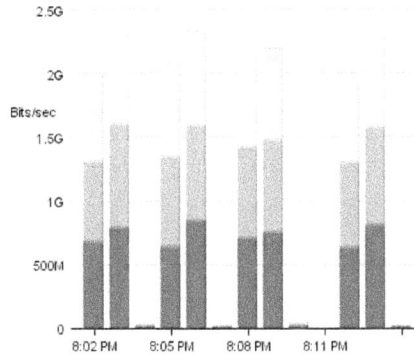

Figure 6: Network Traffic of Windows 8 Booting with Fast startup ON

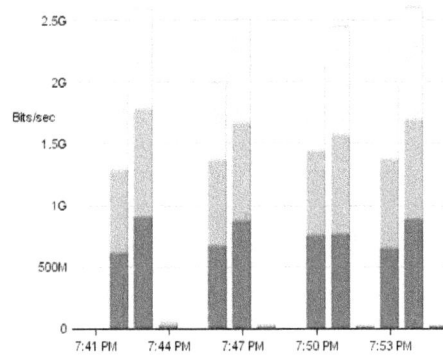

Figure 7: Network Traffic of Windows 8 Booting with Fast startup OFF

# 7. REFERENCES

[1] M.Okumura and S.Fujimura. Construction and operation of diskless pc system of scale that exceeds 1000(in japanese). *IPSJ SIG Technical Reports*, (23):61–66, March 2008.

# "Be Our Guest": Crafting a Magical Client Experience

Rebecca Klein
Valparaiso University
1700 Chapel Drive
Valparaiso, IN 46383
1-219-464-5986
becky.klein@valpo.edu

Kevin Steele
Valparaiso University
1700 Chapel Drive
Valparaiso, IN 46383
1-219-464-6930
kevin.steele@valpo.edu

## ABSTRACT

The Client Services team of Valparaiso University's IT department found inspiration in Disney's guest service models and has been building a culture of superior service throughout IT. Come along on a magic carpet ride to discover how this new world is transforming delivery of technological services to the campus. From Help Desk to training to assessment, we are increasing satisfaction levels among campus constituents as we meet their needs. We will show how we created a guest service compass that guides our decision-making and service delivery. Further, we will share areas where we learned we were creating our own obstacles in empowering staff to provide service to our guests and how we overcame resistance in the quest for continual improvement.

## Categories and Subject Descriptors

K.6.1 [**Computing Milieux**]: Management of Computing and Information Systems – *project and people management.*

## General Terms

Management, Documentation, Experimentation, Human Factors, Standardization

## Keywords

Disney; Client Services; Customer Service; Client Relations; Guest Service; Service Delivery

## 1. INTRODUCTION

Valparaiso University is a selective, independent Lutheran institution consisting of over 3,000 undergraduate and 1,100 graduate students. The university employs just over 1,200 administration, faculty and staff. Within the Office of Information Technology, our Client Services team consists of 7 full time employees who work with university students and employees to satisfy technology needs across 5 undergraduate colleges, the Graduate School, and the Law School. Our Client Services team coordinates efforts through our Help Desk, training, assessment, communication and some technical support services. We work closely with all IT departments to deliver a high-caliber customer service experience.

## 2. CUSTOMER SERVICE PHILOSOPHY REVIEW

Through a series of unfortunate events, it became clear that our current model of customer service was not working. This model was based on everybody fulfilling only their job roles and doing their best to satisfy client needs. Two catalysts can be viewed as the impetus driving the change process.

First, our Help Desk went through several periods of transition over recent years and was struggling to provide the best service possible to our client base. Management of the desk was inconsistent throughout the transitions from one leader to another. The first manager was not instilled with the authority to make and execute decisions. The second manager was not prepared for the transition, and was unwilling/unable to accept assistance from other Client Service team members. The student employees were not receiving the guidance and leadership they needed, thus resulting in a decline in client service levels. The student consultants were inconsistently skilled in both customer service and technical areas, because for years we recruited students with a natural propensity toward providing good service and perhaps lacking in technical skills. We always claimed we could teach them to be techies but couldn't teach a service attitude. We were highly dependent on their personal knowledge and experience without providing the students the proper training and job aides required for the position. These factors all combined to result in the user's quality of service being inconsistent depending on which caller was patched through to which student.

The second catalyst was serendipitously placed on top of the Help Desk transition issues. This situation involved a flawed execution of the Active Directory Migration residing on the technical side of the implementation. The beginning evidence of this project's failure revealed itself in our lab images when computers were taking excessive amounts of time to boot up. Furthermore, the printers were not consistently loading on the machines in the labs, resulting in most users not being able to print anywhere on campus. The biggest issues arose when everybody stepped backward to see who might fix the issue, rather than stepping forward to take responsibility and contribute potential solutions. This resulted in poor implementation, poor client service, and poor customer perception of IT.

By this time, Client Services had already begun a preliminary study of the Disney Institute book *Be Our Guest: Perfecting the Art of Customer Service* [1], which describes the Disney approach to customer service. At first, only a few members of our unit started reading the book. We slowly evaluated the Disney principles within this small group to analyze whether these ideas were a good fit, with our ultimate goal to have the philosophy adopted by our entire department. However, at the point where both of these situations reached their apex, we convened the entire Client Services team to work through the *Be Our Guest* philosophies.

## 3. WHY DISNEY

First, in the desire for full disclosure, two of the team members are full Disney evangelicals, regularly visiting the resorts and theme parks, also having read multiple books on Disney's service and management principles. Additionally, Disney has built an empire on exceptional guest experience and service. If they could build an empire, we could certainly find applicable concepts that could drive our service levels higher. It was a clear fit for our team. The Disney process described in the book is simple, clear, and focuses on exceeding expectations. The approach to create "magic" was a real draw for the team. The common sense approach to knowing guests, developing quality standards, creating delivery systems and pulling it all together emphasized what we desired for our entire IT department. We wanted to become the model for campus in terms of servicing our clients.

Disney's concept of "magic" abducted our thoughts. This was not something tangible that could be purchased; rather something our end users could easily experience. The other concept that Disney uses is the phrase "plus it up." This is the simple concept that you take an ordinary idea and add the details to make it extraordinary.

Each of these concepts was simple, yet profound from anything we had been doing historically. It also would prove to force all of us out of our comfort zones and set higher expectations of service throughout our team.

## 4. PROCESS START

Our start into the Disney model was simple. We convened a small task force of four members from our Client Services team to begin the approach. We were each provided with two items: a copy of the book, *Be Our Guest*, and access to a Google Doc we created titled, "The Dream Document." The task force met bi-weekly starting in late spring 2013. Each time we met, we discussed our reading and "homework" assignments for that week.

The Dream Document was a Google document and was updated during each of these task force meetings and became what was later called the "living agenda." The Dream Document was part of the asynchronous reading tasks. Members of the task force were asked to contribute ideas of how we could apply some of the reading to our service improvements or additions. These additions could be added at any time, day or night.

The "magic" of the Dream Document occurred in our Task Force meetings. All members of the task force would use the Dream Document to guide the meeting discussion. We each had our laptop with the document loaded and we would continuously, and synchronously, add in items as the meeting progressed. The idea was that the document would change from a living agenda to a handbook of sorts that would guide our full IT department's level of service.

## 5. KEY PLAYERS

To give some background, our Client Services team of seven people is loosely organized into three areas as the result of our most recent departmental reorganization. Two staff members fall under each area: assessment and communication, Help Desk, and specialized college support, with a director to guide us all. Before this reorganization, our unit consisted of these same three areas in addition to tech support and classroom technology support. The unit was too large for effective management, so the group was split. Our director worked hard to find different ways to describe our structure so we could easily understand and explain to others why we were grouped together. One of his favorite illustrations is that we functioned like a three-legged stool. The director was the seat of the stool, supported by the three different area "legs." Our work supported his work as director, and in his role, he helped keep us together and working toward the same mission.

From the start, our intention with this project was to make sure it had traction and did not get caught up in theoretical discussions and semantics. The task force was kept small to make sure we were able to get a good, solid start. One person, plus our director, for a total of four members, represented each of the three areas.

At the end of August 2013, we expanded our initiative to invite the entire Client Services team to participate. Each of them was provided with a copy of the book. It was at this point that the previously mentioned issues reached their crossing point. There were a few hard feelings in the progression from small task force to large group discussion. The newer members felt left out of the process, therefore we had to step back and review our first two meetings. The previous task force members also had to spend a little time reinforcing the idea that semantics and theoretical discussions were not to kill the project. This refocused the group on making this a reality-based, task-based, change-based group. Actionable items were discussed and implemented as we worked forward. This implementation would not be completed in just one day …it would be evolving and gradual.

## 6. IMPLEMENTATION

Starting with the Help Desk, we focused our team on providing excellent customer service. We first developed a guest service compass based on Disney's "Guestology Compass." The compass includes three individual areas plus an area for implementation to put all three areas together.

**Figure 1. Guestology Compass**

## 6.1 Guestology

The first area is "guestology," or knowing who our clients are, and what their needs, wants, perceptions, and expectations are. Knowing who our clients are is easy: it boils down to every person with whom we come into contact on campus: they include students, employees, alumni, community visitors, etc. Knowing exactly what their needs, wants, perceptions, and expectations are is trickier. We have long operated under assumptions that we knew what these needs and wants were, and these assumptions may have fallen anywhere from matching the clients' beliefs or being completely opposite. In this process we realized we needed to actually find a way to quantify the answer to the question of what these needs and wants are, instead of continuing to make assumptions.

In our *Be Our Guest* exercise, we developed a comparison chart based on Kinni (2011, p. 40-41) where we compared our own department to Walt Disney World. It was helpful to have Disney as a model for what we would be including in our perceptions /stereotypes and emotions columns. This allowed us to use a concrete example to develop our own client psychographics.

**Table 1. Client psychographics**

| Company | Perceptions/Stereotypes | Emotions |
|---|---|---|
| Walt Disney World | Disney is for kids<br>Long Lines<br>Clean<br>Friendly<br>Expensive<br>Fun | Excitement entering the park<br>Tired feet at the end of the day<br>Thrill of Space Mountain |
| Valpo IT | Don't answer phone/respond<br>Takes forever for tickets to get done<br>They always say no<br>Everyone is so friendly/professional<br>Talk to a full-time employee<br>Unsure of status | Frustrated/Angry<br>Relieved/Grateful for response<br>Hesitation to burden us |

Many years earlier, our campus had joined the Higher Education TechQual+ Project. We decided to use this method again in October 2013 as the best way to gather and quantify information relating to our users' needs and wants. The survey was administered to all campus users, and we have begun the task of analyzing the data to shape our future directions and decisions.

## 6.2 Quality Standards

The second area of the compass was to develop our standards of service. We developed these standards to guide our interactions with our clients, which include several different detailed ways to deliver a good experience, such as eye contact, greeting and welcoming clients, body language, appearance, and genuine thanks and appreciation for the opportunity to serve each individual. These guidelines were taught to the Help Desk students at their two-day training before the school year. All Help Desk staff and Client Services staff are required to adhere to this guideline for service:

1. **Make eye contact and smile!** Start and end every client contact and communication with direct eye contact and a sincere smile.

2. **Greet and welcome each and every client**. Extend the appropriate greeting to every client with whom you come into contact.

3. **Seek out client contact**. It is the responsibility of every staff member to seek out clients who need help or assistance.

4. **Provide immediate service recovery**. It is the responsibility of every staff member to attempt, to the best of their abilities, to immediately resolve a client service failure before it becomes a client service problem. Always find the answer for the client and/or find another staff member who can help the client.

5. **Display appropriate Body Language at all times**. It is the responsibility of every staff member to display approachable body language when visible to clients.

6. **Display appropriate, professional appearance guidelines at all times.** It is the responsibility of every staff member to be within the dress and appearance guidelines at all times when visible to clients.

7. **Preserve the "magical" guest experience**. Always focus on the positive, rather than the rules or regulations. Talking about personal or job-related problems in front of our guests is unacceptable. Use appropriate words and language in all conversations, even personal ones - swearing in front of the client reflects badly on us.

8. **Thank each and every client**. Extend every client a sincere thank you at the conclusion of every transaction. Extend every client a thank you or similar expression of appreciation as he/she leaves your area.

While working on quality standards we identified overarching ideals that would guide every decision we made in offering service to campus. These ideals were prioritized so that we can strive for consistency in determining what is most important as we deliver service. They are also prioritized should one come in conflict with another. In order, these four priorities are:

1. Data Security
2. Courtesy
3. Efficiency
4. Collaboration

In conjunction with developing these standards, we started working on some processes and policies to help us achieve better consistency. One policy we tightened up was our dress code for the students at the Help Desk; we created a uniform for all students to wear to make it simpler for them to dress appropriately and professionally for their jobs. One process we developed was a matrix or rubric that we could use to evaluate each ticket entered by the Help Desk students and assign it a grade.

## 6.3 Delivery Systems

The third area of the compass was to consider the delivery methods systems for our service. This includes our staff, our settings, and our processes. Staff includes the full time employees as well as the students we employ or take on as interns. The term "settings" refers to any venue or method where we come in contact with clients, including our phone line, our physical Help Desk, our website. Our processes include every task or procedure we employ to provide service, from how we answer the phone, to how we gather information, enter tickets, troubleshoot, respond to clients, and much more.

## 6.4 Integration

The final area of the compass is the integration of the other three areas. It is always harder to put it all together, but the great news about our efforts is that we realize we have ongoing opportunities to review and improve. If we find that a particular process isn't working, we will evaluate and revise. If our website needs a change to be more client friendly, we will make the modifications. Ultimately it is the willingness to evaluate and make changes that leads to the service we desire to provide to our campus.

## 7. REINVENTING OUR IMAGE

Recently, we have re-engaged our clients, and internal IT staff, with a new IT logo that speaks to our new renewed focus. While waiting for a meeting to begin in July 2013, we began to discuss our "brand" and what it means to be IT at our institution. We realized that we didn't have a brand and we were losing our focus. Our mission statement was there, but clients don't read those. We needed something visual that provided both internal and external reminders of our departmental mission.

- truth-seeking
- free to inquire
- humble
- compassionate
- service-minded
- purpose-driven
- empowered
- ethical

**Figure 2. Valpo Shield of Character**

Our institution issues to all members a pin called the "Shield of Character" that all are supposed to wear with pride and as a reminder of what it means to be a member of the Valpo community. At the center, there is a flame for the light of truth, but we saw it as a spark or an ignition. We played off the initials IT in the center of the word ignite. We had some discussions of what we were igniting and we settled on innovation. We want IT to be the center and the catalyst for igniting innovation from both on campus and within the community. Our marketing department worked with us on the art rendering and we have moved into trademarking our new logo which is pictured below.

**Figure 3. New IT Department Logo**

We realize we are not Disney, but the tried and true methods are continuously reviewed and implemented where appropriate. We are quicker to address client needs and focus on the project, rather than on the delegation of responsibility. Some of our other divisions have been slower to react, but they are coming along.

## 8. CURRENT STATUS

Starting in June 2013, the entire IT team began taking annual retreats, which will continue into the future. These retreats focus on team building and idea sharing throughout the units. We also work on the overall strategic plan for the department. During these sessions, our Client Services division has started to implement a strategic focus on customer service and "plussing up" the client experience. The aim is to have every member of the IT team focused on the end-user experience in all levels of our institution.

In April 2014, our current Manager of Help Desk Services attended an HDI certification course. Since returning, he has initiated the process of building a service catalog. He has also overseen the replacement of our ticketing system to improve the guest experience. Based on data in both our past and present ticketing systems, customer satisfaction with the Help Desk continues to be high, but because of changing systems, we are unable to draw a direct comparison in order to evaluate improvement.

The results of the TechQual+ survey have been provided to our department leadership, and we are awaiting strategic analysis and recommendations for future decisions and initiatives. Our current plan is to repeat this survey during the 2015-2016 academic year to gauge whether there has been improvement in campus perception of IT and related services.

## 9. FUTURE PLANS

As we expand the concepts further, our goal is to include other units of our IT department more fully in the process. After all, our entire IT department is responsible for creating magic and exceeding expectations. This vision is shared by our CIO. In our planning meetings, we have often discussed the idea that we want IT to fade into the background. This way you almost don't notice us...but this is not ideal either. We want our entire IT staff to be involved in campus activities throughout the university. We want people to know everybody in our group! After all, we have a pretty amazing cast of characters ourselves!

## 10. REFERENCES

[1]  Kinni, Theodore. *Be Our Guest: Perfecting the Art of Customer Service*. Disney Editions, New York, 2011

# Sign, Sign, Everywhere a Sign, BYOD — Build Your Own Digital Sign

William Klein
Valparaiso University Law School
william.klein@valpo.edu

Skip McFarlane
University of Oregon
skipmcf@uoregon.edu

Steve Wassef
Wayne State University
swassef@wayne.edu

Audrey Webster
Willamette University
awebster@willamette.edu

## ABSTRACT
Digital Signage is a resource that many colleges have chosen to deploy in various different solutions and models. The questions of which kind, how much to spend, where to place, and how can we tap into the potential of digital signage have all been asked. Panelists from several institutions will discuss their current digital signage products, deployments, administrative techniques, advantages/disadvantages, and future plans. We will investigate content management software products including: Concerto, Scala, and FourWinds. Several of these institutions are currently in the transitional period for digital signage. The panel's goal is to help inform and advise other institutions that are either in the process of moving forward with a new solution or will be looking to do so in the near future.

## Categories and Subject Descriptors
B.4.2 [**Hardware**]: INPUT/OUTPUT AND DATA COMMUNICATIONS – Input/Output Devices, *Image Display, Voice*

## General Terms
Performance, Design, Reliability, Experimentation, Security, Human Factors

## Keywords
Digital Signage; Displays; Monitors; Concerto; FourWinds; Scala; Rise Vision.

## 1.     GOALS
Demand for digital signage can come from many directions. Reasons for implementing it range from Board of Directors initiatives, individual departments' or users' requests, to campus security concerns. Whatever brings digital signage to campus often becomes only a part of the eventual usage.

Communications, marketing, news, clubs, and special events ultimately take over screen real estate. These uses enhance the

other goals of digital signage, which include conveying safety and location relative (mapping) information, because adding fun or interesting parts to signage outputs can garner more attention.

Digital signage can enhance the experience of students and visitors by displaying news and directions and promoting events on and off campus. Through digital signage, different departments or units can manage communications, promote events, or spotlight someone of interest, such as a professor or distinguished visitor. Featured current and future uses include: announcements, marketing department or activities, displaying news feeds, videos, or live TV, saving money on posters or flyers by using digital signage, and emergency broadcast messaging.

## 2. FOURWINDS

### 2.1 Pros
Centrally managed, Windows friendly. FourWindsInteractive (FWi) is a very well established corporation with large clients like Royal Caribbean Cruise lines, General Motors, and a variety of universities and colleges. http://www.fourwindsinteractive.com/education-digital-signage/. FWi is a market leader and has experience in the space. Clients can stream full HD video using a higher-end PC. Touchscreen and way-finding are also possible with this system. Both Windows and Mac (Native OS and Boot Camp) systems can be used for the client player. FWi also has a web-based player available.

### 2.2 Cons
High-cost, requires a Windows server for the Content Manager, and either a Windows or Mac (Native OS or Boot Camp) for the player. FWi does not serve out content independent of the applications used to build the content, so clients need to have local installs of the application used for the content. The local install solutions create a good deal of overhead and systems administration. Using Windows systems may not be as secure as other options. A higher-end PC costs more, but will allow longevity and capability for upgrades later. FWi Content Manager is a Windows only application. However, the Content Player is not as robust on a native Mac OS X player, in that the Touch Screen functionality, i.e., for use in way-finding, is not supported.

### 2.3 Future at Wayne State University
WSU is currently unhappy with our hardware choice for the players. WSU is definitely considering new and more cost effective playback devices like the Intel Next Unit of Computing (NUC). Also being considered is a non-Windows (Linux), non-FourWinds Interactive (FWi) solution.

## 2.4 Hardware at Wayne State University

At Wayne State University (WSU) several signs are the same, but there are some that are more interesting—for example, the sign at the School of Business in Prentis Hall, which is in a fishbowl shaped, large room surrounded by enormous windows. Prentis Hall has a quad screen array with one PC driving the four monitors. Three of the monitors are used to display RSS feeds from WSU's website including, news, events, and weather. News takes up one screen, events another, weather a third, and a live CNN video feed with closed captions (no audio) fills the fourth monitor.

## 2.5 Current Environment

WSU has a FourWindsInteractive Content Management Server (FWi CMS): version 4.6.1.1772. The MS SQL database is called FWiSignage_Prod on waynesql03.ad.wayne.edu. WSU runs one production server and one development VM server both in the same configuration: Windows 2008 R2 Enterprise server with 6GB RAM, Intel X5650 @ 2.67GHz 2.60GHz (4 processors). 100GB OS partition, 500GB Content partition.

WSU has 60 content player computers (players) running FourWindsInteractive Content Player (FWi CP) version 4.6.1.1772. WSU has multiple player specs. WSU's top-of-the-line spec is an Intel Core i5-2520M 2.50 GHz Processor, 4GB RAM, 80GB solid state disk (SSD) hard disk drive (HDD). The OS is Windows 7 SP1 Enterprise (64-bit). Here is a link to the spec: http://www.digitalsignageplayers.com/DMP-67-Digital-Media-Player-DMP-67.htm

The University of Oregon is currently running the FWi Content Manager on a Mac Pro Tower with a 3.2 GHz Quad-Core Intel Xeon processor, 32GB 800 MHz DDR3 RAM, and OS X 10.9.2 (Mavericks), which runs a virtualized Windows environment consisting of VMware Bootdisk install Windows 7 Pro SP1 Intel Xeon CPU W 365 @ 3.2GHz 3.19GHz, Installed RAM 2GB, 64-Bit OS. The client is MacMini Server (a standard MacMini could be used instead) running OS X 10.8 (Mountain Lion), with a 2GHz Intel Core i7 processor, and 8GB RAM.

## 2.6 Content problems

WSU has a variety of content problems: some minor, others major. The promo section of WSU's website RSS feed is a common problem. The fact that certain content makes the content player stop working on certain content playlists is another. The details of the error in the promo section are related to error handling. The content manager may have a link to content that no longer exists on the website or cannot be found. The way the error is handled by the Content Player (CP) and the Content Manager (CM) is a problem. Both the CP and CM try incessantly to get the data from the webserver.

## 2.7 Network traffic problems

The frequency of requests from the content problem above has been as high as 10Hz (10 requests/second) by one CP or the CM. That type of request frequency borders on a denial-of-service attack on the webserver. This problem is still an open case with FWi and as yet we have no solution other than removing the request for this content from our content manager. WSU still

maintains that this is definitely a poor way to handle these "404 errors" or "page not found" errors.

## 2.8 Windows software configuration

WSU started with Windows 7 Enterprise, added the Content Player software, Dell/Quest Big Brother monitoring software, and RealVNC Enterprise VNC service. WSU can access the PCs in real time using the VNC service. This allows us to see the actual content being displayed not just what the Content Manager guesses WSU will see based on the playlist.

## 2.9 Miscellaneous hardware problems

Content players and monitors can be physically misconfigured or down for a variety of reasons. The main reason is power. The CPs and, obviously the monitors require power. The other big issue is that the monitors are set to the wrong input (should usually be set to HDMI or DVI). In some cases people have played with the monitors and set them to one of the other possible inputs. In other cases there could be a boot error. Boot errors result usually from sudden power loss and a non-clean recovery. These issues require a site visit to the actual display and CP.

## 3. CONCERTO

### 3.1 Pros

Concerto is free. The server can be a virtual machine. It does require a Linux or UNIX OS, PHP, a MySQL database, a web server, and Cron (crontab), so there is some technical skill required for setup. The units in the field only require a web browser with Internet connectivity to serve the content feeds. The feeds system allows for many content management options. Content can be shared and managed by a highly granular system for user group management. Feeds are applied to screens, and screens represent your hardware in the field. Once the server is setup, adding content, feeds, and users is fairly straightforward.

### 3.2 Cons

Concerto is an open source product that is always changing—not only by adding features, but sometimes entire interface changes, which can confuse IT staff and end users alike. Some features are shown in menus as available, but do not actually function. At present there is no way to display a group of items in an order; they only can display in a random order. Frequency can be adjusted on a per item basis. Also, no RSS or immediate emergency notifications systems are available currently. There are forums for troubleshooting, but support is limited.

### 3.3 Future

The future of Concerto is still unknown. It is a good product with an active development community, but feature requests can be slow to be implemented.

### 3.4 Hardware

Concerto runs in a Linux VirtualMachine, along with its own SQL database and Apache webserver within the same VirtualMachine. The device at the display end must be capable of showing a webpage. The layout and control of that web page is what Concerto manages.

# 4. OTHER SOFTWARE

## 4.1 Scala

Scala (www.scala.com) is touted as a "customizable digital signage software" solution. Scala is an incredibly powerful digital signage system that can capture various forms of content, such as images, RSS, video, flash, sound and other third-party content.

### 4.1.1 Pros

Built upon an enterprise model, the Scala system relies upon three components: Designer, Content Manager and Display. The Designer portion has the ability to import content, set display timing, and utilize transitions. Being able to import content seamlessly will allow institutions to maintain a consistent brand across all displays and content. The Content Manager is a separate system that controls the playlists for all the displays. Within the Content Manager, users can organize file types and metadata. The Content Manager also maintains users and their roles within the system. Scheduling also happens at the Content Manager level. The Display portion of Scala operates at the farthest end of the system, updates automatically without interruption, and can maintain screen usage. The Displays continue to operate even if downtime occurs at the Content Manager level or during a network outage. One of the unique aspects of Scala is its ability to "scale" any of the content that is thrown at it and display it seamlessly.

### 4.1.2 Cons

With Scala being as powerful as it is, this product is very popular in the commercial field. Because it is a commercial entity, the system comes at a price. Licensing such a product could come at a steep cost to educational institutions based upon the number of displays needed. The Enterprise model, while stable, does create additional points of possible failure and additional hardware to be put into play for the system to work properly.

### 4.1.3 Future

Scala's future is solid with its strong footing in the commercial arena. This translates to good news to educational institutions that chose to go with Scala. Scala is probably in a better position to acquire other digital signage options rather than to be gobbled up. Scala will continue to develop its product for years to come.

### 4.1.4 Hardware

In this case, the hardware requirements were based on the necessity of having 2 Windows XP desktop machines that ran the Designer and Content Manager. They physically sat next to each other on a desk in the Director's office. The end display units were also Windows XP desktops that were stashed away in ceilings and data closets. The hardware issues were secondary to the fact that XP has been dying a slow death over the past few years with in the influx of Vista, 7, 8, and other Linux flavors that have made the display options far more palatable than previous ones.

## 4.2 RISE VISION

Rise Vision (http://www.risevision.com/platform/). Rise Vision is a free, "cloud" based system that allows clients to expand to unlimited displays and presentations.

### 4.2.1 Pros

Built on the Google App engine, Rise Vision is best used with Google Chrome. A Google account is not necessary to use Rise Vision, but could be useful in the future. Adding users to the system is fairly easy, and assigning roles gives a hierarchical means of developing and distributing content. Using the terminology that Rise Vision uses, a display is both the physical monitor and the computer that pushes out the content to the monitor. Rise Vision's "dashboard" gives the content managers a quick and easy overview of what is happening on the system at any given moment. They will see active, disabled, and non-published presentations, addresses and resolution of displays/presentations. All of the user interfaces exist in the cloud on Rise Vision servers. This creates dependence on an Internet connection for both the administration and for drawing the content to the displays. The good news is that the displays will continue to run the assigned presentations if connectivity has been severed. The content can be displayed on Rise Vision servers as well, but as of later this year, clients will be charged for storage. This has prompted clients to host their own content or look at other storage options, such as Google and Amazon. This could lead to creative ways to share content between departments. One of Rise Vision's strengths is the ability to add in free "gadgets" to enhance the display experience and create additional content. These "gadgets" range from inserting Flash files (SWF) into presentations, following Twitter feeds, to viewing web page content. What Rise Vision does best is leverage Google content and allows Calendaring, Maps and Spreadsheets to be displayed. Templates can be configured ahead of time and information can be added in real time if needed. Rise Vision also incorporates the ability to have displays in an interactive mode for touch screen content.

### 4.2.2 Cons

Having a clear understanding of how Rise Vision assigns displays and presentations is crucial to the setup and deployment of the system.

### 4.2.3 Future

Rise Vision is open source, which comes with its own challenges. The future of the product depends on who picks up the project for continued development. It could simply cease development at any moment. How long will it take for one of the larger corporations to realize the impact that projects like Rise Vision are making in the industry?

# 5. INFRASTRUCTURE, DEVICES, AND DISPLAYS HARDWARE

## 5.1 Infrastructure Considerations

### 5.1.1 Wired versus wireless

Wired network connections are recommended for digital signage installations to ensure consistent connectivity and bandwidth. Wireless installation can work, but would not be recommended when streaming video or live content is an intended function.

### 5.1.2 Power considerations

Power can be an issue if clients need to ensure 100% uptime or want to remotely restart the device. Not every device can inexpensively have power cycled. While a UPC can also be costly, if the desire for emergency broadcasting is there, then it is necessary.

### 5.1.3 Devices to displays ratio

There are multiple ways to push content to displays in terms of how many devices per display are needed. A one-to-one, device-to-display, ratio allows for individual sign management. A one-to-multiple, device-to-displays, ratio requires splitting the device's output. That means additional cost for items like a matrix switcher (can cost several thousand dollars) or signal repeater (about $500 for a good quality one). For this reason, a 1:1 ratio could be the most cost effective. If clients also need a UPC for their device, then a 1: multiple setups could be more fiscally logical.

## 5.2 Signage displays

There are two schools of thought: cheap and replaceable or commercial grade. Which implementation would work best depends on the university's priorities. Cheap displays allow clients to get into the digital signage business with less financial burden. If the display lasts several years then it was a good deal, and if not it doesn't matter. When it does breakdown or the quality diminishes so much that it must be replaced, clients could be left with some unanticipated downtime while replacing it. Commercial grade displays allow for a more reliable implementation. However, the cost is much higher. Some universities could consider issues like power requirements and eco-friendly ratings when buying displays.

Wayne State has chosen to go with the commercial grade. For better or worse, they have had great luck -- three years with 95% success. WSU has only had 3/60 screen failures (5%). That is amazing. They could have gone with cheaper displays and had the same success or possibly had to replace half of them.

These are the newest versions of what WSU chose (NEC P553): http://www.necdisplay.com/p/large-screen-displays/p553

## 5.3. RaspberryPi

### 5.3.1 Pros

The small form factor, low power, quiet, very inexpensive price, and customization available to the RaspberryPi hardware made it a great starting point for digital signage deployment. There are many case options available on the market, so securing or hiding it is easy. There are no fans, so it does not add noise to quiet spaces. The device costs less than $40 alone, and with the needed power cable, display cable, and SD card, it still comes in at less than $100. There is a large community built around the RaspberryPi device. As a result, there is a specialized Linux version, and there are guides for almost any situation.

### 5.3.2 Cons

As with anything deemed "cheap," the RaspberryPi device has its share of problems; primarily in terms of video processing. Even simple slideshow animation effects can become jittery.

### 5.3.3 Future

The hardware may change to grow with the industry. It seems unlikely that more functionality will be added, such as a more powerful GPU. The use of Raspberry Pi in digital signage could be very low for this reason. According to the Frequently Asked Questions section of the Raspberry Pi website (http://www.raspberrypi.org/help/faqs/), "As of the end of 2013, there are no immediate plans for the next model; a new model may be released in 2 – 3 years, but this is not a firm schedule."

### 5.3.4: Hardware specifications

The RaspberryPi model B with upgraded RAM (512MB) and its 700MHz processor does not handle video playback and has trouble with visual transitions, such as fade effects. A RaspberryPi with the HDMI and power cables, a case, a 4GB SD card for the local OS (Raspbian), and a power-over-ethernet splitter all costs less than $85.

## 5.4 Intel NUC

The Intel Next Unit of Computing (NUC) line could be the inexpensive, viable hardware solution. For less than the cost of a Mac Mini, a university can have a small form device with all the functionality of a full desktop. Its graphical capabilities are greater than that of a RaspberryPi, there are models with wireless built-in, and client can run the OS off of a USB. Prices for an NUC range from $150 to $450.

### 5.4.1 Hardware component specifications

The low end of those players are Medius DMP-7000 boxes including a Pentium Dual CPU T3200 @ 2GHz; running Windows 7 Pro SP1 32-bit with 2GB RAM. They also include a 160GB 2.5" SATA HDD, RS-232 (serial port) for controlling the monitor (on/off/advanced features).

The high end of those players consist of a Medius DMP-67 box including an Intel Core i5-2520M @ 2.5GHz; running Windows 7 SP1 Enterprise 64-bit with 4GB RAM. They also include a 64GB SSD HDD, RS-232 (serial port) for controlling the monitor.
Here is a link to the high end CP: http://www.digitalsignageplayers.com/DMP-67-Digital-Media-Player-DMP-67.htm.

### 5.4.2 Pros

The performance is better and more options are available than with a Raspberry Pi. Video playback is possible on these devices. The price still comes in as less expensive than a standard desktop computer, while remaining small enough to hide behind a typical digital signage display.

### 5.4.3 Cons

The computers are small, but not overly powerful. The lowest tier model is still significantly more expensive than a Raspberry Pi and has problems displaying flash or video content.

### 5.4.4 The Future

This product is fairly new to Intel's lineup. The market for inexpensive, single use devices has exploded since the release of the RaspberryPi. Continued development by a reliable, big name company like Intel is expected and welcomed. Smaller devices are necessary for continued growth in many areas of technology, and that overlaps with the growth of digital signage.

### 5.4.5 Use experience

One threat to reliability with the Intel NUC that other hardware devices do not suffer is the hard drive. It ships with a standard mechanical hard drive. Institutionally, Wayne State

University saw a failure rate of 15 standard hard drives within the full deployment of 60 devices. Since switching the hard drives over to solid-state technology, that failure rate has dropped to zero.

## 5.5 Other small hardware considerations

Valpo Law has been using Acer Veriton N260Gs with Intel Atom™ processor N280s and 2GB RAM. The hard drives are sitting at 160 GB, but hard drive capacity is not the issue here, only the ability to access the network, run the RiseVision player and download the images. These units are at the low end of the spectrum in terms of hardware. They were left over from a project that didn't pan out. It was a matter of low-hanging fruit for us. A general recommendation would be for these computers to be used only for display use and in a general desktop environment. Depending on the environment and content that is being pushed out to the displays, using a low-end computer should not be out of the question for institutions looking to save costs in a project of this scope.

## 6. USER MANAGEMENT AND EXPECTATIONS.

The following considerations can help with managing usage, content, and expectation when implementing digital signage.

## 6.1 Content generation

Commonly, university communications or marketing departments end up interested in the output of digital signage. A scheduling or events department can be a great resource for generating interesting content. Faculty or administrative staff may have content to display. The worst-case scenario is when the IT department is left with the task of generating content.

WSU's Marketing team manages their content. They allow their users in the departments to publish their data to central webserver's Content Management System (CMS). This allows the FWi Content Manager to pull the data from the RSS feeds. In some cases they have used Excel CSV files as the data source for the FWi CMS to grab menu data—for instance, the cafeteria.

Valpo Law's content is mainly driven by its Marketing Department, whose job it is to provide the slides and content. In some cases, the slides and art have been shared with the IT department to be able to create some content on the fly, but not on a consistent basis and mostly in emergency cases.

## 6.2 Policing content.

At some point, with any system, there is a gatekeeper. By default that person (or persons) also becomes the content police. Whoever ends up in that role would be best served by a written policy, to ensure guidance when deciding what will be displayed and unity of content to ensure displays are interesting. A good method for ensuring content is display-worthy, is to incorporate its management with another system, such as webserver content. Common security practices that allow access only to those that directly need it are prudent.

## 6.3 Expectations

Who is demanding digital signage? What is its primary purpose or goal? What are anticipated secondary or tertiary uses? Who are the stakeholders? What is the expected "up time," maintenance or replacement, and lifecycle of hardware? Are there any statistics or stories from end users that justify the use of digital signage? How long is the expected time of IT staff?

### 6.3.1 Wayne State Expectations

No one is "demanding" digital signage. It has become an expectation of students, staff, and faculty. It provides a more modern look and feel to the campus. It gives the university's marketing department yet another opportunity to promote the university, its events, and achievements for its audience. The secondary uses are for the visiting public. A tertiary use, which we plan to test soon, is to use the signs to broadcast emergency messages to the entire campus. That was a major selling point to the campus stakeholders. The campus stakeholders are, of course, the university administration, the computing division, the marketing department, and, to a much lesser extent the audience (students, staff and faculty). Expected uptime has been 3 years. We have made it 4.5 years. Maintenance and replacement has been a nightmare. Due to the fact that we have several customers who have purchased the equipment using "one-time" funds, they didn't consider that the equipment would age past their warranty expiry date (3 years). So now we have had some out-of-warranty failures and found no one to foot the bill. The lifecycle of the hardware for the PCs has been 3 – 5 years. The lifecycle of the monitors (commercial grade) has been easily 4.5 years so far. There is no direct feedback mechanism built in to digital signage because it is a one-way medium. Like a billboard, we cannot assess the effectiveness without providing a feedback loop (such as with a questionnaire).

### 6.3.2 University of Oregon Expectations

At the University of Oregon, research programs were "requesting" Digital Signage to promote their research. That led to Central IS investigating and determining a greater use and opportunity for campus as well as a chance to standardize the system in use, which in turn led to the adoption of FourWinds. This was implemented initially as a buy in to get the ball rolling, but it is now available to all of campus. Reasons for adopting digital signage vary. One unit, Academic Extension, found the "sell" came with the utilization of the Emergency Management outreach. It was felt that it was their responsibility to their constituents to provide this type information in an accurate and immediate fashion. From there, it was an easy way for the leadership in Academic Extension to understand the potential use, and then to expand on what this system could offer to their constituents.

## 6.4 Lessons learned

### 6.4.1 Sign placement

One of the main things we would recommend is effective sign placement. Be sure to place signs where they make sense to be placed. In other words, don't just put up signs everywhere. Consider where they will have the largest impact. We've done so in a few strategic locations. The School of Business sign is a prime example of how to utilize multiple screen deployment. It is a 2x2 quad screen array. The first quadrant is for the date/time/weather, the second quadrant for a live CNN feed, the third quadrant is for university events, and the fourth is for university news.

### 6.4.2 Hardware
Due to the small size of digital signage devices, they cannot house multiple hard drives for redundancy, so solid-state drives are essential. They allow for less downtime spent replacing standard mechanical hard drives, which do not handle running 24/7 very well without venturing beyond the desired price point for most installations. Similarly, the digital signage displays need to be able to handle continuous use without overheating, burning in images, or otherwise failing. That is one area where spending more really adds a tangible benefit in terms of user experience.

### 6.4.3 Content
Have something worth displaying! Content needs to be timely and attractive enough to catch the audience's attention, yet brief enough not to bore the audience, while remaining long enough to communicate the message. It must be relevant enough to keep viewers coming back to look, and fresh enough to attract new viewers

## 7 ACKNOWLEDGEMENTS

The authors would like to thank Brian Yulke, from the NYU School of Law, who will be joining our panel at the SIGUCCS 2014 Support and Service Conference in Salt Lake City, Utah, later this fall.

# Needs Analysis for Instructional Technology Projects

Trevor M. Murphy
Williams College
22 Lab Campus Drive
Williamstown, MA 01267
011.413.597.2231
tmurphy@williams.edu

Judy Teng
Albany College of Pharmacy and
Health Sciences
106 New Scotland Ave
Albany, NY 12208
011.518.694.7210
judy.teng@acphs.edu

Randy Matusky
The George Washington University
2121 I St NW
Washington, DC 20052
011.514.998.8276
randolph.matusky@gmail.com

## ABSTRACT

Instructional media production in the higher education environment is often rushed. Faculty propose instructional technology solutions to help deliver content to students or to teach in novel ways, and instructional technologists may create media or systems to meet the faculty member's specifications. Often this process does not fully consider the needs of the students who ultimately use the finished product. Instructional tools and media can be enhanced by including a needs analysis process before the development process begins. The role of needs analysis process is to use information gathered from the intended users of the product to inform the product's design and implementation. The authors will share examples of how needs analysis is conducted at their institutions (Williams College and Albany College of Pharmacy and Health Sciences), how needs analysis has shaped the products they create for instruction, and how not including a needs analysis can result in a less effective finished product.

## Categories and Subject Descriptors

K.6.1 [**Management of Computing and Information Systems**]: Project and People Management – *systems analysis and design.*

## General Terms

Management, Human Factors.

## Keywords

Instructional Design; Needs Analysis; Instructional Technology; Project Management; Higher Education.

## 1. INTRODUCTION

### 1.1 Williams College and Albany College of Pharmacy and Health Sciences

Williams College is a residential liberal arts college located in the northwestern corner of Massachusetts in the town of Williamstown. The college has 2,000 students and 300 faculty. The Office for Information Technology at Williams College consists of four groups including Networks and Systems, Desktop Systems, Administrative Information Systems, and Instructional Technology. The Instructional Technology group provides faculty with pedagogically informed technology support.

Albany College of Pharmacy and Health Sciences (ACPHS) has a strategic focus on pharmacy and health care degree programs with two campuses; one campus is in Albany, New York, and the other is in Colchester, Vermont. The college has about 1,700 students and 150 full and part time faculty. The Center for Innovative Learning is committed to implementing research based teaching and learning solutions by following an instructional design process.

### 1.2 Instructional Design Models

Instructional design is the systematic process of assessing the needs of a learner, determining the goals of instruction, and then composing teaching methods, resources, and assessments that will best facilitate effective learning. The instructional design process can be a team collaboration that involves faculty/subject matter experts, instructional designers, developers and multimedia specialists.

Instructional design models offer guidance on the processes and tasks that are part of any instructional project. At their best, models guide project managers through steps that if completed result in successful and efficient products that are effective in transferring knowledge and skills. At their worst, a model can bring added administrative costs in the form of extra bureaucracy and paperwork leading to project implementation delays and inefficiencies.

The ADDIE model is an instructional design model that breaks down the parts of a project into five distinct phases: Analyze, Design, Develop, Implement, and Evaluate. Each phase has related tasks, but it is often possible to work on more than one phase at a time concurrently. In addition, there are often opportunities to revise various parts of the project as new information is gathered.

There are other models to consider such as the Dick and Carey model, which has more phases:

- Identify instructional Goals
- Conduct Instructional Analysis
- Analyze Learners and Contexts
- Write Performance Objectives
- Develop Assessment Instruments
- Develop Instructional Strategy
- Develop and Select Instructional Materials
- Design and Conduct Formative Evaluation of Instruction.
- Revise Instruction
- Design and Conduct Summative Evaluation.

For smaller projects, a simple model with fewer phases like the ADDIE model might be ideal. Larger projects might benefit from a more elaborate model such as the Dick and Carey model. These models can be followed formally, or they can be adapted to the needs of the teams that use them.

## 1.3 Instructional Design at Williams College and Albany College of Pharmacy and Health Sciences

Both Williams College and Albany College of Pharmacy and Health Sciences have staff who assist faculty in the creation and implementation of technology rich learning tools. At Williams, a course in Russian may require students to create digital stories as a portfolio piece that emphasizes enunciation and fluency for example [5]. Astronomy faculty may want students to work with planetary nebula spectra [6]. At the Albany College of Pharmacy and Health Sciences, staff may assist a faculty member in moving from a lecture-based course on immunology to video based case studies followed by interactive exercises to emphasize group learning. Instructional design staff may also assist a faculty member to include a well-designed learning strategy in a module on diabetes.

One of the strengths of the Albany College of Pharmacy and Health Sciences is that the staff conduct formative and summative evaluations of their projects so they can measure increases in motivation, teaching effectiveness, and learning. At Williams College, there are seldom enough students in a course to have meaningful and statistically significant studies, but student surveys are conducted to collect qualitative information.

Albany College of Pharmacy and Health Sciences tends toward formal processes of instructional design projects. Williams College has a more informal process that depends on the project scope.

## 2. BENEFITS OF CONDUCTING A THOUGHTFUL NEEDS ANALYSIS

Needs analysis is an important step in the instructional design process. It provides a systematic process for determining the gaps between existing conditions and desired conditions. A needs analysis can inform the choices that will be made about the design and delivery of instruction. Overlooking or conducting a superficial needs analysis can result in instructional projects that do not meet the needs of teachers or students. Such projects are likely to be abandoned.

Needs analysis informs any work with faculty on instructional materials. While there are more steps in the process than just needs analysis for creating effective materials for teaching and learning, a needs analysis is often overlooked and is the focus of this paper.

An example of overlooking needs analysis is giving an academic department a department website redesign that does not match their ability to maintain and update the site. A dynamic site is requested that is written in PHP. The staff member who will edit the site pledges to learn enough PHP to maintain the site. The finished site is delivered, but the staff member does not learn PHP. The site is immediately broken and abandoned. The department is not pleased and blames the technology implementation rather than the lack of training. In retrospect, it becomes clear that WordPress or some other tool would have been a better match to the web site manager's demonstrated skills and interests. The site manager had never learned a programming language before, nor had they attended or attained any technology skills training. Such information could have been gathered, considered, and used to inform the final implementation of the

website. A needs analysis would have revealed the flaws in going forward with a website requiring programing. With this extra background information in mind, a more efficient path to a working end product could have been pursued.

A common situation is a faculty member coming to an instructional technology staff member with an idea based on a technology they have heard of from colleagues. Through discussion, it is found that the technology the faculty member proposes implementing would not meet the intended outcomes, but some other solution would be more appropriate. Such a discussion is an example of an informal needs analysis. Making the needs analysis more formal can help tailor work on instructional projects to meet the needs of faculty and students.

## 3. NEEDS ANALYSIS TECHNIQUES

### 3.1 Gap Analysis

One of the many goals in conducting a needs analysis is to determine the learning gap for the individual learner, which is sometimes referred to as Gap Analysis. Gap Analysis is important for the instructional designer because it shows them what skills and competencies they need to build their instructional material and learning situations around. Dick, Carey and Carey [2] recommend breaking the process down into three steps:

1. Establish a standard or goal you want to achieve with your training. This is often referred to as the desired status
2. Determine the actual status or the level that the students currently hold
3. Identify the gap between the desired status and the actual status

The significance of this procedure is the financial cost that can be saved. If a large gap is discovered following a proper Needs Analysis report, then the IT department can confidently move forward with creating the necessary training. But if it turns out that there is no gap, then there is no need for any training, meaning the IT department can use those financial resources elsewhere.

For example, students in a laboratory conducting research took three to four weeks to learn how to remove the brain from larval fruit flies. The faculty member wanted the students to be able to contribute to the research in the lab in less than a week. The gap was determined to be the difference between what the students observed in the microscope during the dissection as compared with the static, hand-drawn illustrations and instructions that the students used to learn the technique. A training video was developed that used real footage from a camera attached to the microscope. In this way the instructional materials closely matched the performance goals for the students. The very best footage that showed the techniques step by step were compiled and augmented by voiceover describing the process as it was seen in the video. New students now only take a few days to learn the technique and can contribute to research much faster.

However, if the videos were instead focused on how fun it is to work in a lab where students can dissect larval fruit flies, it would not address any identified gap and thus not contribute to the goals of the faculty member. The IT department can justifiably turn down such a project.

### 3.2 KASH Analysis

Guglielmino and Guglielmino [3] advocate comparing the knowledge, attitudes, skills, and habits (KASH) of leaners with the desired KASH. Describing the gaps in the KASH analysis can inform the approach to instruction.

**Table 1. Example format for a KASH analysis**

| Current KASH | Desired KASH |
|---|---|
| Current Knowledge | Desired Knowledge |
| Current Attitudes | Desired Attitudes |
| Current Skills | Desired Skills |
| Current Habits | Desired Habits |

KASH. Analysis is one of the possible ways an instructional designer can measure the gap between the actual status or level of understanding of a student, to the desired status that the designer wishes the student to attain following the training. In order to properly measure the actual status and the desired status, the designer must use some form of assessment, such as a pre-assessment and a summative assessment. These assessments must not place inappropriate amounts of stress on the learners, since it may lower their overall motivation for the training. Michael Allen [1] believes that proper assessments will show if the learners are beginners, intermediate performers, or advanced performers. Most importantly, assessments show learners what sorts of tasks they will be able to perform once they have completed the training.

For example, a lab requires students to collect and identify aquatic insects as indicators of water quality. By interviewing students and performing a KASH analysis, it was found that students were motivated, but struggled with the text-based instruction. Image based materials were comprehensive and often had so many species that it would be difficult to identify the correct species from their samples. By specifically identifying the shortfalls in student knowledge, attitudes, skills, and habits, learning materials could be crafted that directly addressed the needs of the students. Targeted video tutorials that included close-ups of locally collected and classified aquatic insects replaced the text-only instructions.

## 3.3 Learner Analysis

One of the major reasons for conducting a Needs Analysis is to ensure that the students receive the exact type of training they need. An instructional design project that does not have a Needs Analysis risks ignoring the needs of the students, or the target population. A large component of the Needs Analysis must be the Learner Analysis. Walter Dick, Carey and Carey [2] state that a Learner Analysis will provide the instructional designer with useful information on the target population, such as entry skills, prior knowledge of the topic area, attitude toward content and potential delivery system, academic motivation, educational and ability levels, general learning preferences, attitudes toward the organization giving the instruction, and group characteristics.

There are various ways to collect the needed data for a learner analysis. If resources permit, the instructional designer can visit the location and conduct interviews with either the subject matter experts (SMEs) or current and former students. If it is not possible to visit the location and conduct surveys, then the designer could carry out surveys and questionnaires in order to gather information about learners' goals, interests, and skills. Finally, pretests can also be administered to the students in order to obtain all the previously mentioned information.

It is easy to assume that after meeting and working with students year after year that such analysis is not necessary. However, students can be surprisingly diverse and spending some time to talk to the students about their needs and preferences can be revealing. For example, a faculty member had a course with two graded exams that formed the sum total of assessment. Many students dropped the course, not for lack of interest, but for the practical reason that if they have a bad day and perform poorly on either one of the exams, they could very well fail the course. No other assessments, homework, or participation opportunities were available in the course to allow the student to correct for one bad test experience. Instead of wondering why the course always had such an exodus of students during the drop/add period each semester, the faculty member could have talked with students. This is one of those cases where an assumption about students (students want fewer assignments) results in surprising student behavior. The grading system could easily be changed to address student concerns. This type of information can be gained by interviewing students with an open mind. It can be a mistake to assume that students in a particular class will have the same character traits that we associate with all students. Furthermore, some observed behaviors might lead to assumptions that do not apply to all contexts. For example, students might use text messaging on their phones to communicate with friends, but not want to use text messaging to communicate about coursework.

## 4. NEEDS ANALYSIS AT WILLIAMS COLLEGE

Williams College does not have a formal process for applying needs analysis techniques to instructional projects. There is active interest in improving outcomes and efficiency of technology work. The whole of the Williams College Office for Information Technology underwent a two-day training on project management. Needs analysis was not touched on in the training. Project management training starts with a project in hand. Ideally, a needs analysis occurs first to define the project.

## 4.1 Needs Analysis Success

A music technology lab at Williams College consists of unique hardware and software that involve audio signal routing from software application to software application, from software application to hardware output, and from hardware input to software application. Students have historically struggled with these topics even after they are covered in class.

To address this need, a KASH analysis was conducted that consisted of interviews of the professor as well as two students. It was found that written documentation was largely ignored. Students would search out YouTube videos for troubleshooting advice. Students would also go to great lengths to avoid using some software and hardware. For example, one student would record all audio on her iPhone and import the audio into the software rather than learn how to route a microphone input signal into a software application. The most difficult content was clearly working with MIDI data. Also, students struggled with poor computer use habits such as starting projects just before they were due or not properly backing up work. These poor habits may seem irrelevant to technology use, but it does explain why students do not consult with the professor about their difficulties. The students don't know the troubles they will encounter because they haven't started working on their projects yet. Documentation needs to be clear and available even late at night before an assignment due date when students are doing the work.

In the past, the student struggles with basic electronic music concepts were seen as a failure of the documentation. In response, the information was posted in the technology lab in poster format with many images to help make the concepts clear. No needs analysis was conducted. No students were consulted. Posting the information seemed logical, yet the new poster did not seem to change student behavior. Students were just as confused about the concepts after the poster was made as they were before..

The KASH analysis revealed that the documentation was not used because it lacked sufficient visual cues to guide the students through the content. The visually rich software and hardware interfaces with their many buttons and knobs required a more visual medium. It was decided that video and screen capture documentation would better address the needs of students. The videos were distributed to students through the course management system for the class. The instructor often referenced the videos as they became relevant to the student work and projects for the course. An example of the video documentation can be found at http://youtu.be/lDPDjaiF95A.

| Current KASH | Desired KASH |
|---|---|
| **Current Knowledge**<br>• The students had no previous music technology experience, and lacked a strong understanding of computer technology.<br>• The students could not do basic troubleshooting work when audio routing was not working.<br>• One student completely avoided using a microphone and also made no use of MIDI in their composition projects.<br>• The students struggled with MIDI data, the software logic of inputs and outputs, and converting MIDI data into audio. | **Desired Knowledge**<br>• The students will be able to manage the set up of music lab station software and hardware to produce audio.<br>• The students will be able to troubleshoot the music lab station software and hardware by following a procedure if the audio routing is not working.<br>• The students will record audio using a microphone and the external mixer and incorporate that audio in their composition projects.<br>• Students will be able to create MIDI content and convert MIDI to audio. |
| **Current Attitude**<br>• Both students were highly motivated to work with sounds, and took responsibility for their own learning.<br>• Both students said that the Microsoft Word Documents about how to use the software were descriptive, but nevertheless difficult to interpret and not helpful.<br>• One student would search YouTube for videos that might offer help.<br>• One student avoided consulting the teaching assistant or instructor when confronted with difficulty.<br>• Both students were willing to put in whatever amount of time was necessary to be successful in the course. | **Desired Attitude**<br>• The students will be motivated to learn how to use the music lab software and hardware to complete assignments.<br>• The students will have the confidence to use all the software and hardware needed for the course.<br>• The students will seek assistance from the course resources, instructor, or teaching assistant as needed. |
| **Current Skills**<br>• Both students could create electronic composition work within the time constraints of the course.<br>• One student improvised a way of recording audio that used her iPhone rather than the microphone and the mixer.<br>• Both students found some software that they really enjoyed and used sounds from that application extensively in their work.<br>• One student worked exclusively with recorded audio and avoided MIDI entirely in their final composition project. | **Desired Skills**<br>• Students should be able to create audio from all software titles covered in the course and apply them in their electronic music composition projects.<br>• Students should demonstrate their ability to incorporate audio recorded from a microphone and audio created from MIDI data in their compositions. |
| **Current Habits**<br>• One student would quit a composition instead of troubleshooting the problems. As a consequence, she created and threw away four compositions before having one that she submitted as her finished work.<br>• Both students spent a great amount of time working on the projects for this course including the night before assignments were due.<br>• Students seldom restored the computers or backed up their work. Both students lost work that had not been saved. | **Desired Habits**<br>• Students should restore (reimage) computers often.<br>• Students should save and back up their work.<br>• Students should gradually work on compositions a little each day. |

As the course was taught, it was observed that fewer students had difficulties working with the music technology hardware and software. When students did have challenges, they often received help from their peers, the video documentation, and from the teaching assistant for the course who was better able to handle technical questions.

## 4.2 Skipping Over the Needs Analysis
The goal of a needs analysis in the higher education context is to jump directly to a successful implementation on the first try thus saving resources as well as preserving trust with the college community. Here are two examples of failures to conduct a cursory needs analysis.

### 4.2.1 A Simple Video Project

In 2009 a video was created to illustrate for first year students some concepts of sustainability and how to be green. A student was tasked with creating the video and given great freedom over the content. The student understood the goal of the project. Some student workers were asked to stand in as actors.

A video was produced without a needs analysis. No one assessed first year students to see what they knew about sustainability and where their understanding of sustainability at the college fell short. Stakeholders in the various campus systems that are part of sustainability were not involved in the project. In good faith, the student did her best and worked within the parameters she was given. The lack of a needs analysis resulted in a lack of focus for the video. The video was ineffective at addressing the gap in knowledge that first year students have about sustainability because that gap was never described or measured.

The video failed to meet the needs of the project sponsor. It could be that the failure of this project is a failure of communication and also basic project management. Project milestones may have revealed signs that the video was not progressing well. A needs analysis would have helped both student and project sponsor address key needs of the project from the beginning.

### 4.2.2 Implementing a Classroom Polling System

A more spectacular needs analysis failure at Williams College chronicled the first implementation of polling response systems [4]. The needs analysis was limited to the observation that other schools have polling response systems; we should have a polling response system too. Though every effort was made to make the implementation of a polling response system successful, it failed because the hardware and software purchased did not meet the needs of the faculty who used it to teach, or the staff who support and maintain the computer hardware and software in classrooms.

A second effort was made to implement polling technology at Williams College that was informed by the lessons learned by the failure of the first system. Now, polling systems are used with great success.

## 5. NEEDS ANALYSIS AT ALBANY COLLEGE OF PHARMACY AND HEALTH SCIENCES

### 5.1 Needs Analysis Techniques

At Albany College of Pharmacy and Health Sciences, the Office of Instructional Design Services (IDS) undertakes and conducts design and redesign projects by working together with faculty members. One of the responsibilities of the office is to provide pedagogical support to faculty and to promote student-centered active learning by engaging students in the learning process using creative methods and technologies. The office helps faculty on course and learning activity design utilizing sound instructional design principles and practices with strong learner-centered approaches. The office adopted the project-based model in summer 2012 to provide support to teaching and faculty development. Instructional designers of the office reach out to faculty members to find out their support needs, but the faculty members initiate their projects. Although there is no set specific model that the office adopts for needs analysis, the analysis step is never omitted and the project concludes with an evaluation procedure, which in turn serves as analysis stage for the next cycle of the revision of the project.

### 5.2 Needs Analysis Success

Every project starts with a faculty interview meeting. The meeting serves as an analysis of content -the course, end users -learners and instructor(s), and technologies. At the meeting the designers collect as much information about the course/module, the group of students, the instructor(s), and the technologies used as possible. This includes the type of course: require/elective, the time required/allocated of the course, course goals, module objectives, redesign goals, existing materials, and assessment strategies of the course. The student experience and their learning techniques may vary depending on the type of the course: lab course, didactic course, or a professional year course. The instructor may have various teaching styles, teaching philosophies, and various comfort levels of using technology.

There is a project evaluation stage for each project as well. At the end of a project, a full project evaluation involves a student survey, a student focus group interview, faculty interview, and analysis of the students' learning outcomes which consist of analysis of students' test results of the redesigned module. The final course exam results are analyzed as well. The evaluation data is served as part of needs analysis for when the project is revisited or expanded for future redesign.

So far the office conducted a total of 18 projects with a few returning projects for more expansion. The general feedback is positive. Professors who conducted the redesign project felt that they benefit from the project and the process. They accomplished what they planned to achieve with their teaching goals. In addition, they felt that they are more conscious about teaching strategy. The process helped them with their research in teaching. They have also developed their scholarship of teaching via working with instructional designers on the redesign project.

An example of a success story is the institutional IPPE rotation student workbook that was redesigned to an asynchronous interactive discussion board assignment. The workbook used to be paper based and the issue was that students did not use the workbook as part of their rotation experience assignment. The students often left the workbook exercises to the last minute. Faculty did not grade it until the students' rotation was over. If students had any misunderstanding about the workbook questions they left the rotation with the mis-concept still in place since it was not corrected at the time. The workbook questions were not on target to what students must learn. They were not up-to-date either. When the experiential education (EE) faculty came to IDS we sat down to analyze what the issues were with the content of the workbook questions, the process of the assignment, and what the EE faculty would like to accomplish from the redesign. The instructional designers guided the EE faculty to update the workbook questions. We removed all the questions that were not what students must know. Instead, we concentrated on refining the questions to make sure that the workbook questions align with the students' actual practice and experience when they were on site. A rubric was also created to guide the students on completing their workbook. The discussion board also allowed the faculty and students to interact 'real time' when students were on the practice site. If any misunderstanding was found it was corrected immediately. Students were exposed to rotation sites that their group members were at. For example, if a student was in a rural area hospital he/she was able to learn what his/her classmates who were in a metropolitan hospital were up-to each day. This was done through peer interaction. Through EE faculty and student interaction the faculty were able to direct the students to appropriate sources if any errors occurred in the students' responses. The faculty was also able to stimulate students into a deeper discussion about certain topics while the students were on site. The project concluded with a great success. Students responded that the assignment helped them to be more active asking their preceptors questions, and helped them to review and connect the practice to what they've learned in other didactic and lab courses. The preceptors were very happy with the assignment because it stimulated the students to ask questions and actively participate in the practice while on site. The preceptors reported their satisfaction to the faculty via a survey. The faculty were very satisfied because they saw the students' learning outcomes being improved. More students completed the rotation with a great experience.

The project was evaluated with a student survey, preceptor survey, student focus group interview, and a faculty interview. A few suggestions were integrated with the second round of implementation of the project for the summer 2014 student IPPE institutional rotation. An example of feedback integration is that the rubric has some rewording to encourage student interaction rather than critique. The workbook questions were revised as well.

Due to the success of the project the community IPPE rotation was also redesigned based on this model.

## 5.3 Lessons Learned
The feedback that the office received from student focus groups indicated that sometimes there were cases when no needs analysis is in place.

Some instructors added pre-class recordings to "flip their class". Flipping a class is a practice where lecture type materials are presented to students online in the form of video so that class-time can be focused on problem sets or group activities. However, students reported that the recordings tend to be too long. They also felt that the modules added extra information with the pre-class recording in addition to the regular class lecture. This has become a burden to students because they felt overwhelmed by the added content. The students lost focus while viewing the long videos. The students didn't feel that they absorbed the information well either. The office encourages professors to work with instructional designers who help them implement the needs analysis stage to ensure that the redesign project meets the needs of their students and achieve the goal(s) of the professor in terms of their teaching objectives.

## 6. CONCLUSIONS
In conclusion, as you can see from the examples of the two colleges needs analysis is the very first important stage in instructional design processes. It informs stakeholders in the process, i.e. the designers, developers, and media specialists, and subject matter experts of directions, models, and other relevant

activities in the design stages. Yet so many times it might be ignored. The models of needs analysis might be different but the stage should not be omitted. One way to think of needs analysis is that needs analysis is that project work that is done to ensure efficient and effective skill and knowledge transfer. Looking at needs analysis in that light, it becomes apparent how fundamental needs analysis is to the work of instructional technology staff who work with faculty in higher education environments.

## 7. ACKNOWLEDGMENTS
Thanks to Dinny Taylor, Chief Technology Officer of OIT, and Jonathan Leamon, Director of Instructional Technology, who support the author's professional development at Williams College.

Thanks to IDS staff at ACPHS who successfully conducted projects with the project-based model of instructional design support to ACPHS faculty, and to Dr. Ian Douglas under whose vision the project-based model was adopted.

## 8. REFERENCES
[1] Allen, M., Michael Allen's guide to e-learning: building interactive, fun, and effective learning programs for any company. John Wiley & Sones, New Jersey, 2003.

[2] Dick, W., Carey, L., and Carey, J., The systematic design of instruction. 7th ed. Pearson, New Jersey, 2009.

[3] Guglielmino, P. J., and Guglielmino, L. M. Are your learners ready for e-learning? *The AMA Handbook of E-Learning.* AMACOM American Management Association, New York, NY, 2003.

[4] Murphy, T. Success and failure of audience response systems in the classroom. In*Proceedings of the 36th annual ACM SIGUCCS fall conference: moving mountains, blazing trails* (SIGUCCS '08). ACM, New York, NY, USA, 33-38, 2008. DOI=10.1145/1449956.1449969 http://doi.acm.org/10.1145/1449956.1449969

[5] Murphy, T. A tale of 101 digital stories. In *Proceedings of the 35th annual ACM SIGUCCS fall conference* (SIGUCCS '07). ACM, New York, NY, USA, 269-271, 2007. DOI=10.1145/1294046.1294109 http://doi.acm.org/10.1145/1294046.1294109

[6] Murphy, T. Williams instructional technology: summer students working on faculty projects. In *Proceedings of the 35th annual ACM SIGUCCS fall conference* (SIGUCCS '07). ACM, New York, NY, USA, 272-276, 2007. DOI=10.1145/1294046.1294110 http://doi.acm.org/10.1145/1294046.1294110

# Security BYOD – Be Your Own Defense

Cate Lyon
Whitman College
345 Boyer Ave
Walla Walla, WA 99362
1-509-527-5764
lyoncd@whitman.edu

Mike Osterman
Whitman College
345 Boyer Ave
Walla Walla, WA 99362
1-509-527-5419
ostermmg@whitman.edu

## ABSTRACT

How does a small higher education institution implement security controls to protect sensitive data and at the same time not make end users feel as if they are losing ownership of their computer? Whitman College grappled with this problem for several years and finally found a solution where we can (almost) have it all. Using existing technology and one additional vendor solution we are able to realize our goal of a secure computing environment while maintaining a flexible, friendly user environment.

## Categories and Subject Descriptors

K.6.5 [**Management of Computing and Information Systems**]: Security and Protection – *Authentication, Invasive Software Unauthorized Access.*

## General Terms

Security.

## Keywords

Security, Group Policy, AppLocker, Viewfinity

## 1. INTRODUCTION

Whitman is a private, independent, co-educational, non-sectarian residential liberal arts and sciences undergraduate college, founded in 1882. We are located in the southeast corner of Washington State, about 4 hours east of Portland, Oregon. Whitman has an enrolled student body consisting of 1541 students from 42 states, 2 US territories and 25 countries. Whitman College employs approximately 600 staff and faculty, each of whom has at least one institution-provided computer.

## 2. CULTURAL CONTEXT

Until very recently, staff and faculty computers at Whitman College are deployed with the primary operator having local administrative rights. This had been necessary due to the lack of centralized patch management on endpoints, as many applications require administrative rights to update.

A byproduct of this deployment decision is that operators had the ability to install any software of their choosing, often times for personal use. They could also highly customize the look and feel of their workstation essentially making it more their "own".

Given this context, removing administrative rights to secure against malware would be potentially demoralizing for operators.

## 3. IMPETUS FOR CHANGE

Given the cultural context, implementing controls would be both politically and logistically challenging, however several forces contributed to our decision to take on this issue.

## 3.1 PII Loss

Personally Identifiable Information (PII) is broadly defined as "any information about an individual maintained by an agency, including [1] any information that can be used to distinguish or trace an individual's identity, such as name, social security number, date and place of birth, mother's maiden name, or biometric records; and [2] any other information that is linked or linkable to an individual, such as medical, educational, financial, and employment information."[1]

In the Whitman context, we consider PII to be any information that falls under state or federal breach notification laws, such as the Revised Code of Washington[2][3] or HIPAA-HITECH.

Prior to advances in malware that trivialized exfiltration of data, the biggest PII loss was due to a lost or stolen laptop or removable media device.

## 3.2 Zero-Day Vulnerabilities and Drive-By Malware

With the rise of zero-day vulnerabilities and drive-by malware, a tipping point was reached. Our standard tools – desktop antivirus and user education about the risks of opening unexpected attachments and carefully selecting applications – were no longer effective.

Zero-day vulnerabilities are software vulnerabilities that are actively being exploited the same day of (or prior to) their discovery. In this scenario, antivirus vendors do not have enough lead time to identify and ship updated signatures before users are at risk. Antivirus software is designed to block "known bad" programs, a strategy that is ineffective in the face of zero-day threats.

---

[1] http://csrc.nist.gov/publications/nistpubs/800-122/sp800-122.pdf

[2] http://apps.leg.wa.gov/rcw/default.aspx?cite=19.255.010

[3] http://apps.leg.wa.gov/rcw/default.aspx?cite=42.56.590

Drive-by malware differs from previous threats in that it does not necessarily require any interaction to download and execute programs. Because of this, relying on the good judgment of computer operators was no longer a viable option. As drive-by infections frequently occur via syndicated ads on legitimate, mainstream web sites further put our community's data at risk.

## 3.3 Tool Availability and Maturity
Our standard tools were no longer adequate given the risk facing the institution. As we embarked on this project we were able to find software that helps to mitigate most of the problems we were encountering.

## 4. EARLY ATTEMPTS
Prior to finding the "right" solution, we made several attempts at various solutions, all of which had unacceptable limitations for a large-scale deployment.

## 4.1 VM's on Client Machines
One of our first attempts at a solution was to separate sensitive functions to virtual machines (VM's) running on each operator's computer. This allowed for the expected ease of use in the day-to-day environment, while allowing for a more restricted "safe" environment within the virtual machine.

This solution did not function well over time as each virtual machine needed to be patched on a regular basis by IT staff with administrative credentials. Additionally, because the VM "host" (the operator's computer) was still running with administrative rights – malware could be installed and capture potentially sensitive information on the local computer or mapped network drives.

## 4.2 Terminal Services
The next stage consisted of moving sensitive functions to terminal servers. Rather than a completely separate environment that needed patching per computer, this approach allowed for a single point of configuration and system maintenance (i.e. patches) as each terminal used the same underlying operating system.

While this made the system more maintainable, it became apparent that operators needed multiple terminal environments to perform different job functions, quickly adding to the capital and resource cost of this solution. This approach also did not prevent against the risk of keyloggers or exfiltrating malware.

## 4.3 Ad Hoc Local AppLocker Policies Running as User
Acknowledging that the primary computer needs to be protected to prevent against keylogging and exfiltration, the team experimented with Microsoft's application whitelisting software, AppLocker. Introduced in Windows 7, AppLocker is the replacement technology for Software Restriction Policies. Unlike antivirus software which blocks "know bad" programs, application whitelisting maintains a list of "known good" programs and only allows those to be executed.

The second component of this phase involved switching operators to running within the user role rather than as a local administrator. Without this change, leveraging User Account Control (UAC) or performing the "Run As" function on a program would bypass AppLocker as configured. Additionally, if malware were to

bypass AppLocker, this approach would limit the scope of what it could do to the operating system.

These approaches are listed in both the Australian Signals Directorate top 4 security controls[4] and SANS "First Five"[5] (aka "quick wins") as effective security controls to greatly reduce risk.

While this addresses the greatest outstanding risks of the prior attempted solutions, there were two major impediments:

1. As the AppLocker rules were being managed in the local context instead of centrally, updates to the rules had to be done manually on each computer. As we increased the "secure configuration" onto more computers, this resulted in increasingly onerous and complicated administration.

2. Application whitelisting does not take user privileges into account; it only determines whether or not an application is allowed to execute. Many programs require administrative privileges to install updates and some older programs require administrative rights to execute. These limitations required technicians with administrative rights to visit individual computers and perform updates on a regular basis – not an effective use of time and resources. Additionally, we were unable to deploy this solution to any computers that needed to run programs that required administrative rights to execute.

## 5. THE "GOOD ENOUGH" SOLUTION
After much trial and error, we arrived at a solution that met the core requirements of the project: effective malware prevention, ease of deployment and administration, and minimal impact on computer operators.

## 5.1 Technologies
One technology was insufficient to meet the all the project requirements. While Windows 7 provided the foundational application whitelisting technology, we needed additional tools to improve ease of management of AppLocker policies and to overcome the limitations of AppLocker with regard to privilege elevation.

### 5.1.1 AppLocker via Group Policy
Prior to this project, Group Policy had not been utilized extensively by Whitman College to centrally manage workstations. To overcome the shortcomings of locally deployed AppLocker policies, we worked with our network administrators to create specific Organizational Units (OUs) delegated to project leads, allowing us to narrow the scope to computers using the secure configuration. This allowed us to make configuration changes and deploy the policies once. It also simplified the setup of workstations, resulting in quicker deployment of a more complex configuration.

### 5.1.2 Run as User
To reduce the impact of any malware that might bypass other controls, and to prevent system changes that might undermine the

[4] http://www.asd.gov.au/infosec/top35mitigationstrategies.htm

[5] http://www.sans.org/critical-security-controls/guidelines

secure configuration, it was necessary to switch computer operators from the Administrators group to the Users group.

### 5.1.3 Privilege Elevation
In order to allow computer operators to install legitimate software, and, more importantly, patch existing application vulnerabilities, we needed a tool that would allow someone with limited privileges to elevate to an administrative role. We compared 4 products when looking for a privilege elevation solution and decided on software named Viewfinity. This software gives administrative rights to a user so key functions can be performed without running as an administrator.

Viewfinity activates when the user tries to run an application that requires elevated privileges or for the installation of a new device or software, typically the User Access Control (UAC) phase. For software that has been previously approved, an administrative token is granted and the software runs with elevated permissions. For software that has not been approved, the operator is presented with a dialog that asks for information about the device or application. That request is logged in the central console and can then be approved or denied by designated administrators. Additionally, Viewfinity policies are applied whether or not a workstation is connected to the network/domain, a key requirement for those traveling who may not be connected to the VPN.

### 5.1.4 Viewfinity Reloaded

While Viewfinity met the requirement of privilege elevation, we ran into some issues with an early version that impeded our progress and frustrated both operators and IT staff. Primarily, it wasn't consistently functioning as expected, and IT staff went through several iterations of testing and fixing configured policies. Computer operators would not always know whether or not they were going to be able to run a piece of software or if it was going to ask them, yet again, to create a justification request. Additionally, we were unable to create policies based on publisher signature, a capability we had with AppLocker, which resulted in the need to approve every software update as it was released.

Given these limitations, we began to explore alternatives as we found the status quo to be unsustainable and undermined confidence among computer operators.

Soon after we began our search for alternatives, Viewfinity released a new version that resolved all our issues and concerns, and it has been functioning well ever since.

### 5.1.5 Encrypt Mobile Devices

Washington State Law RCW 19.255.010 requires disclosure if any "unencrypted personal information was, or is reasonably believed to have been, acquired by an unauthorized person."[6] While whole disk encryption has been in use for administrative staff laptops at Whitman for several years, it remains a core component of our "secure config".

## 5.2 Implementation
The implementation of our current solution is on-going.

---

[6] http://apps.leg.wa.gov/rcw/default.aspx?cite=19.255.010

### 5.2.1 From Panic to Planning
In the early stages of the project, computers were given the "secure config" after one or more malware incidents. While this helped us identify willing beta testers – those who had experienced an unexpected malware infection and potential loss of PII first-hand – it also created an environment in which we were rushed to deploy in order to get the operator up and running and back to work as quickly as possible.

As the project matured, we reached the point where the technology is stable enough to effectively "sell" the solution as it was intended to function, rather than needing to work out the kinks as we did with our early adopters.

### 5.2.2 Expectation Management
The expectations of both our internal IT staff as well as our end users needed to be managed effectively and travelled different avenues. Our main focus was to remain as transparent and as open as possible when communicating with both parties.

### 5.2.2.1 Language Use
Probably one of the most important things we learned was that the language we used affected the end users attitudes. When installing this solution for our early adopters, we originally referred to it as a "locked down" configuration. This equated to the end user feeling as if they had done something wrong and were subsequently being punished for it, which is antithetical to our goals. To better align our goals with our choice of language, we have since changed to referring to this as "secure configuration" both externally and internally.

### 5.2.2.2 No Rush Jobs
The procedures for computers with secure configuration needed to have specific expectations set – not just for end users but also for IT staff members. The turnaround on computer repair or reallocations for computers with secure configuration needed to be expanded an additional 2 to 3 days. Because of this delay in turnaround, we have created a secure configuration laptop that can be loaned out while a computer is in for repair or reimaging.

### 5.2.2.3 Internal Staff Impact on Operating Procedures
Because of the specialized nature of the software, the domain-specific knowledge used in vetting exception risks, and the need to have various people changing the configuration, the ability for any IT staff member to service a computer with the secure configuration is sometimes limited, requiring assistance from the project team. This has underlined the need for open and frequent communication with internal customers (other IT staff) as well as with computer operators using the secure configuration.

## 5.3 Remaining Challenges
Although we are in a much better situation now, both technically and risk-based, than we were at the beginning of this project, challenges remain.

### 5.3.1 Two Sets of Policies
Both the AppLocker and Viewfinity policies are now sufficiently complete to address the majority of computer operators' needs. Nevertheless, when new applications must be added, it typically involves creating exceptions in both AppLocker and Viewfinity, which is less than ideal. A better solution would be one that addresses both application whitelisting and privilege escalation, and uses a single unified policy set. To date, we have been unable to find such a solution.

### 5.3.2 No Self-Submission for Group Policy Blocks

When an application has not been whitelisted in AppLocker, a generic Group Policy error message is returned to the operator. Unlike Viewfinity, we have no automation to collect these events, nor do we have the contextual information from the operator to help us evaluate the safety of making an exception. We therefore rely on operators alerting us to the block, which often requires inspection of the event logs to identify what was blocked.

### 5.3.3 Classification of Endpoints

While some cases are obvious and straightforward, it's not always clear where the threshold exists that makes an operator a candidate for the secure configuration. It is very important to the goals of the project to not overreach and apply this configuration where it is not warranted, at least not at this stage of the project.

### 5.3.4 What's Safe?

Much like classification of endpoints as candidates for secure configurations, the risk threshold of requested software exceptions is not always clear. It's a delicate balance between avoiding a culture of "No" and creating too much risk.

### 5.3.5 No Centralized Patch Management

One of the primary drivers for the requirement of privilege escalation is the need for computer operators to patch applications. Were we to have central patch management, particularly for third party applications such as Adobe Flash, Oracle Java, and Adobe Reader, we would not be nearly as reliant on privilege escalation technology to meet our goals. Centralized patch management would also save valuable time for computer operators, as they would not need to spend time installing individual updates themselves.

### 5.3.6 Not a Cross Platform Solution

Although many of our administrative staff use PCs, we do have exceptions. This solution only addressees the Microsoft Windows 7 operating system.

## 6. LESSONS LEARNED

### 6.1 Framing is the Key to Success

Setting expectations was our greatest lesson learned. This meant that we had to take into use the feelings of our end users. We needed to frame this solution NOT as "protecting the user from themselves", nor as a "lock down" but rather as a partnership where everyone participates in being good stewards of data.

### 6.2 Avoid Analysis Paralysis

What can you live with? There came a point where we needed to make a decision, even if it wasn't a 100% complete solution. We had a pretty clear idea that we wanted to mitigate risk and be in regulatory compliance. But we also felt very strongly about not making our end users feel as if we were watching/judging them or taking anything away.

### 6.3 Focus on the Endpoints that Matter Most

We have configured some workstations securely because they have been infected often. In these cases, unless they work often with PII, it is at the operator's request. We are limited by licensing and resource allocation and came to the realization that we needed to prioritize which endpoints display the most risk.

### 6.4 Quality of (Work) Life

The primary objective of this project is for every constituent to be good stewards of other people's private information, and giving our staff tools to help us succeed, not to place restrictions on computer operators. We do not see our role as being "Big Brother" or the IT cops. We also do not feel it is necessary to configure these computers so stripped down as to be demoralizing.

While it is necessary to control what applications can be installed on the computers to safeguard people's private information, we place a premium on "quality of (work) life" to offset the necessary diminished access to the configuration of the system. As such, we gladly approve requests for legitimate applications that allow for personalization and those that contribute to a positive working environment, such as Spotify. By doing so, we hope to further convey the values of this project as means of rational protections of personal information rather than a means of exerting control.

## 7. CONCLUSION

At this point, Whitman College is better equipped than at any time in the past able to protect sensitive data. We feel that with the software that we have employed as well as the sensitive manner in which we have deployed it, that we've (almost) got it all.

# Making Sense Out of Information Chaos

Mark Fitzgerald, MBA
OIT Director of Customer Care, Boise State University
1910 University Drive
Boise ID, 83725-1413
01-208-426-4127
markfitzgerald@boisestate.edu

## ABSTRACT

Support centers have been overrun by information. Categorization and cataloging have failed to help us keep up. A new method is required. As we have entered the age of data we need a more human aspect to our training, knowledge management and day to day assessing of knowledge.

This paper discusses practical learning ideas and key ideas such as the Pie Principle, socialization of knowledge and information bubbles.

## Keywords

Searchability; information models; pie principle; information bubbles; knowledge management

## 1. INTRODUCTION

Society is drowning in information and this information overload is growing exponentially year by year. With so much data, we struggle to make sense of it all, resulting in misunderstandings, missing what is important, and slowing down our ability to react. We struggle to differentiate between what is irreplaceable information and what is disposable.

Information problems are not unique to our age. Every society and age has had to cope with various problems of knowledge management. At its core, education is about how a society manages knowledge and passes it along to the next generation. In that way, knowledge management drives our economies and directly affects our lives. As we look to history we can better understand solutions for our current information problems.

## 2. THE AGES OF INFORMATION

Dr. Bill Rankin, director of educational innovation at Abilene Christian University, has researched heavily the impact of technology on information throughout the ages. His premise is that each age has its own information problem and that technology is used to solve that problem. He goes on to express that technologies created to solve one information problem create the problem of the next age. (Rankin, 2011)

He breaks information history into 3 distinct ages:

The Age of Hands
The Age of Books
The Age of Data

According to Rankin, for most of the history of the earth, we were in the Age of Hands. We learned things through word of mouth and used a system of apprenticeship. Knowledge was in the hands of a master and through relationships with this master, it was passed down to apprentices. People had to travel to the information to learn, thus the information problem of the age was access.

Guttenberg created the solution with the printing press. While books existed in the age of hands, they were expensive, hard to duplicate and considered very precious. Small libraries were prized possessions. The technology of the printing press allowed libraries to grow and to be shared. Information now could travel to the people.

What Rankin calls the Age of Books could be more aptly described as the age of machines. Everything in society, including learning, became mechanical and repeatable. Teaching methods changed from apprenticeship to memorization. People were now required to read books, commit the facts to memory and recall them for a test. This was a coping mechanism to the information problem of the day - searchability. Now that people could access information, they had a hard time searching and finding the right bits of information.

Teachers in this age were considered a fountain of knowledge; it was easier to ask someone that had memorized the facts than to search them out yourself. Technologies started to change as well. Society started to classify and categorize information. This can be seen in the Dewey Decimal system, book indexes and early databases. Just as books existed in the Age of Hands, computers existed in the Age of Books. As computers and search engines solved the information problem of searchability, it created the problem of today - assessment.

An internet search engine will yield millions of documents in seconds. As consumers of this information, we need assessment skills and technologies to help us know what to trust and what to apply to our unique situation. An internet meme attributed a quote from Abraham Lincoln which sums this challenge up nicely: "Don't believe everything you read on the internet just because there is a picture with a quote next to it." Assessment skills depend on us learning and teaching models of information rather than memorizing facts and relying on personal experiences.

## 3. INFORMATION MODELS

Information models teach us the semantics of situations and allow us to search more precisely in order to find credible and applicable information. It was not long ago that an IT support organizations would request one of every type of device they were expected to support. As the number of devices grew making it difficult if not impossible to obtain one of every type, there was a call for standardization, categorization and classification. Despite the call, devices became ever more numerous and fragmented.

A quick poll in my office yielded interesting, yet not surprising results. I went around cubicle to cubicle holding out my phone asking, "What was I holding."

Answers ranged from an Android, to "Not an iPhone", to a Nexus, to "a cell", to "a brick." No one said I was holding a smartphone. But what term would most IT support systems use to describe this piece of equipment? Hence, searching for knowledge and the use of correct terminology proves the difficulty in finding common language when searching for knowledge.

Support organizations had to find other ways to keep up with the expectation to support these devices. People learned patterns of how devices worked. Models were built on how to support cell phones in general rather than specific phones. The models taught us how to use common languages to search for features and issues and how to apply them to the unique devices you were dealing with. Finding common language has proved to be difficult.

Proof that categorization fails with fragmentation can be seen in the Android cell phone market. In July 2013, Open Signal reported that they had seen 11,868 distinct types of devices running Android each with their own distinct software versions, hardware features and performance issues. There are potentially more options for categorization than the support organization user base (Open Signal, 2013).

## 4. POINT OF VIEW

The Pie Principle, by Brian Fitzgerald, also illustrates the breakdown of categorization and classification. The Pie Principle asks does 1 pie + 1 pie = 2 pies or 12 slices? Depending on how you see the world, 1+1 can equal 12. You could have 2 people argue about the answer of 1+1, but the truth of the matter is that they

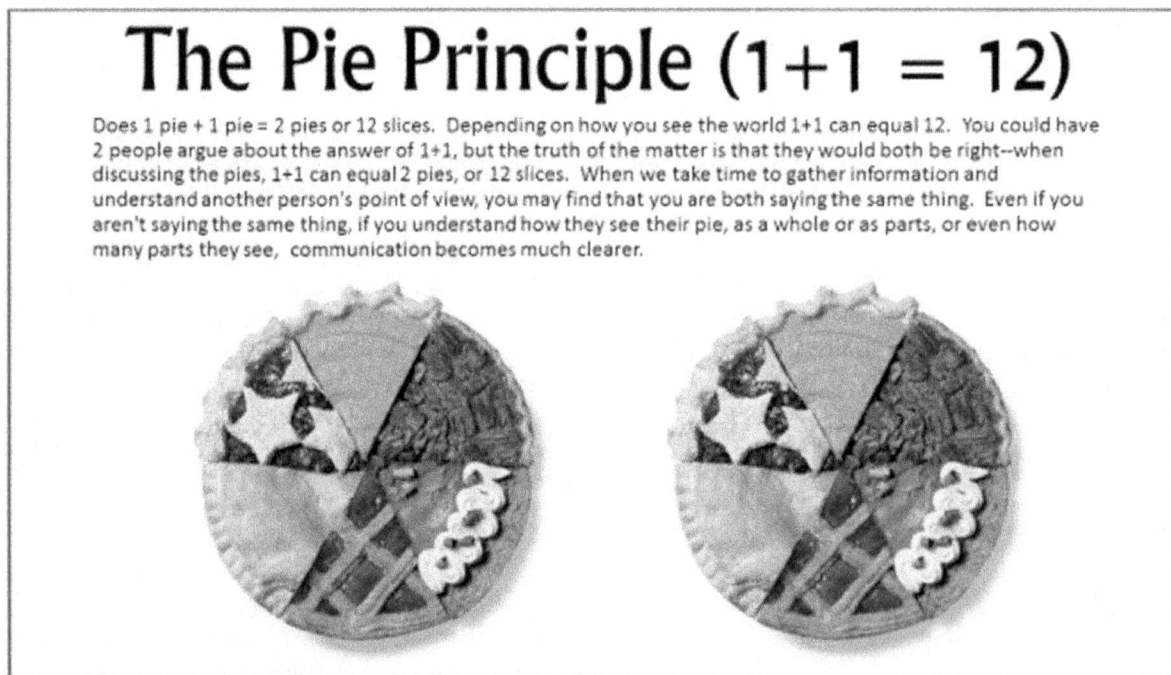

# The Pie Principle (1+1 = 12)

Does 1 pie + 1 pie = 2 pies or 12 slices. Depending on how you see the world 1+1 can equal 12. You could have 2 people argue about the answer of 1+1, but the truth of the matter is that they would both be right--when discussing the pies, 1+1 can equal 2 pies, or 12 slices. When we take time to gather information and understand another person's point of view, you may find that you are both saying the same thing. Even if you aren't saying the same thing, if you understand how they see their pie, as a whole or as parts, or even how many parts they see, communication becomes much clearer.

*Figure 1©Brian Fitzgerald*

would both be right--when discussing the pies, 1+1 can equal 2 pies, or 12 slices. The point is that it is completely dependent on your point of view (Fitzgerald, 2013).

With massive amounts of information, point of view completely reveals or obscures the data you are looking for. Information models aid by shaping points of view into a common vocabulary. Some would term this the semantic web. This is the concept of using defined libraries of information to limit or scope searching (Wikipedia, 2014).

Leaders in the IT industry need to better understand the concepts of information models and work to teach them to knowledge workers. Information is highly fragmented and very individualized, but as we mature our organizations often increase the amount of time spent working with collaborative teams. Helping individuals select models and use them in the proper context will lead teams to be more efficient and work together better.

# 5. RELATIONSHIPS WITH INFORMATION

Even with information models, we struggle to keep up. It is human nature to begin to compartmentalize information. Eli Pariser in his 2011 book coined the phrase "filter bubble." He explains that by personalizing our searching we are narrowing our world view (Pariser, 2012). We begin to search for information only from people we trust and agree with. If there is one thing that becomes clear, it is that credibility comes from relationships.

One can view this filtering as a good or a bad thing, but these filters are based on an element of trust. Those around us influence us positively or negatively. Family, friends, managers, subordinates, civic groups and the media all shape our opinions. We begin to trust those we have had positive experience with and distrust those with negative experiences. In the future we are presented information from those sources, we judge the value of the information based on that trust.

Search and information providers are using that personal relation to project confidence in the data being provided. Look to a Google search for examples. You will see the name of the author and perhaps a picture in the search return. It will associate the author with other works or bodies of knowledge they may be associated with. Based on social media, it will return searches more relevant to your personal circles (Raphael, 2013).

In absence of a personal connection, voting systems have been used. This can be seen with stars, reviews, likes or view counts. The theory behind this is that if no one you associate with has experience with the information you seek, at least you can trust the masses. This works with opinions, such as the quality of a restaurant. It can also work with facts that can be publicly

verified. It breaks down when it is the assessment of research.

For example the American Library Association (ALA) has been quoted many times on the Internet as saying that "By 2020 information on the internet will double every 15 minutes." While I believe this concept to be true, I would like to understand the premise better. Is this a reference to file size, the amount of articles or number of users of the internet? In searching for this quote, I have yet to find the original source. I have not found this quote anywhere on the ALA's website nor in any bibliography. I am left asking, what research did they use to draw this conclusion, who really said it, was is actually the ALA or another source and what problems am I creating by perpetuating this quote?

By knowing original sources we can find out more about their credibility. By expanding our own relationships we can discuss and understand how people have come to conclusions and how they have assessed the data. Personal relationships bring us trust and common understanding because we understand the characteristics of an individual, word choice and past background.

# 6. CHANGING THE KNOWLEDGE BASE

There are direct correlations to be learned when one applies this to knowledge management. Managers that implement knowledge bases need to evaluate how social their tools are. These small visual cues can lead to much higher and greater confidence in the data.

- Does the tool you use display the author of the article and their picture?
- Can the end user turn around and rate the data and provide comments?
- Is it open to the entire organization to produce knowledge?
- Are the most used articles floating to the top of the search?
- Is information being searched by common organizations being analyzed and used in the search algorithms?

Knowing how to use a computer is not limited to IT employees and there are many benefits in building a knowledge support structure throughout your organization. Comments and contributions from the organization helps IT produce better data but also gives other consumers information to relate and helps to build a knowledge base that is closer aligned to the needs of the business.

# 7. CONCLUSION

When contemplating information chaos there is far more to think about than just knowledge bases. After all, these are just stores of information. Returning to Bill

Rankin, his contention is that a teacher simply providing information rather than teaching someone to assess information may be causing more harm than good. Part of teaching people the skills of how to assess, is teaching them to think for themselves. We need to be constantly learning, searching and growing as we teach those around us to do the same.

When sharing information, our most basic measures of categorization more often than not hide information. We need to learn how use to use information models to document and share. Like a key unlocking access to a building, using the right model will fully unlock and explain our information in a manner much quicker and deeper than simple classification and categorization.

Many only trust in the masses to assess data and with certain types of information this can easily lead them to be fooled or miss important explanatory details. Relationships help us find and trust information quickly but are limited to the scope of experience of our peer groups. To combat this we need to expand our relationships, seek for understanding of more information models and libraries.

Assessment truly is the information problem of our day. What are you doing to help your organization overcome this problem?

## REFERENCES

[1] Fitzgerald, B. (2013, May 23). The Pie Principle. (A. Fitzgerald, Interviewer)

[2] Open Signal. (2013, July). Android Fragmentation Visualized. Retrieved from opensignal.com: http://opensignal.com/reports/fragmentation-2013/

[3] Pariser, E. (2012, March 26). Retrieved from The Filter Bubble: http://www.thefilterbubble.com/

[4] Rankin, D. B. (2011, January 1). Mobile Learning at ACU: Full Presentation. Abilene, Texas, United State of America: ACU.

[5] Raphael, J. (2013, August 20). Getting around Google+: Expand your circles -- and your influence. Retrieved from computerworld.com: http://www.computerworld.com/s/article/9241653/Getting_around_Google_Expand_your_circles_and_your_influence

[6] Wikipedia. (2014, May 2). Semantic Web. Retrieved from Wikipedia: http://en.wikipedia.org/wiki/Semantic_Web

# Digital Orientation for New Students: Hiding the Tech Behind the Fun...

Phinehas Bynum
St. Olaf College
1510 St. Olaf Avenue
Northfield, Minnesota 55057
+1 507 786 3840
bynum@stolaf.edu

## ABSTRACT

An IT-attended move-in experience offers the opportunity not only to provide technical assistance, but also to introduce every new student to the services and resources provided by IT. Arming students with this knowledge lays the groundwork for a rich and positive academic computing experience. However, it is difficult to pique interest with talk of academic technology, device configuration and digital security. Applying game-based learning can make engaging with academic tools, setting up a computer, and learning the campus IT rules more interesting and maybe even fun. Moreover, existing tools can be used in new ways to efficiently accelerate IT outcomes. Examples include using a survey to gather statistics about incoming client devices, creating a virtual hunt for the Helpdesk in Google Maps Engine, and using a "what you and your roommate(s) are bringing to campus" Google Document to show the power of collaborative editing. Organized in an LMS like Moodle with badges and incentives, these disparate elements become a social organism that encourages participation, educates incoming students, and offsets the week one IT rush. With the ever growing technological needs of college campuses and the comparative shortage of IT time, perhaps drawing from learning paradigms like game theory can help up maximize what time we do have.

## Categories and Subject Descriptors

A.m [**MISCELLANEOUS**]: The ACM Computing Classification Scheme: http://www.acm.org/class/1998/

## Keywords

Gamification, Helpdesk, Orientation

## 1. INTRODUCTION

St. Olaf College piloted an IT new student orientation in 2014 for incoming students using a combination of game-based learning and IT student work. This effort, though not without its hurdles, was well received and achieved positive outcomes.

IT orientation can help students discover campus resources, learn how to connect to campus services and reduce onboarding confusion and frustration.

IT orientation can help IT initiate a positive first interaction,

*SIGUCCS '14*, November 2–7, 2014, Salt Lake City, UT, USA.
Copyright 2014 ACM 978-1-4503-2780-0/14/11…$15.00.
http://dx.doi.org/10.1145/2661172.2661187

increase visibility, and provide proactive support while saving time in the future.

## 2. PLANNING

The team was formed; a Helpdesk Manager, an Instructional Technologist, a Web Developer, and a Systems Programmer. Our goals: provide information critical to getting connected to campus resources, show students where and how to get help, and offset the week one Helpdesk rush.

After a period of brainstorming with colleagues, student workers, and IT counterparts at other institutions, we settled on implementing four items that would have the greatest impact in terms of providing support, increasing visibility, and engaging the incoming student body. They were: a responsive IT Intro webpage, an international student IT session, a digital scavenger hunt, and student-run dorm sweeps. Each of these events would hopefully address an aspect of orientation week that would normally consume a great deal of IT staff time at the beginning of the year.

## 3. DESIGN CONSIDERATIONS

New ventures can place extra pressure on fulfilling existing responsibilities, particularly during the brief summer that serves as preparation for an upcoming school year. Therefore, every minute of time spent on this orientation was designed to save time in the future, and all work done was designed to incorporate as many pre-existing resources as possible. Furthermore, work with maximal impact was completed before attention was given to less important items. These considerations would ensure that we achieved the most bang for our buck. For example, the first content creation session was spent crafting a web-friendly week one IT logo to brand all of our output. The logo was reused on posters, T-shirts for student workers, web buttons, and documentation and contributed to the cohesion and visibility of the entire project. Another high-impact step performed near the beginning of the project was reaching out to other departments involved in the student orientation process in order to coordinate and collaborate, preventing overlapping programming and learning from groups with a depth of experience in the new student orientation process. Notable groups contacted included ResLife, Admissions, the Bookstore and the office of International Student Affairs.

Coordinating with these four offices gave us the opportunity to include our event calendar to in the week-one student handbook and gave us insight into planning our event lineup. We also worked with these departments to coordinate communication with the incoming students and reuse already-open lines of communication instead of creating new ones for IT.

## 4. IT INTRO PAGE

The IT Intro page was one of the items produced that continues to be helpful every day at the Helpdesk. At its core, it is simply a list of links to existing documentation, facts about IT services, and the various avenues to get IT help. Although any IT landing page contains similar links to documentation, crafting a "getting started" document to house the most often requested links was incredibly helpful and made directing clients to relevant documentation both over the phone and accessing it in person simple. Special attention was given to make the page responsive and mobile-friendly, so it could easily be accessed from portable devices while troubleshooting and connecting consoles and other devices to our network services.

## 5. INTERNATIONAL STUDENT SESSION

The Internet is the typical college student's primary form of communication with friends and relatives, and that goes double for international students. Also, from a purely logistical standpoint, devices configured in other languages with unfamiliar software installed often take extra troubleshooting to connect to campus services. Holding a dedicated IT orientation and connection session for incoming international students is a good way to introduce them to campus services, get them connected on their first day on campus, and offset the inevitable "trouble laptop" that might hold up the Helpdesk during a rush. In coordination with Instructional Technology, we gave a brief talk about academic tools used on campus and followed up with a configuration session to get everyone connected to campus wireless, printers, and network storage, and left them with information about getting further help and advice.

## 6. MOODLE SCAVENGER HUNT

Moodle was an ideal teaching tool to organize our digital orientation hunt as it is used by nearly 70% of professors on campus and contains tools for enrolling students and tracking activity completion. Conveniently, it also allows conditional logic that facilitates the creation of a game-like course. Our design considerations led us to create scavenger hunt "challenges" that used a social or school-related concept to promote the educational tool used to create the activity. For example, one summer student worker used Google Maps Engine to create an interactive campus map with annotated pins and embedded links to the Street View of each dorm, and a Moodle quiz was used to track completion. Another created a Google Document template formatted to coordinate what items to bring to campus with your roommate. Technical skills silently addressed in the Moodle Scavenger Hunt included:

- Authenticating using school credentials on multiple systems.
- Downloading and uploading files from and to Moodle.
- Navigating, searching, and using online IT resources.
- Taking an online, timed test and filling out a survey.

Moodle's built in messaging system was used to communicate information about the other IT events to all new students and was a convenient way to remind students about our in-person analogue to digital orientation: the dorm sweeps.

## 7. DORM SWEEPS

The physical extension of the digital orientation was a student-run dorm sweep in which IT students visited every first-year dorm on the first night of classes and helped students troubleshoot and configure their devices. Given that we had approximately 25 student workers, about 800 new students, and only 5 hours allocated (5 PM to 10 PM) to complete the sweep, efficiency was critical to the success of this venture. To that effect, a number of technologies were leveraged to simplify the challenge.

First and foremost, we printed flyers with information about IT, instructions for connecting to the wireless and wired networks, and URLs to other important documentation. These flyers were hung on every doorknob on move-in day. At the bottom of each flyer was printed, "Want help getting connected? Leave this flyer on your door and we'll drop by!" along with details about the date and time of the dorm sweeps. The advantage of the flyers was threefold; clients who most wanted help could be prioritized before we made general rounds through the building, every student was exposed to IT documentation and the most important configuration steps, and the path to get more help was made very clear.

For the event proper, configuration scripts (mostly shell script) for the most common Helpdesk operations were developed and bundled over the summer for Mac OS X, Windows 7 and Windows 8. These included installers for the campus printing system (Papercut), troubleshooting utilities such as a DNS reset tool and a wireless setup utility, and scripts to mount network drives. Scripts were copied to 128MB flash drives (an ideal size for scripts and cost effective) and one drive was given to each student. On average, time saved was nearly 15 minutes per laptop, and without this level of automation, the dorm sweeps would have been impossible to complete in one evening. The scripts will continue to save time at the Helpdesk over the course of the year.

Finally, our Instructional Technology team lent us one classroom set of iPads to facilitate communication and manage the logistics throughout the event. Using a list of all new students and room numbers from ResLife, a master Google document was created to track visits to every room and shared with every student on the Google Drive iPad app. An Apple ID was created for each iPad and each student could video call one of the three full-time staff stationed at the Helpdesk for advice throughout the evening. Moreover, each student worker could pull up relevant documentation if so needed while out in the field.

## 8. OUTCOMES

Every incoming student was given the opportunity to get help getting connected, and many did want and receive it. IT visibility to new students was greatly improved, and nearly a quarter of new students completed the scavenger hunt. Approximately 10% of incoming students left their flyers on their doors to request help, but more than twice that number were actually helped during the dorm sweeps. Our greatest hurdle was that there is no way to be fully prepared for the idiosyncrasies of every personal computing device and there were a few instances in which we had to refer students to more in-depth help at the Helpdesk, but this is one of the inevitabilities of supporting a wide range of personal devices. However, we needed no extra staff to keep the Helpdesk afloat during week one this year, and we now have a number of resources in the scripts and the IT Intro page that facilitate faster service at the Helpdesk and will continue to evolve and improve.

# Nurturing a Culture of Collaboration

Kristen Dietiker
University of Washington
Box 356410
Seattle, WA 98195
(206) 616-9066

dietiker@uw.edu

## ABSTRACT

In 2012, the Department of Surgery at the University of Washington implemented Atlassian's Confluence wiki product as a department intranet and collaboration space. Use of the product among various workgroups has grown organically and has contributed to improved information sharing and knowledge management. This paper will discuss the department needs and the issues that led to the adoption of Confluence; a brief technical overview of the architecture and design; the rollout process, including communication and training; and an examination of lessons learned and ideas for how our rollout could have been improved. Additionally, tips for increasing team collaboration and knowledge management, regardless of the system or application chosen, will be discussed.

## Categories and Subject Descriptors

K.4.3 [**Organizational Impacts**]: Computer-supported Collaborative Work. K.6.3 [**Software Management**]: Software Selection.

## General Terms

Design, Documentation, Management.

## Keywords

Collaboration; Knowledge Management; Knowledge Transfer; Intranet; Wiki; Atlassian; Confluence

# 1. INTRODUCTION

## 1.1 Organizational Overview

The Department of Surgery is an academic department in the University of Washington's (UW) School of Medicine, and employs over 400 faculty, staff, researchers, and affiliated clinicians across several locations and at multiple affiliated institutions. Research, Education, and Clinical Care are the three primary foci of the department. While the department is an academic unit, it is under the umbrella of "UW Medicine" and thus has strict data security requirements that govern the use of all departmental computing resources.

## 1.2 Information Technology Overview

The Department of Surgery's IT infrastructure is maintained by a team of eight employees within the "Surgery IT" unit. This team manages the network, domain, server, and workstation environment for other department personnel. The environment is a heterogeneous mix of different operating systems, software applications, and other technologies primarily determined by employee desire and role requirements (for example, a clinical or research role typically determines need for specific hardware and software). This environment has roughly a 75% Windows 7 to 25% Macintosh split, with most Windows 7 computers configured with older versions of Microsoft's Internet Explorer to maintain compatibility with certain UW Medical Center applications.

There are multiple campus IT groups that also provide services to the department; the primary ones are UW-IT and UW Medicine Information Technology Services (UWMITS). UW-IT is the central university technology unit and provides network infrastructure and core IT services such as email, HR, and financial applications to the entire campus. They also provide both Google and Microsoft Office 365 cloud services to the campus, although UW Medicine employees, including Department of Surgery employees, cannot use the campus Google cloud offering because of the lack of HIPAA compliance. UWMITS provides the medical centers, School of Medicine, and other affiliate groups with clinical applications such as electronic medical records, and also manages the computing infrastructure in the medical centers. The Surgery IT team works with the range of IT services and groups on campus to provide a single point of contact for department employees.

# 2. PROJECT IMPETUS

## 2.1 Background

The Department of Surgery had maintained a department-wide intranet web site for over 10 years. It had gone through many different "owners" and content editors over the years, and thus was a hodgepodge of disjointed page structure and content. Typical end-user complaints about this intranet revolved around the existence of outdated and conflicting information; the lack of an integrated search function, and the lack of a Content Management System (CMS), requiring knowledge of HTML to edit or add pages. In addition, the intranet was designed to present the "common denominator" content most useful for administrative staff. Specific content and functionality useful for research scientists or faculty was not included, nor were guidelines and procedures for specific workgroups.

Meanwhile, the Surgery IT Services Group maintained their own documentation, guidelines, and procedures specific to internal workflows. This documentation was typically created and stored in various Microsoft Word documents on a Windows fileshare. Like the department intranet, it was cumbersome, had outdated and conflicting information, and was difficult to search.

## 2.2 Initial Efforts

In 2012, the author, who serves as the Manager of Department Computing for the Department of Surgery, began formulating a plan to improve internal team documentation and collaboration. The author had familiarity with wikis in general as well as with Atlassian Confluence, which was already in use by UW-IT for systems documentation and project planning. The cost of a 10-user license, more than adequate to cover all of Surgery IT, was inexpensive enough to determine that it would be easy and relatively cheap to implement within the existing budget cycle. The author downloaded a trial, set up a test Confluence server on a unique Windows 2008 R2 Server on the department VMware cluster, and imported a few sample documents as a proof of concept. This was done within a day.

Also underway at the same time was an ongoing project to convert the department intranet into a CMS, with the goal of providing a better user experience by allowing easier content editing, streamlining and updating the content, and providing a search function. Several CMSes had been considered, with WordPress determined to be the easiest and quickest to implement, and suited for the task. An initial "sandbox" site had been set up to test the environment, determine content migration strategies, and test design and template ideas for the content. The author was responsible for setting up the WordPress environment in the UW-IT hosted server cluster and configuring it with accounts for the content management team to begin their work migrating content. This content migration had been in process for several months at the time of Surgery IT's initial Confluence Wiki trial.

## 2.3 Turning Point

The Surgery IT group was encouraged by the initial results of testing the Confluence wiki environment and planned to go forward with purchasing a 10-user license. In fact, the trial run was so successful that the team immediately envisioned the tool would be useful and applicable to others in the department.

The author presented a short demo of the Confluence tool to the department's administrative leadership team and advocated that the wiki would be a better option for a departmental intranet than WordPress because of the ability to create workgroup-specific spaces to hold collaborative content, which was beyond the scope of the then-current department intranet. For example, research labs could maintain a space for their unique procedures, lab protocols, and other content not relevant to the department at large; while committees could create and share agendas and notes among committee members. In addition, the product was cross-platform and worked flawlessly on Macintoshes and had an identical feature set between Mac and Windows platforms, unlike other workgroup collaboration tools such as Microsoft Sharepoint. This final point had been a stumbling block in previous discussions to replace the department intranet with Sharepoint.

The department determined that the wiki option was superior to the original CMS plan for reasons beyond the ability to provide custom spaces to labs, administrative units, committees, and

more. The strong search feature was well liked, the intuitive editing interface was easy to use, and the ability to add Word or PDF documents as attachments to wiki pages made Confluence more attractive than the original WordPress plan. The WordPress installation was abandoned, and resources were focused on Confluence instead. A 500-user license of Confluence was purchased, enough to cover the entire department.

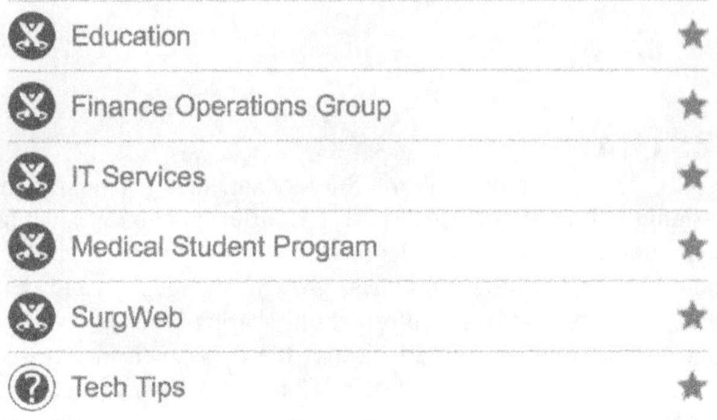

**Figure 1: Partial List of Available Spaces**

## 3. PROJECT ROLLOUT

### 3.1 Architecture

The decision to adopt Confluence occurred quickly, and a project plan was developed by Surgery IT for internal use, as the implementation requirements were primarily determined by a small subset of the IT team. Several questions needed to be answered before the wiki could be configured for production use. Chief among these was the authentication mechanism. Confluence has an internal directory for user accounts, but it can also connect to Active Directory and LDAP directories. The department maintains its own Active Directory domain, so this was a strong option. However, the previous web-based intranet leveraged the campus-wide NetID authentication scheme. Leveraging NetID for this Confluence installation was desirable because several department research groups collaborate with external users in other departments. Leveraging NetID authentication would allow Surgery IT to easily configure lab wiki spaces to permit access by specified non-departmental users elsewhere in the University of Washington system.

UW-IT's Confluence installation uses Shibboleth to leverage NetID, so Surgery IT originally tried to duplicate this scenario for the departmental Confluence installation. However, we ran into problems, such as a lack of documentation on how UW-IT's Confluence system was customized to support this, a lack of familiarity with Shibboleth within Surgery IT, and a major difference in Confluence versions between the UW-IT installation and the departmental installation. This meant the basic guidance that UW-IT was able to provide did not work for this project.

After several weeks of trying to work through these problems, Surgery IT determined that leveraging the department's Active Directory was a better course of action. Expediency was the primary driver of this decision, but the fact that it would be easier to maintain in the future was also important. As for the ability to permit users from elsewhere on campus to access our wiki, it was decided that the number of people this would cover was sufficiently small enough that manually adding accounts to the

Confluence internal directory when needed was a workable solution.

Once the decision was made to use Active Directory, the new wiki server was ready soon after. Two spaces were immediately created; the first, for the Surgery IT team, to host internal documentation and procedures, and the second one to serve as the department-wide space for intranet use. This second space was created with the name "SurgWeb", to mimic the name of the old intranet that it would replace. The idea behind the naming was to make it more obvious and intuitive for a new wiki user to find the space and the documentation they were looking for. Finally, user groups were set up and the intranet content team started migrating content to this new space.

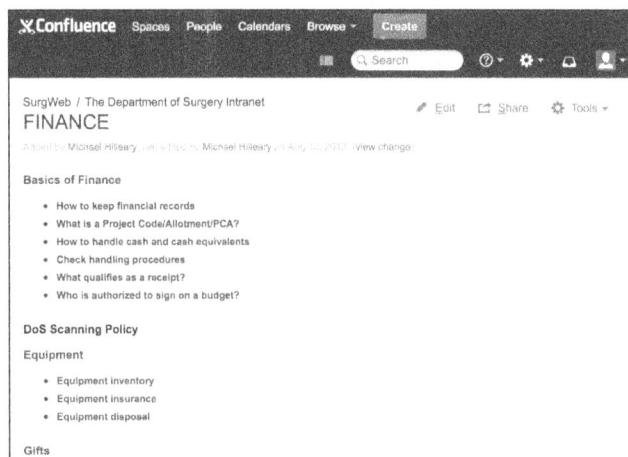

**Figure 2: Sample Page from SurgWeb Space**

One question that came up early was whether to allow all department users to edit the new SurgWeb space. One argument for this was that mistakes and changes could be quickly identified and fixed as knowledgeable staff viewed content. Another argument in favor of staff editing capabilities was that by distributing the ability to edit the intranet, it reinforced the concept that it was a shared responsibility to contribute knowledge, share best practices, and help other department personnel. The main argument against allowing all department employees the ability to edit the SurgWeb space was that the content was primarily specialized (Human Resources, Finance, and Information Technology) and that managers in these respective areas needed to curate the content. There was a fear among some decision-makers that by allowing other staff to edit these pages, mistakes could be introduced. A compromise solution was adopted, where all department personnel could comment on any SurgWeb space page, but only a handful of content owners could edit the page content within that space.

## 3.2  User Training and Education

While the intranet content team was busy migrating and revising content for the wiki, two members of Surgery IT and one member of the intranet content team participated in some advanced training provided by Atlassian. The idea behind this was that these three individuals would be able to provide additional, high level support to other departmental users in a "train the trainer" model. That being said, it was recognized early on that hands-on, in-person training on how to access and use all the features of the wiki could not feasibly be provided to every member of the department since it does not have dedicated training staff or

spaces, and Surgery IT did not have the resources to provide 30 or 60 minute training sessions for over 400 users. However, it was believed that the majority of department personnel would be able to navigate and search for content with no training, and units and labs that wanted unique spaces could request training tailored to their workgroup. In addition to this, some high level demonstrations, links to the new wiki, announcements, and articles were provided to department employees in a number of ways, including at faculty and staff meetings, in newsletters, email announcements, and through the department manager's group. This "soft rollout" provided some breathing space to the content team and Surgery IT.

## 3.3  Soft Rollout

The author also advocated for the organic, bottom-up growth of the wiki, rather than a top-down approach where users and workgroups were forcibly moved to new a new documentation platform and procedure for all their work. The basis for this reasoning came from the book "Wikipatterns" by Stewart Mader [1].

By moving the then-current intranet content to the new wiki platform, it would help department users consuming that information "get their feet wet" with the new platform. It was believed that those users who were more comfortable with change and the new abilities would naturally reach out and inquire about getting additional wiki spaces for their personal or workgroup use.

## 4.  WIKI USE AND COLLABORATION

### 4.1  Expectations

One of the hopes leading into this project was for increased collaboration and knowledge sharing between department personnel. By providing up to date content, and then making it easy for end-users to keep that content current, the department hoped that staff would see the wiki as a place they could add helpful tips, corrections, new findings, and best practices to share with other department personnel. There was a desire to capture and refine this knowledge, and build a knowledge base that helped staff and improved efficiencies. In addition, it was expected that as staff began using the wiki to access the intranet space, there would be increased desire for additional spaces to accommodate the specific needs of research labs, workgroups, and committees. This would improve knowledge retention within those groups. Finally, as demand for more wiki spaces grew organically, use of the wiki as "the place to go" for daily needs would increase.

### 4.2  Findings

In actuality, knowledge sharing between staff has indeed increased by using the wiki as a platform for collaboration. However, this is primarily achieved within individual workgroups and not across the department at large. Because the SurgWeb space is configured to only allow a handful of people to edit pages, sharing of tips and best practices in department wide matters such as Human Resources and Purchasing is artificially constrained. That being said, the number of wiki spaces has increased as expected. And, as workgroups get their own spaces, collaboration within those workgroups has improved somewhat.

**Most popular spaces (Views)**

1. SurgWeb (724)
2. Education (332)
3. IT Services (266)
4. Tech Tips (212)
5. Finance Operations Group (133)
6. Medical Student Program (124)
7. GSD (69)
8. HMC Staff Page (34)
9. ISIS (22)
10. Cuschieri Research (20)

**Most active spaces (Edits)**

1. Education (80)
2. IT Services (58)
3. SurgWeb (53)
4. Tech Tips (26)
5. Finance Operations Group (9)
6. Research (7)
7. HMC Staff Page (5)
8. Cuschieri Research (5)
9. GSD (4)
10. Gibran Lab (3)

**Figure 3: Space Views and Edits, January 2014**

However, the majority of wiki use is still consumption of information, such as reading news and instructions. For example, in January 2014 the top three viewed spaces had a combined 1,322 page views, while only 191 comments, contributions or changes were recorded [Figure 3]. While the difference between page and space views and edits appears to be vast, they seem to track together; when a page gets edited, views of that page increase over the next couple of days [Figure 4]. This indicates an interest on the part of staff to learn new information and keep current.

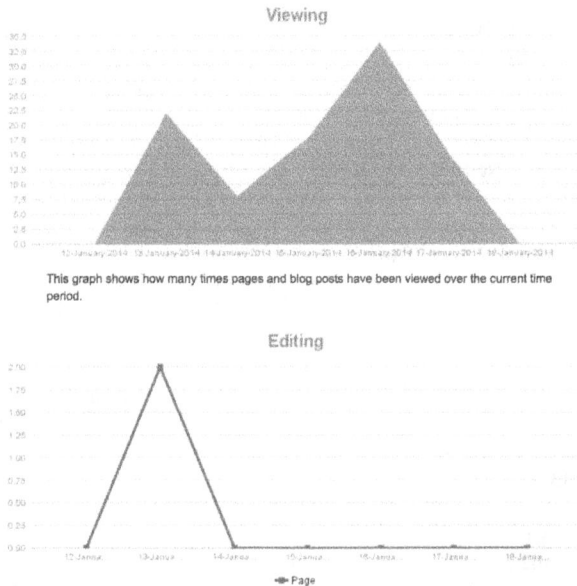

Viewing

This graph shows how many times pages and blog posts have been viewed over the current time period.

Editing

**Figure 4: Increased Page Views Following Edits**

### 4.3 Future Plans

There has been much discussion within the department on how to best utilize the potential of the wiki. As of this writing, a tool is being developed to survey department staff on their opinions and ideas for the wiki. The results of this survey will be used to plot future directions, including whether additional outreach and training is needed. Other changes that have been suggested include rebranding the wiki and renaming the SurgWeb space.

## 5. CONCLUSION

After almost two years of use, the adoption of a wiki platform for our department intranet is seen as both a success and an opportunity for improving departmental collaboration. It seems clear that the correct tool was chosen to support this collaboration short term, as already we have seen uses that would not be possible had we adopted WordPress for our intranet. However, after seeing the benefits of improved collaboration within various workgroups, we are dedicated more than ever to the goal of improving collaboration across the department at large. Our next steps are to examine opportunities to refine and tweak our Confluence configuration to support this goal.

## 6. REFERENCES

[1] Mader, Stewart. Wikipatterns. 2008 Wiley Publishing Inc., Indianapolis IN.

[2] Madox, Sarah. Confluence, Tech Comm, and Chocolate. 2012 XML Press, Laguna Hills, CA.

# Riding the iOS Rollercoaster: Design, Implementation, Circulation and Support of iPads at Penn State Libraries

Alexa Spigelmyer
Penn State University
E1 Paterno Library
University Park, PA 16802
(814) 863-7098
Ajs44@psu.edu

Jeffrey Shawver
Penn State University
E3 Paterno Library
University Park, PA 16802
Telephone number, incl. country code
Jms24@psu.edu

## ABSTRACT

The circulation of iPads is a goal for many universities and colleges as they emerge as a major player in tablet technology. Unfortunately, there is very little research or documentation available to technical specialists trying to provide this service. There are a variety of tools available and each tool has its own nuances and challenges.

Penn State has been circulating iPads for two years, and has developed many successful processes along the way. This presentation will cover the project from design to implementation as well as the shift from build to maintenance as the project has matured.

## Categories and Subject Descriptors

C.5.3 [Computer System Implementation]: Microcomputers–Microprocessors, Personal Computers, Portable Devices, Workstation

## General Terms

Management, Documentation, Design, Standardization

## Keywords

iPad; Configurator; Circulation; Apple; Supervision; Mobile Device Management

## 1. INTRODUCTION

iPads have created quite a stir since their introduction in April of 2010. Many universities have been scrambling to figure out if and how to manage the growing demand for these devices for both students and faculty/staff.

At Penn State Libraries we provide iPads to our faculty and staff, and are currently circulating over 300 iPads to students and staff in campuses all across Pennsylvania.

## 2. Project Scope

Before choosing a product to manage your iPads, it is important to first determine the scope of your management. Some prefer a

more hands on approach, keeping updates and accounts central. Others may decide a less structured form of management is the best choice. At Penn state we use a variety of solutions, all tailored for the location or use.

## 3. Management Tools

Although there are a variety of management tools available, there are three different groupings that all of the Penn State Libraries iPads fall into. The choice for which management tool to use involves a variety of factors, but the most important are the number of iPads to be circulated, frequency of ownership change, and the technical expertise of the staff supporting the devices.

### 3.1 Configurator

For our most robust implementations of student circulation, we decided on Apple Configurator. Apple Configurator is Mac only software that has been released for free by Apple through the app store. This is a high cost solution because although the software is free, peripherals needed include a dedicated Mac computer, internet connectivity, and some form of storage/charge cart. We only use this solution when iPad numbers are above 30 and there is at least one technical staff on site, as setup and support can sometimes be both time and research heavy.

The configurator is a powerful piece of software that is deceptively clean and simple. All iPads are first supervised, placing a supervision profile on the device that binds it to the machine issuing the profile. Once supervised the configurator adds both applications and other profiles per user specifications. The profiles can be used for a wide range of purposes including adding web links, limiting access to content, and providing authorization credentials or framework for wireless, email, and calendars.

Once an iPad has been supervised and configured, it can be released to the public for use. When an iPad is returned, reimaging is as simple as connecting the iPad to the configurator origin machine. The iPad will have all temporary data, cookies, cache files, user installed applications, and user data wiped. After, the image is reapplied to overwrite any aesthetic changes.

With iOS7 Apple introduced a feature called Activation Lock, which is a series of default settings designed to prevent thieves from turning of security features such as Find My iPad and Erase and Reactivate your device. Configurator allows seamless bypassing of Activation Lock where other imaging methods require more work.

Configurator is also very versatile, allowing for different groupings of iPads. Abington campus provides a configurator station that services both student general use circulation and a more specific image used for a Digital Arts class. When an iPad is connected, configurator knows which group it belongs to and applies the data accordingly.

## 3.2 iTunes

At our smaller campuses and branches, the price of hardware and personnel time associated with using a configurator setup is prohibitive. We needed to look at Windows-based solutions to fit with our current computer infrastructure. The only tool available in this case is iTunes. Although much less robust than the configurator, iTunes can still be used to store and reapply images.

The drawback to this style of configuration is the time investment. Each iPad will have to be manually erased, plugged into iTunes, and then restored to the image that has been built and backed up. This process is very manual compared to the plug and play reimage of the configurator. Any time major iOS updates are released your image must be updated to reflect these changes. Additionally, proper Apple ID use is encouraged as activation lock can present issues when there is no supervision profile being applied.

## 3.3 Unmanaged

For our staff and faculty, things work a little bit differently. When an iPad is designated to a staff or faculty member, it's assumed that the device will only be returned when the employee leaves, or when the device dies. Because of this, we decided to take a fully hands off approach. The devices are inventoried upon arrival, keeping track of both serial number and MAC (Wi-Fi) address.

They are then given to the recipient, usually with a quick consult about passcodes, configuring email, setting up Wi-Fi, and some other general best use tips.

We've found our staff and faculty have responded very well to our hands off approach. All are informed to contact support if they feel uncomfortable updating or troubleshooting but very few need a repeat visit. Because these devices are unmanaged and therefore cannot be remotely wiped, staff and faculty iPad users are directed to keep sensitive data on managed workstations instead of the device.

## 4. Design and Configure

Now that you've figured out HOW you're going to manage your devices, it's time to actually make them work. An image for an iPad is slightly different than an image for a computer, and is made up of four pieces: your Apple ID/supervision, apps, aesthetics, and profiles.

## 4.1 4.1 Apple ID

The Apple ID is the Apple account associated with your devices. These accounts can be free or associated with a prepayment card or credit card. We use free accounts for our configurations, and each campus/branch has their own. To alleviate issues of personal emails attached to company accounts we use listserv emails for registration. This allows multiple people to receive information about the account, and leaves it open to change hands.

In the configurator you will need an Apple ID if you plan on purchasing any applications, even though the device isn't configured using the Apple ID.

## 4.2 Apps

For our student circulating iPads, we allow each area to build their own app list. Our campus/branch setups using iTunes tend to keep the app list slim to assist with long imaging times, while the Apple Configurator setups normally have large app pools as apps are not removed and reinstalled every reimage.

For our main circulation instance we decided to provide a full app experience so that anyone without an Apple ID could still get a robust experience without the hassle of creating an account. Productivity apps such as QuickOffice, Evernote, Photoshop Express and Dropbox remain our most popular apps based on student feedback polls. Non-productivity applications such as Facebook, Skype, Pandora and Twitter keep a close second.

## 4.3 Aesthetics

To provide a way to easily identify our iPads we focused heavily on consistent Aesthetics. Using configurator we were able to set and quickly change visual aspects of the image such as lock screens, backgrounds images, banner text, and the contents of the dock.

To keep our iPads fresh, and also to let our students know that these are updated frequently, we change our lock screen at least twice a year to a seasonally appropriate image. Often these images come from staff or students who have checked out an iPad and used the camera to snap a picture of the library grounds under heavy snowfall or framed with spring flowers.

## 4.4 Profiles

Profiles are the true configuration tool for the iPads. Profiles can be used to restrict access to content, provide a series of web links or bookmarks, set basic configuration information for mail and calendar setup, or to provide security certificates needed for campus wireless.

Although much can be configured with profiles, we keep our profile list slim. Our goal in circulating these devices is to allow the students to test and see if these devices are helpful to them in their academic pursuits, and setting restrictions seems counter to our goals.

## 4.5 Wireless

As many of us know, campus wireless can be a tricky issue. Many wireless networks require some variety of security certificates, and Penn State is no different. When starting this project we were faced with the issue of taking wireless 802.1x security certificates that install on demand and giving them the ability to be preloaded and editable.

After much trial and error a strategy of using placebo values for user credentials, a false user id and per connection password, allowed for a pre-installation of our wireless saving our users the long and frustrating process of finding and downloading wireless certificates.

## 5. Implementation

Once everything is ready it's time to roll out your project. For our first major release of the Pattee/Paterno Library iPads we only advertised at the main circulation desk with one 8.5x11 sign and a small social media blast.

Despite the minimal advertising, our original 65 iPads quickly had a queue twice that big behind them. To alleviate this, ten more were promptly added to the pool.

Now that the project has been in place for longer our pool has grown to over 90 iPads in Pattee/Paterno Library alone. Our branch libraries circulate three to five iPads each, and our 20 satellite campuses range anywhere between a full cart of 125 devices to a more modest three or four.

## 6. Circulation and Support

After the initial rush of implementation, circulation becomes steady and you'll start evaluating your common issues. Some of these issues can stem from the process of circulation; some are unavoidable and can only be mitigated at best.

### 6.1 Circulation Process

Our iPads circulate for a week-long loan period, with the exception of devices used for specific classes and are on semester loans. Devices are checked out with a charge brick and the appropriate cable.

When returned the iPad is simply plugged into the configurator. This strips away all user data while preserving core application data. This helps minimize imaging times. Once an iPad has finished it's imaging process the configurator shows the iPad as ready to circulate. Any iPad that runs into issues during imaging is flagged with a symbol in the configurator and is removed for service.

### 6.2 Support

Support of our iPads is done in a tiered approach. Initial triage is handled by circulation supervisors who have all gone through basic training for troubleshooting. The most frequent issues can be resolved by performing a factory reset, and having local staff

able to perform this step helps keep iPads in circulation and not bogging down the queue.

Occasionally we will get something more remarkable, a broken screen, a student that has found a way to fully wipe away our supervision and activation lock the device, and everything in between. These are handled on a case by case basis, but any damage or lost iPads are charged back to the patron for full replacement value.

### 6.3 Maintenance

Regular maintenance of the iPads is needed, especially during large iOS upgrades. It is recommended that any staff in charge of updates also has a personal iPad so they can be alerted to any changes in iOS, and can perform a test install before making a sweeping change.

Scheduled monthly updates of both the configurator software and your applications are suggested. Although you can set the configurator to automatically update the iOS on your devices, your applications will still need to be updated manually.

## 7. Conclusion

Taking the plunge and deciding to add iPads to your support or circulation workload can be incredibly daunting. Understanding your institutional goals, the amount of time and money available to the project, and having a clear plan before you order your hardware all help make a pile of iPads into a successful implementation.

# Unrestricted Secure Computing

Greg Madden
Information Technology Services
Penn State Harrisburg
Middletown, PA 17057
gem19@psu.edu

John B. Tyndall
Information Technology Services
The Pennsylvania State University
University Park, PA 16802
jbt8@psu.edu

## ABSTRACT

Information technology (IT) departments have historically enforced security on end-user computers through a combination of software agents that restrict what the computer can do, mandate particular actions on the part of the user, report various pieces of information back to IT, and regularly check for and apply updates, as well as policy restrictions that tell the computer user the various ways in which they are not allowed to use their own machine. From a user perspective, this can be summarized as: IT takes a perfectly good computer and refuses to let you use it until they load it up with bloatware and tell you what you aren't allowed to do. Because of this, IT is often seen as making computers less useful rather than more useful, i.e., IT is the "Department of No."

In this paper we attempt to provide a framework by which IT can overcome these historical tendencies while still maintaining the security that we must necessarily have in order to protect the proprietary and sensitive data in use by our campuses, colleges, and departments. We recognize the primacy of importance of data protection (as opposed to device protection). We discuss the various agents that are installed on end-user computers and suggest means by which those agents might be removed (i.e., bloatware reduction). We discuss frameworks currently in place for data protection (e.g., SharePoint, Citrix) that might be utilized to begin removing usage restrictions from our end-user computers (i.e., restriction reduction). Finally, we propose a model in which both the software agents and the usage restrictions take place at the network level rather than at the level of the end-user computer, thereby freeing the end-user computer from the clutches of IT and releasing it into the wild to be used to its fullest by the end user.

## Categories and Subject Descriptors

K.6.5 [**Security and Protection**]: Invasive software

## General Terms

Economics, Experimentation, Design, Human Computer Interaction, Management, Security, Social Informatics, Standardization

## Keywords

Data protection; security; unrestricted secure computing

## 1. INTRODUCTION

Information Technology (IT) departments in higher education find themselves at a crossroads as a result of two primary converging trends in the computing and networking industries.

On the one hand, we face the rapid commodification of a wide variety of services we have historically provisioned locally. These include wired networks, wireless networks, visitor networks, data storage platforms, server platforms, application services, software, and standardized desktop services; and often, these services are not only more cost effective but usually better designed and implemented than anything we have previously attempted to (or currently) offer. We are nearing the end of the era in which we created value for our organizations by providing locally hosted, powerful, stable computing platforms; instead, we are entering the era in which powerful, stable computing platforms can be inexpensively purchased and deployed with a minimum of local infrastructure. This shift will eventually have a profound impact on IT staff as they transition to "new" roles that address this type of paradigm: local liaison between the business unit and the service providers, local interface to the service, and local customization experts of the service.

On the other hand, we face a rapid proliferation of a wide variety of personal devices in the hands of our customers, coupled with increasing expectations of flexibility and convenience, as well as a growing impatience with restrictive security measures that impede the ability of the customer to use his or her device to its fullest. It is this second trend, towards end-user device flexibility, which will require the greatest measure of institutional change on the part of IT departments.

In this paper, we present the idea that common information security practices—which typically secure individual *devices* by enforcing varying levels of restrictions to intended usage—are no longer relevant and/or feasible as solutions to two evolving information technology trends.

## 2. RESTRICTIVE HISTORY

The history of IT departments is coincidental with the history of limiting and restricting the use of computers. Since at least 1961 [2], passwords have routinely been in use specifically on computer systems to restrict their use to authorized persons. The advent in the 1980s of local area networks consisting of desktop and laptop computers from various manufacturers running various operating systems led IT departments to an ever-escalating push for conformity and security across the expensive enterprise. In the quest to be efficient and use our limited resources wisely, we slowly colonized every pocket of our organizations and insisted that all computers be treated equally. This made sense. We were, in many ways, forced in to this position by the priorities of our organizations—if the budget is insufficient to support mass customizations, then standardized environments are the only answer. There is also a solid logic behind the IT position: through standardization we can create environments with extremely limited downtime, on extremely limited budgets.

Today, the pain accrues to our customers. Administrative rights are routinely denied, following the Saltzer-Schroeder least-privilege model [7]; we premise our relationship with end-users on their fundamentally assumed untrustworthiness. We make them agree to terms and conditions every single day even though they work for us. We restart their machines when they least expect it. We make them identify themselves and use passwords. We impose a mandatory moral dilemma on every single person by forcing them to change their passwords far too often, compelling them to write it on a piece of paper against their better judgment. We lock their screens when they turn their back. We impose our virus protection upon them. We ask them to certify their machines free of personally identifiable information. We run software update-checkers and operating system patch-updaters at inconvenient times without their permission, and when we do not do it well they cannot run the update even if they want to. They cannot install easily available software for themselves, even if it is completely appropriate for their job functions. Their personal devices are denied access to our networks.

Thus, it is no surprise that our customers frequently bear us ill-will—even though each of the restrictions listed above is not only justifiable, but often is mandatory as a result of policies and auditing guidelines developed outside IT. In our organization, for instance, one way of reading our foundational IT policy is that it creates a fiduciary duty for IT departments to render each and every computer less useful before we release it for use by our customers. We have become "Mordac, the Preventer of Information Services [8]."

IT departments find themselves at a juncture where it will be necessary to reject decades of best practices in order to remain relevant. We need to recognize that our best practices can now be implemented and distributed inexpensively by remote services. We need to lead the push to utilize these services. We can either allow this to drive us into irrelevance (Once the device is managed and supported remotely, once the data is managed and protected remotely, once the network is contracted, once your applications and services are hosted in the cloud, what will be left for you to do? Printing?—in that case, it is time for a new career.), or we can turn our attention to providing specifically those services which must be provided locally: the customizations, excep-tions, and special requests that we have historically treated antagonistically, labeling them as inefficient expenditures of our limited resources.

## 3. FORWARD

While our arrival at this point in the history of IT is understandable, if local IT departments are going to survive the coming era of commodification of services, we need to become the "*Enabler* of Information Services." We need to recognize that all of our effort in creating tightly restricted, highly standardized, easily replicated computing environments—efforts which might have had us applauding ourselves for our efficiency and contemporary thinking as recently as two or three years ago—are, if not already irrelevant, soon to be irrelevant. We have perfected the art of delivering standardized IT at just the right time to hand off that art to a set of vendors, who are busy preparing a dizzying suite of options for us to choose from. For most use-cases, our customers will soon be well-served without us. We will come to need very few hard IT skills in our IT departments, e.g., perhaps nothing more than a liaison service with technical expertise, a service desk, and experts in local customization.

This last point is key. Our collective futures as IT departments lie in (a) our ability to source our commodity services wisely; (b) the ongoing need to provide hands-on local assistance and education to our customers; and (c) our ability to provide them with the flexibility and customization we have spent the last three decades denying them. We must focus on providing specifically those services which cannot be provided by others, for any service which can be provided by others will be provided by others in the immediate future, and these service providers will be more cost-effective than we will be.

## 4. ELIMINATING OUR FOOTPRINT

Given this convergence of trends (e.g., easy availability of standardized services, an endless proliferation of devices and operating systems, the desire for flexibility among our customers), IT departments will need to reconfigure our mix of skills. Instead of building staff to answer the question, "How can I operate stable, secure systems efficiently?" (this will be done by our service-providers), we will need to build staff to answer the question, "How can I maximize the utility of the devices in my customers' hands while maintaining the security of their data?"

We note that the latter question actually comprises two separate questions:

1. How can we maximize the utility of the devices in our customers' hands?

2. And how can we do so while maintaining the security of our customers' data?

To the first, we answer by rejecting the history of IT as a history of IT restrictions. Let us maximize the utility of our customers' devices by leaving them alone to do as they are designed to do. We call, in essence, for the planned elimination of IT restrictions and requirements on end-user devices. This implies that the security measures which have traditionally been employed—if we still find them valuable—will need to be implemented somewhere other than on the end-user device. We must change our focus from securing the *end-user device* to securing the *proprietary data* accessed by the end-user device. Through the adoption of this principle of non-interference with the device, IT can simplify its responsibilities in many ways, still allowing for efficient operations.

To the second, we need to functionally separate our security from our devices, so the users can use the devices to their fullest capacity. If we are to end our reliance on our end-user devices as the sources of security, we need to carefully study the types of security we are offering, and find a way to take each class of security off of the *end* device and onto some sort of *security* device, through which the end device communicates to access the network. Ultimately, this should lead to security at-least-as-strong as what we currently have (security with a different set of flaws and limitations than we currently have, but security nonetheless). As an example, consider an environment with 1500 end-user computers: we re-implement our security measures 1500 times, once per device.

If we could replace this system with a centralized security appliance of some sort, we could implement our security measures once (on the security appliance) and be done with it. With this model, we are not simply diverting restriction to another location (i.e., instead of the bloatware preventing users from what they want to do, the appliance prevents the users from doing what they want to do). Instead, we minimize our footprint on the end-user device, which allows us to free its resources that are normally dedicated to redundant tasks, more intelligently and comprehensively (not to mention more transparently) handle *securing* the device (which, this paper argues, is differentiated from and can be done without *restricting* the device), and ultimately leave our customers with unrestricted secure computing.

## 5. COMMON IT RESTRICTIONS AND REQUIREMENTS

If we are to eliminate the IT footprint from end-user devices while maintaining security, we need to examine the types of usage-restrictions we place on these devices and find a plausible alternative to each. There are two main classes of restrictions and requirements that today's IT departments commonly employ on end-user devices:

1. The wide variety of beneficent software agents deployed for various purposes by IT, each of which potentially uses compute-cycles that are then unavailable to the user

2. Policy-based restrictions such as administrative rights restrictions and Internet restrictions that are specifically designed to restrict the user.

More specifically, in the first category (which we may think of as restrictive in the sense that they potentially result in performance degradation) we note at least the following set of agents:

1.1 Hardware authorization agents that confirm a specific device is entitled to connect to a network.

1.2 User authentication agents that prevent a device from being utilized unless a pre-authorized user identifies him- or herself to the authentication server.

1.3 Anti-malware agents that keep a device free from viruses, trojans, and other malicious software.

1.4 Backup agents that ensure a customer's data are kept safe from accidental (or, perhaps, intentional) deletion.

1.5 Update-checkers that periodically interrupt a device and check for software and hardware updates via the network.

1.6 Other updaters that may intrude on the user, frequently asking questions he or she is not qualified to answer (and, when poorly implemented, cannot run anyway because the user does not have administrative rights).

1.7 Personally identifiable information remediation engines, theoretically protecting the privacy of both the user and anyone else whose data are on the user's machine, but in practice is highly intrusive and borderline worthless.

1.8 Hardware and/or software firewalls that restrict network traffic to and from a device.

1.9 Patch management services (i.e., high-end centralized updaters) that may intrude on a user and/or restart his or her device with little or no notice.

1.10 Inventory agents that typically report back to a central IT database system.

1.11 Remote support agents that allow IT staff to connect to a device from a remote location and provide support.

1.12 Software distribution agents that enable the remote installation and/or uninstallation of applications to and from a device.

1.13 Other agents depending on the particular circumstances of the IT department and the corporate environment.

In the second category, we note at least the following set of common policy-based restrictions:

2.1 Denial of administrative rights, which means an end-user becomes dependent on IT for even the most routine change to his or her device, both in terms of software and hardware peripherals.

2.2 Requirement to change passwords at a defined interval (though not particularly effective [5], nonetheless recommended somewhere in the range of every $[a, b]$ days, where $a, b | a, b \in \mathbb{N}, a \geq 30, b \leq 365$), which means that a user becomes locked out of his or her device every $[a, b]$ days (which, itself, is another policy-based restriction, i.e., to deny access after $n$ failed logon attempts, where $n | n \in \mathbb{N}, n \geq 0, n \leq 10$).

2.3 Website restrictions (in higher education, uncommon on single-user faculty/staff devices, but perhaps common on multi- and single-user student devices), which enact corporate censorship.

In general, these common security practices ultimately hinder productivity [5] and disregard the *availability* aspect [4] of the *Confidentialty-Integrity-Availability* information security model.

In higher education the negative effect of these restrictions falls heaviest on those with the greatest need for computing autonomy: researchers, creatives, and experimental pedagogists, particularly among the faculty. To the extent that this set of our customers most neatly embodies the mission of our universities and colleges, our willingness to impede their computing represents a willingness to explicitly undermine the fundamental purpose of our institutions. In our zeal to protect the institution, we destroy it from within. (An anecdote: in a recent consultation with a University School, the dean described the IT department as "behaving maliciously" and "undermining our ability to do our research," when in reality IT was simply implementing policy-based usage-restrictions as required by audit and recommended by the University's central information security department. This IT department had made the mistake of identifying one trend (i.e., adoption of cloud services) while missing another: flexibility and customization.) When a high-functioning IT department with a solid infrastructure and forward-thinking sourcing policies can be described as malicious, something has to change.

No value-judgment is intended towards the set of restrictions and requirements described above. Everything being done in the name of security is justified in some way. We are not suggesting that security should be reduced or eliminated, simply that it should be moved.

## 6. UNRESTRICTED SECURE COMPUTING

Having identified those restrictions and requirements that need to be removed in order for IT to eliminate its footprint on end-user devices, the question becomes, "How can we do so?"

First, we recognize that not every one of our customers currently requires unrestricted secure computing. There are many job functions in higher education that are well-suited to a restricted, standardized, highly secured environment. (This presumes we are in agreement that "work" devices are to be used in the pursuit of "work business" only, and that all non-work related uses are banned. In practice, this is rarely the case in higher education; not only is the separation of what is *work* and what is *personal* a gray-area at best, but even "malicious IT departments" consider it humane to allow the continuation of such practices even if they result in the need for customization of the work environment.) For those of our users who can be served well by standardization, we should select the appropriate provider of standardized services (perhaps ourselves for now, perhaps a cloud provider later) and effectively provision that service.

That said, many of our users (e.g., faculty, researchers, creative professionals, educational innovators, frequent travelers) would be served well by less standardized environments. For these people we need to take as our goal the complete elimination of usage-restrictions; thus, we need to explore how each type of restriction can best be eliminated. Without undertaking an exhaustive inventory of the restrictions and requirements listed above, we will provide a preliminary sketch of what computing might look like in the absence of end-user device usage restrictions.

### 6.1 Securing Content, Not Devices

Gartner [3] predicts a tenfold increase in the number of Internet-connected devices—to 30 billion—by 2020. Consequently, as Romer [6] suggests, managing device-specific security is becoming too cumbersome, if not vacillating, particularly as these devices (each with their own vendors, platforms, architectures, operating systems, etc.) seemingly pop up at an unprecedented rate.

Consequently, we propose that the first step to creating an unrestricted secure computing environment is recognizing that, ultimately, data protection is more important than device protection. Services such as Sharepoint and Citrix (even, for that matter, Box and Dropbox) already provide secure access to non-local data storage. While we have no choice but to put in place restrictions that prevent the download and repurposing of proprietary information, we do believe that such protection can take place in the network, not on the device.

### 6.2 Extending Network-Based Security

We recognize that many types of security take place in the network: firewalls implement access restrictions, network access control appliances identify devices on our networks and block unauthorized devices, switch ports allow or deny access to the network based on various condition, spam filters pre-examine email to weed out the most egregious spam. Thus, there is precedent for providing security services through the network, and there are working examples of devices that provide high-volume security efficiently and effectively. In some ways, it is surprising that we have not already recognized the capacity of these devices to perform more security functionality for us and that we have not yet moved some of our security functions to these devices.

Given that network-based security appliances are already common, it is largely irrelevant whether in the future we add additional capabilities to existing security appliances (e.g., an improved firewall, a virus-checking switch), or whether in the future we create wholly new security appliances devoted specifically to end-user device security. What would be necessary is that any device that connects to our network speaks via the security appliance, however the implementation takes place.

The point of the matter is that as we dedicate ourselves to maximizing the customer experience and eliminating the restrictions on what our customers can do, the end-user device security has to go somewhere. We need to imagine a future in which our users are not only able to take delivery of a new device directly from the device vendor—with no intervention on the part of IT—and then freely use our network, but also use that device to its maximum potential—with no intervention on the part of IT. (In our ideal world we might be able to install a single security agent on the device to take the place of the myriad of agents and restrictions we currently impose.) If our users choose to implement device-specific restrictions (e.g., passwords) on their own behalf, we could certainly encourage that—and, to the extent that they choose to implement their own restrictions, we must be able to support them in the event that anything goes wrong.

### 6.3 Extending and/or Constricting the Operating System

There is no doubt that the current crop of operating systems is uniformly incapable of ceding the full extent of their security responsibilities to the network, and that there is currently no appliance which could provide the large variety of desirable security functions described above. Without the cooperation of operating system designers, unrestricted secure computing in the sense outlined here will not be possible. Ideally, our security appliance would be operating system agnostic, would speak a common security-specific language, and could be implemented in a manner that requires minimal-to-no intervention (e.g., in the form of an agent) on the end-user device. In practice, we envision the rise of a class of security appliances that begin by offering a service like malware protection and then ramp up from there, adding other services until they provide replacements for every possible end-user device security situation.

Additionally, we may find that while some security functionality is best provided by a network appliance, other functionality is best addressed with a thorough reimagining. For instance, Apple Inc. have at least somewhat solved the problem of virus infections by certifying software at the source [1], i.e., by centralizing iOS and Mac OS software distribution, they can improve device security without having to employ a additional mechanism on the device itself. While this does have the undeniable chilling effect of making it difficult to write and release software to one'âĂŹs own device without extensive prior planning, it does provide the undeniable benefit of removing the virus protection *from the device*. While it is certainly debatable whether or not this is a desirable direction to take, the point is that we have options, and that creative thinking around the problem of security will lead us to solutions that work.

## 7. CONCLUSION

Information technology (IT) departments commonly respond to the need for security by imposing usage-restrictions on devices. Our is a history of making these devices work less-well than they would have otherwise worked without our interventions. Our ability to continue in this direction is being rendered obsolete by our customers' newfound attachments to devices of every size, shape, and operating system, as well as by their desires to use those devices to the fullest of their capacities—without the limitations put in place by IT departments. Rather than fighting our customers, it is time we adapt to the new reality: recognizing our need to protect proprietary data and to do so, while allowing them to use their device to its fullest extent.

## 8. ACKNOWLEDGMENTS

The authors wish to thank The Pennsylvania State University for providing the opportunity to work together on this paper.

## 9. REFERENCES

[1] Apple Inc. App store review guidelines. https://developer.apple.com/app-store/review/guidelines/ (Accessed 2 September 2014).

[2] P. Crisman, editor. *The Compatible Time-Sharing System: A Programmer's Guide.* The M.I.T. Press, 2nd edition, 1965.

[3] Gartner, Inc. Gartner says it's the beginning of a new era: the digital industrial economy. http://www.gartner.com/newsroom/id/2602817 (Accessed 2 September 2014), October 2013.

[4] J. Granneman. Information security strategy: Stop punishing end users - network computing. http://www.networkcomputing.com/careers-and-certifications/information-security-strategy-stop-punishing-end-users/a/d-id/1234457 (Accessed 2 September 2014), Sept 2013.

[5] C. Herley. So long, and no thanks for the externalities: The rational rejection of security advice by users. In *Proceedings of the 2009 Workshop on New Security Paradigms Workshop*, NSPW '09, pages 133–144, New York, NY, USA, 2009. ACM.

[6] H. Romer. Best practices for byod security. *Computer & Fraud Security*, 2014(1):13–15, Jan 2014.

[7] J. Saltzer and M. Schroeder. The protection of information in computer systems. *Proceedings of the IEEE*, 63(9):1278–1308, Sept 1975.

[8] Universal Uclick. The official dilbert website with scott adams' color comic strips, animation, mashups and more! http://www.dilbert.com (Accessed 2 September 2014).

# Simulation of Power Saving in Private Cloud Environment

Yukinori Sakashita
School of Information Science
Japan Advanced Institute of Science
and Technology
Nomi, Ishikawa, Japan/
Yokohama Research Laboratory
Hitachi Ltd.
292 Yoshida-cho Totuka-ku
Yokohama, Kanagawa, Japan
sakasita@jaist.ac.jp

Kanae Miyashita
Research Center for Advanced
Computing Infrastructure
Japan Advanced Institute of Science
and Technology
Nomi, Ishikawa, Japan
k-miya@jaist.ac.jp

Shuichi Kozaka
Research Center for Advanced
Computing Infrastructure
Japan Advanced Institute of
Science and Technology
Nomi, Ishikawa, Japan
kosaka@jaist.ac.jp

Satoshi Uda
Research Center for Advanced
Computing Infrastructure
Japan Advanced Institute of Science
and Technology
Nomi, Ishikawa, Japan
zin@jaist.ac.jp

Mikifumi Shikida
Research Center for Advanced
Computing Infrastructure
Japan Advanced Institute of
Science and Technology
Nomi, Ishikawa, Japan
shikida@jaist.ac.jp

## ABSTRACT

Power shortages during the summer season have become a serious problem in Japan. At JAIST (Japan Advanced Institute of Science and Technology), students and staff received more than 25 requests to cut down on their use of power in July and August 2013. As a result, reducing the amount of power consumed by the data center in JAIST has become a pressing issue. The data center centrally manages 24-hour computing resources for all students and staff. Consequently, reducing power usage at the data center requires that infrastructure equipment be shutdown, with only a minimal impact on services. However, it is difficult for administrators to understand whether the power can be reduced and the influence on services is a minimal impact. The data center installed virtualization techniques and the connection between servers and storage is complex. This paper describes a technique for simulation of migration resources to reduce power consumption while minimizing the impact on services in a private cloud environment in the data center. We will make a plan for power saving in the private cloud environment by using it.

## Categories and Subject Descriptors

K.6.4 [Computing Milieux]: System Management [Centralization/ decentralization]; H.3.2 [Information Storage and Retrieval]: Information Storage; C.5.5 [Computer Systems Implementation]: Server

## General Terms

Measurement; Performance; Power Saving; Data Center

## Keywords

Private Cloud; Storage System; Data Center

## 1. INTRODUCTION

Since the Fukushima Daiichi Nuclear Disaster caused by the Great East Japan Earthquake in 2011, there have been a number of requests for reduction of electric energy in IT infrastructure in Japan. The reduction of electric energy poses a problem for JAIST. To reduce power usage, unnecessary IT Infrastructure needs to be idled or turned off. However, Quality of Service (QoS) to a user cannot be lowered. It is difficult to do both of these actions at the same time. Thus, this paper proposes a method for reducing the electric energy of the storage of IT infrastructure. This method uses virtualization technology that can provide a service without the dependence of physical hardware while maintaining the QoS. Furthermore, we describe a simulation of the electric power reduction effect using the I/O access data in JAIST Private Cloud Environment.

## 2. OUR IT INFRASTRUCTURE

This section describes JAIST IT infrastructure and its electric power problem.

### 2.1 JAIST IT Infrastructure

Figure 1 shows an overview of IT infrastructure in JAIST. JAIST centrally manages the IT infrastructure, which about 1500 school staff members and students use. The main services are terminal services, an e-mail server, storage services using the high availability file servers, parallel computers, etc.

*SIGUCCS '14*, November 2–7 2014, Salt Lake City, UT, USA.
Copyright 2014 ACM 978-1-4503-2780-0/14/11...$15.00
http://dx.doi.org/10.1145/2661172.2661184

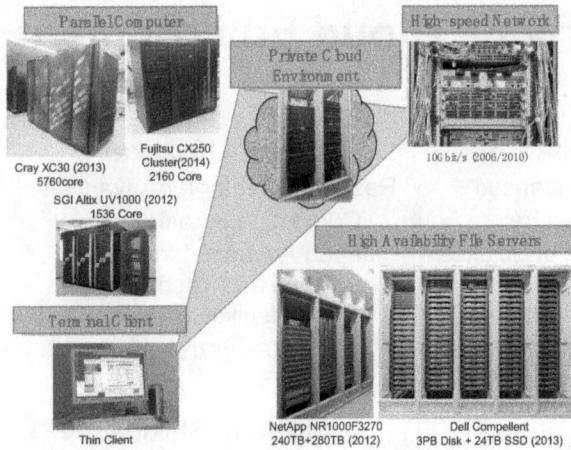

**Figure 1 Overview of JAIST IT Infrastructure**

The terminal service is used by not only students but also the school staffs(professors, office staff, etc.). The data center in JAIST provides these services 24 hours a day, and 365 days a year.

## 2.2 JAIST Private Cloud Environment

In JAIST, three virtualization technologies of different layers are installed into the terminal, and a private cloud environment is provided [1][2][3][4][5]. Table 1 and Figure 2 shows the machines and composition of the JAIST Private Cloud.   In addition, the storage in Table 1 and Figure 2 stores only OS images. User data is stored in another high-availability file server.

**Table 1 Machines of JAIST Private Cloud**

| Category | Product |
|---|---|
| Physical Server | Fujitsu PRIMERGY RX200 S2 and BX620 S2 |
| Storage | Fujitsu Eteruns DX80 S2 |
| Virtualization | <Server> VMware VSphere <Session> Citrix XenApp <Application> Microsoft Application Virtualization |
| OS | Windows2008 (Japanese/English), Solaris10 |

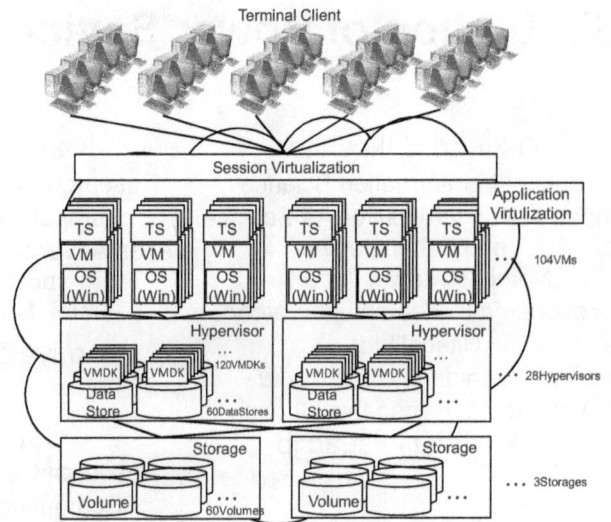

**Figure 2 JAIST Private Cloud Environment**

The users (students and school staff) can use the terminal service provided in the JAIST Private Cloud when they are on or away from the campus. Moreover, there are also many students from overseas. Therefore it offers not only Japanese but also an English version of Windows. When users login, they choose a Japanese or an English OS, as shown in Figure 3.

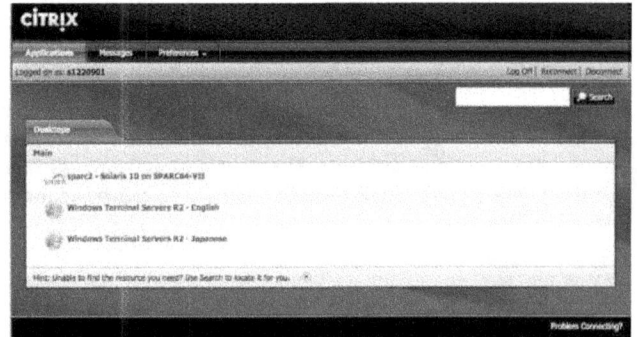

**Figure 3 Login GUI in Terminal Service**

Furthermore, session virtualization is realized in the JAIST Private Cloud environment. Whenever the user is logged in to it, the load of VM is judged, and the user  is connected to VM with the least load. This makes it possible to avoid concentration of the load of VM. And, even if obstacles occur in VM, such as failure and power down, the user can continue using the service by login and the user environment is maintained.

## 3.  ELECTRIC POWER PROBLEM

In Japan, electric power shortages have posed problems since the Great East Japan Earthquake, which happened in March, 2011. Especially in summer, the use of air-conditioning increases and thus so does the amount of used electricity. According to information made public by the Tokyo Electric Power Company (TEPCO), the peak accrual times each year are 14:00-15:00 every

54

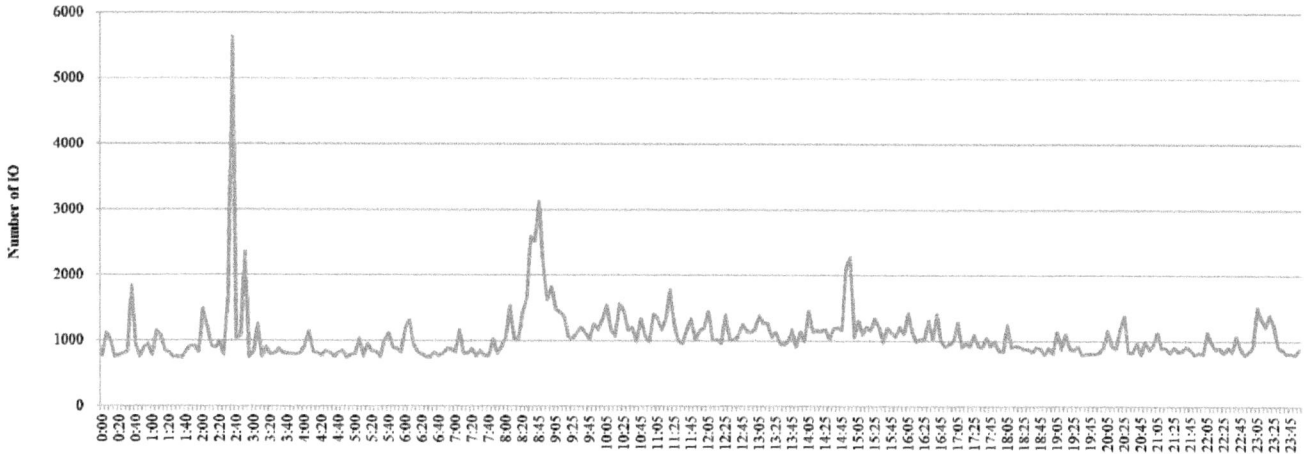

**Figure 4 Total Number of I/O in Hypervisors**

day in in August, when about 60 million kW are consumed. However, at 3:00-5:00 in August, when is the lowest time zone at night when temperature is lowest, only about 29 million kW are consumed. In JAIST, 25 power-saving requests were made by the facilities division in July and August 2013. Students and staff cope by turning off air conditioning in work rooms or turning off the power supplies of unnecessary items to reduce power consumption. Figure 5 shows power consumption of a building of JAIST Data Center in 2013. This building has not only the data center but some laboratories. Students are on summer vacation in August and September, therefore there is less electric energy. However, as a whole tendency, electric energy is increasing from April to July. Thus, power consumption has been a serious issue especially in summer.

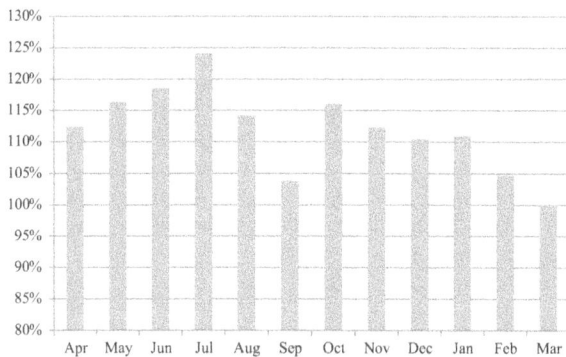

**Figure 5 Power Consumption of JAIST in 2013**

# 4. PROPOSAL FOR POWER SAVING

As described in Section 3, to solve the problem posed by electric power shortages, we reduced the power consumption of JAIST IT infrastructure. There is research of Beloglazov team, which reduces the power consumption of virtual environment [7]. In this research, VMs are migrated according to the total utilization of CPU, and power consumption is reduced. However, VM migration requires load for the server and storage in a both migration source and target. Thus, migration of VM cannot be carried out unless there is sufficient remaining utilization of CPU, memory, etc. Therefore, we propose the reduction of electric

energy by considering the JAIST Private Cloud environment where the physical infrastructure is concealed by virtualization technology. So, in this paper, we propose the method of performing electric power control of VM, which are managed virtualization of session, without migration. This method loses I/O access from VM, and decreases the power consumption of not only servers but also storage. According to SNIA Emerald, power consumption of storage differs depending on whether there is an I/O load or not (idle) [8].

Therefore, this method estimates number of VMs from managing XenApp without down grade of service level. So, VMs are shut down belong same a storage. As a result, the storage without I/O is selected. Next, the storage is turned off. Thus, the power consumption of storage is cut down without VM migration.

# 5. EVALUATION

This section describes a simulation method of this proposal and its results.

## 5.1 Simulation Method

The simulation was carried out in the following procedure using the average data of I/O in hypervisors, as shown in Figure 4. The environment assumed in a simulation is given in Table 1 and Figure 2.

(1) The maximum number of I/O per hypervisor is computed by dividing the maximum I/O number by the hypervisor number.

(2) The maximum number of I/O per VM is computed from the number of hypervisors that are VMs.

(3) The data in Figure 4 and the number of VMs that may stop in Step (2) are computed.

(4) The time and the amount of storage that may stop I/O load in Step (3) are computed.

(5) The results in Step (4) are used, and the amounts of electricity used when storage is set to idle and when the power supply is turned off are computed.

In Step (5), in consideration of the shutdown time of storage and start-up time, the power supply of storage was treated as a state

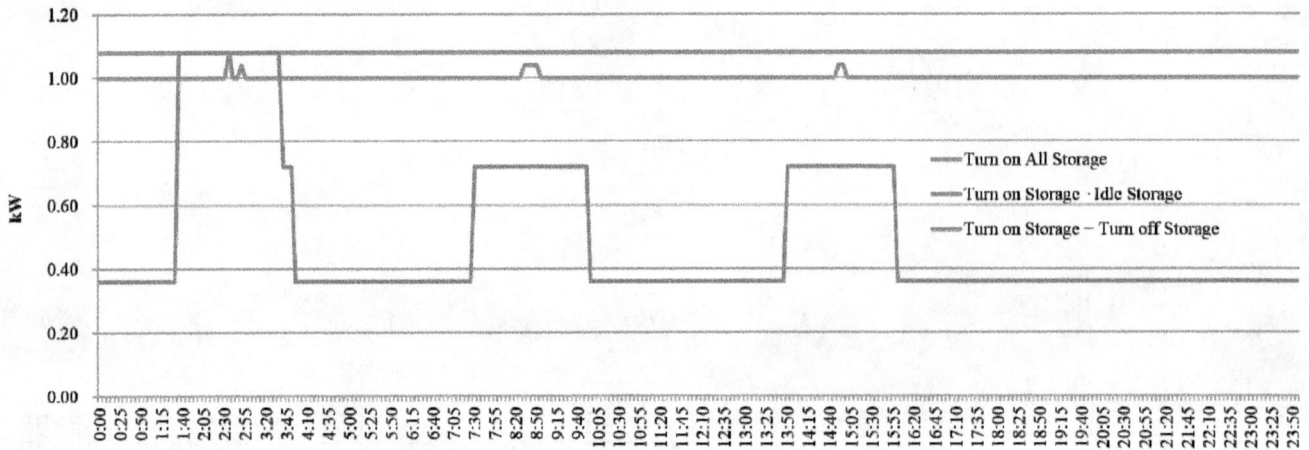

**Figure 6 Result of Power Consumption Simulation**

with I/O load and was simulated as being on and off for one hour. Moreover, the power consumption of the storage used by this simulation is shown in Table 2. This amount of used electricity was calculated using the Fujitsu Storage ETERNUS DX Disk Storage Array Consumption power calculation tool [9].

**Table 2 Power Consumption in Storage in JAIST Private Cloud Environment**

| Status | Power Consumption [kW/Storage] |
|--------|-------------------------------|
| Idle | 0.32 |
| I/O Load | 0.36 |

## 5.2 Results

Figure 6 shows the results of the simulation. The highest number of accesses comes at 14:30-15:00, when electric energy is higher than in an idle state. However, on the whole, power consumption is lower when power supply is turned on and off than in an idle state. Figure 7 shows the total amount of used electricity for one day. From these results, when idle storage is used instead of leaving all storage turned on, electric power is reduced by 7%. Also, when the power supply of storage is turned on/off, electric power is reduced by 54%.

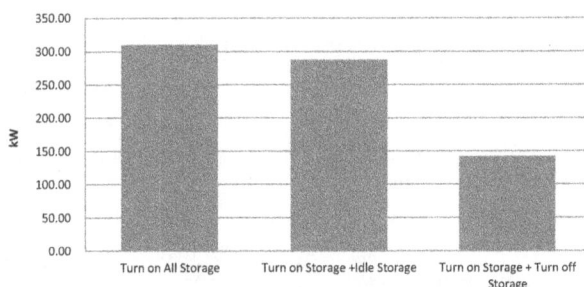

**Figure 7 Total of Power Consumption in One Day**

## 6. Consideration

The results of the simulation showed that electric power can be more than halved when the power supply of storage is turned on and off. Changing storage to an idle state reduces electricity only slightly. Thus, we consider the operation in which the power supply of storage is turned on/off. To operate the storage, the administrator has to turn the power supply on/off using the specialty management GUI. Quite a few administrators are resistant to automating the turning on/off of the power supply of storage. Therefore, we also consider the case where an administrator turns the power supply on/off manually. According to the results in Figure 6, the power supply is turned on/off seven times: 1:35, 3:40, 3:55, 7:30, 9:55, 13:50, and 16:00. An administrator's office hours are assumed to be from 8:30 to 17:30, so an administrator can manually turn a power supply on/off only three times: 9:55, 13:50 and 16:00. As mentioned in Section 3, little power is consumed at night in Japan. Therefore, we assume the administrator turns the power supply off at 8:30 immediately after coming to the office and turns it on at 17:30 before going home. The power status of storages by administrator's manually operation is shown in Table 3. Thereby, the amount of electricity used in one day is 248.04kW. This operation case can reduce electric power for the power supply of all the storage by 20% more than leaving all storage turned on.

**Table 3 Power Status of Storage by Manually Operation**

| Time | Storage1 | Storage2 | Storage3 |
|------|----------|----------|----------|
| 8:30-9:55 | On | On | Off |
| 9:55-13:50 | On | Off | Off |
| 13:50-16:00 | On | On | Off |
| 16:00-17:30 | On | Off | Off |
| 17:30-8:30 | On | On | On |

## 7. CONCLUSION

Since the Great East Japan Earthquake in 2011, all nuclear power plants in Japan have been closed. This has made necessary a reduction of power usage of IT infrastructure. However, saving energy is especially difficult in summer. In past research, VMs have migrated according to the total utilization of CPU, and power consumption is reduced. However, VM migration requires load for the server and storage in a both migration source and target. Thus, this paper proposed a management method that reduces the power consumption of storage by adjusting the number of running VMs. So, As result of a simulation of this proposal method by using the log data in JAIST private cloud, it reduced power consumption by 54%. Even when operation was not done automatically but manually by an administrator, power consumption was reduced by 20%. Therefore, there is no load of VMs migration to a server and storage, and it has reduced power consumption. Thus, simple operation can also reduce power consumption by combining the virtualization technology of a different layer. In power saving, it is only one virtualization technology, and the combination of two or more virtualization technologies is important. For future work, we are going to control power supplies of network and research systems that reduce power consumption.

# 8. REFERENCE

[1] Mikifumi Shikida, Kanae Miyashita, Motostugu Ueno, Satoshi Uda. An Envaluation of Private Cloud System for Desktop Environments, In Proceedings of the 40th annual ACM SIGUCCS conference,131-134, ACM SIGUCCS (2012)

[2] Mikifumi Shikida, Hiroaki Nakano,Shuichi Kozaka, Masato Mato, Satoshi Uda. A Centralized Storage System with Automated Data Tiering for Private Cloud Environment, In Proceedings of the 41st annual ACM SIGUCCS conference, ACM SIGUCCS(2013).

[3] VMware,Inc. VMware vShpere http://www.vmware.com/products/vsphere/, (2014)

[4] Citrix Systems, Inc. Citrix XenApp, http://www.citrix.com/products/xenapp/overview.html, (2014)

[5] Microsoft Corporation. Microsoft Application Virtualization, http://www.microsoft.com/en-us/windows/enterprise/products-and-technologies/mdop/appv.aspx, (2014)

[6] Tokyo Electric Power Company,Inc.,The Tokyo Electric Power which sees by a mathematical table　http://www.tepco.co.jp/corporateinfo/company/annai/shiryou/report/suuhyou/index-j.html, (2013)

[7] Anton Beloglazov, Rajkumar Buyya, "Energy Efficient Allocation of Virtual Machines in Cloud Data Centers," Cluster, Cloud and Grid Computing (CCGrid), 2010 10th IEEE/ACM International Conference on , vol.577, no.578, pp.17-20, (2010)

[8] SNIA, SNIA Emerald, http://www.snia.org/emerald/ , (2014)

[9] Fujitsu Storage ETERNUS DX DiskStorageArray Consumption power calculation tool. http://storagesystem.fujitsu.com/jp/tool/power/#note01, (2014)

# My Life as an Information Technology Sous Chef: Managing to Grow Professionally While in the Same Job

Kathryn Fletcher
West Virginia University
Information Technology Services, PO Box 6500
Morgantown, WV 26506-6500
(304) 293-8769
kathy.fletcher@mail.wvu.edu

## ABSTRACT

Most career development articles present advice on how to advance into management roles. I am among those information technology professionals who do not aspire to become supervisors and directors and are content with their current jobs. Choosing to stay in a role presents its own challenges, as there is a fine line between contentment and complacency. The information technology manager needs the plateaued employee to remain a productive member of the work team, to be willing to learn new skills for new projects, and to adapt to different organizational structures over time. The employee needs to maintain a professional network and keep skills updated in case a reorganization or budget crisis leads to an unexpected job search. In this paper, I will discuss what I am doing to remain a satisfied and productive employee in the hopes that others might benefit from my experiences. I will also share tips from a few information technology managers who supervise one or more plateaued employees. The paper presentation will include time for discussion with those attendees who also find themselves in a career plateau either by choice or by circumstance and with those supervisors who manage plateaued employees.

## Categories and Subject Descriptors

K.6.1 [**Management of Computing and Information Systems**]: Project and People Management – *Management Techniques, Staffing.*
K.7.1 [**The Computing Profession**]: Occupations.

## General Terms

Human Factors, Management.

## Keywords

career development; plateau; professional development.

## 1. INTRODUCTION

After a major reorganization of the campus unit formerly known as the WVU Office of Information Technology, I found myself reflecting on my career past and future. I decided to participate in the mentorship program that was recently started as a service to members of ACM SIGUCCS. I requested a mentor to help me reinvent myself. After the reading, reflections, and discussions involved in this mentoring process, I was inspired to share my journey with others while I continue to learn more about myself as an information technology professional.

### 1.1 About West Virginia University and ITS

West Virginia University is the state's public land-grant institution with over 29,400 students on its main campus. It has seventeen colleges and schools, including four off-campus divisions in other regions of the state. Information Technology Services provides infrastructure, enterprise applications, and technical support for all WVU campuses [6].

### 1.2 About Me

I am a graduate of West Virginia University, having finished both a Bachelor of Science and a Master of Science degree in statistics. As part of my graduate assistantship, I provided walk-in assistance for students taking computer science classes. After a year of teaching statistics as an adjunct, I was hired by WVU Computing Services to provide technical support to students, faculty, and staff. Over the years, the topics I am able to support have changed and increased in number, I have been promoted twice, and I have been a part of numerous staff reorganizations and departmental name changes. At the time of writing this paper, as in 1985, my job includes a mix of end-user technical support and training tasks.

### 1.3 Why Do I Want to Stay in the Same Job?

I feel that I am on a career plateau by choice. Although I never wanted to be a manager, I did agree to supervise a full-time employee and a student employee in order to meet organizational needs at that time. I learned from this experience that I am not comfortable trying to accomplish work through delegation and that I did not excel in "coaching for performance." Although I attended a lot of management workshops and my skills improved somewhat with some coaching from my own supervisor, supervision was always the least favorite part of my job.

My supervisor recently modified our team's organization chart to move the full-time subordinate position, once it was vacant, to report to a different supervisor for job classification reasons. I do not miss supervisory duties; I enjoy being responsible for my own work instead of being partially evaluated on the performance of a subordinate.

## 1.4 Why *Sous Chef*?

You might be wondering what an information technology sous chef is. In the kitchen, a sous chef is the second in command to the head chef de cuisine, delegating work, supervising line cooks, assisting where needed, keeping track of inventory, and more. Our IT project management office recently closed our project to upgrade our existing course management software to Blackboard Learn 9. At that ceremony, I received a certificate of appreciation from the WVU Associate Vice President for Academic Innovation, naming me a *sous chef* for my efforts on the project.

My duties on this project included learning how to use the Blackboard Learn 9 software, creating and updating training workshop handouts, and training over 500 faculty and staff on how to use the new system and how to rebuild courses as we did not migrate course content from Vista 8. I was responsible for teaching other trainers and our eCampus Points of Contact how to use the new software, much as a sous chef trains new employees in the kitchen. I spent a lot of time on my feet training (sometimes in a computer lab that was as hot as a kitchen) and kept track of questions and software quirks to resolve and share with the project team and campus instructors, just as a sous chef must serve as a problem solver. I sometimes served as an intermediary between the instructors and the application administrators, explaining technical solutions to the instructors while freeing up the technical staff to focus on their system chores, just as a sous chef works between the kitchen workers and the wait staff and between the head chef and the kitchen staff.

In real life, sous chefs in a commercial kitchen have a lot more managerial responsibilities than I do in my current role as they are responsible for hiring and disciplining workers, delegating tasks, and purchasing. However, I feel that both jobs are supporting roles that ensure the work gets done, with a sense of responsibility for creating a quality product, and are critical to organizational success.

## 2. CAREER PLATEAU

## 2.1 Definitions

This definition is similar to what appeared in several articles and blog postings: "A career plateau is a point in the career of an employee where the possibility of vertical promotion within the official hierarchy becomes very low or absent altogether [5]." Some articles linked a plateau to the number of years without achieving a higher position, such as five years. Patrick Lee's research included determining the employee's own perception of being on a career plateau.

While researching the literature on this topic, I found a paper by Patrick C. B. Lee where he discusses job plateaus in addition to career plateaus. "Job plateau is defined as the point whereby the individual finds the work boring and that it provides no opportunities for learning new skills." His work goes on to remind us that information technology professionals often have a high need for learning new skills and enjoy challenges [1].

His later paper introduces a new term, "professional plateau," where the concern is whether or not employees are maintaining and improving their skills to avoid obsolescence: "… it may be

possible that employees are plateaued in their careers but they are progressing professionally in their jobs. [2]"

## 2.2 Possible Causes

### 2.2.1 Organizational plateau

Sometimes a higher-level position is not available in the organization. Organization charts resemble triangles with fewer positions at each higher level of responsibility. There is competition for these positions with searches often including external candidates. Sometimes hiring freezes prevent organizations from filling vacant positions.

### 2.2.2 Career plateau

The employee might not be suitable for a higher role. Some employees might not have the technical skills or managerial skills needed for advancement. Others might not present themselves well as candidates for open positions.

### 2.2.3 Personal choice

Not all information technology workers aspire to managerial positions. Some employees must stay in the local area for family reasons. Sometimes an employee is staying in the organization to retain health insurance or other personal benefits.

## 2.3 Possible Negative Effects

### 2.3.1 Outdated skill sets

If plateaued employees do not continue acquiring new technical skills, an organization might have to fill new vacant positions with external candidates or risk not being able to respond sufficiently to new technical projects. Employees need to overcome a sense of inertia and keep their skills up to date in case they need to initiate a job search unexpectedly or to compete for new technical positions in the organization.

### 2.3.2 Decreased productivity

Plateaued employees and their managers should watch out for a "retired on the job" phenomenon. Complacency can lead to an employee doing just enough work to stay out of trouble. Sometimes long-term employees are less open to new ideas and new ways of doing things; their resistance to change could impede progress on projects and efforts to improve efficiency.

### 2.3.3 Morale issues

If an employee is on a career plateau but not by choice, he or she might experience some resentment of new hires or co-workers' promotions. There is also a risk of boredom—less likely in information technology but still possible for those who work in the same position for several years.

## 2.4 Possible Benefits for Organization

### 2.4.1 Retention of skilled employee

When employees with years of experience and needed technical skills remain in a role, the organization benefits by retaining that knowledge and by not needing to invest resources in replacing the incumbent. When an employee leaves a role, the vacancy can lead to increased work for those remaining; additional resources are spent on a job search, assuming the organization is allowed to fill that vacant position.

### 2.4.2 Stability

Although an organization will want to avoid stagnation, plateaued employees can offer a measure of stability with their institutional knowledge and long-term relationships with colleagues and customers.

## 2.5 Benefits for Plateaued Employees

An employee who deliberately decides to not seek other positions (or at least not for a while) or one who is resigned to being on a career plateau can often benefit from staying in that role.

### 2.5.1 Time to Learn New Skills

Once an employee masters the current role, he or she can invest in acquiring additional skills that can be used to compete for a new position later on or to become more valuable to the organization in the existing position.

### 2.5.2 Time to Self-Evaluate

"If you're constantly on the move to the next promotion, you don't have much time to sit down, acclimate, and evaluate. Use the career plateaus you encounter to assess your situation: Are you happy on your current path? [4]" This advice was included in a blog posting to recent college graduates entering the work force. However, I feel that this advice could apply to information technology professionals of all ages, to evaluate where you are right now and determine what makes you happy in your work life.

### 2.5.3 Work Life Balance

A plateaued employee might be able to spend more free time with family and on outside activities that lead to personal growth. An employee might incur less stress by staying longer in a position where he or she is somewhat comfortable with the tasks, especially if the tasks are interesting or evolve over the years. Sometimes management roles, especially at higher levels, require an employee to work longer hours or to complete work at home.

## 3. GROWING IN PLACE

Starting in my early years of full-time employment, I took personal responsibility for my professional development. I decided that no one else in the organization could care as much about me and my learning as I did. Over the past thirty years, I have actively sought out learning opportunities even though I did not seek other jobs. I am listing some of my past and current activities that contribute to my success at work and my strong sense of job satisfaction.

## 3.1 Learn New Software

I manage our institution's lyndaPro multi-user training accounts and take advantage of this access to lynda.com to learn new software skills. I attend any vendor training sessions associated with software implementation projects and frequently attend workshops presented by my colleagues. I take advantage of the ACM Learning Center resources. I attend free online webinars and MOOCs. I install new software packages and "learn by doing" as I try to apply any formal training that I attended. Learning new software has enabled me to teach additional workshops and webinars as part of my job.

## 3.2 Participate in Conferences

Over the years, I have been fortunate enough to attend several conferences related to my job. I try to present a paper or poster session at these conferences since working on the presentation provides another opportunity for learning; making a presentation at the conference helps me justify my request to attend.

### 3.2.1 ACM SIGUCCS Annual Conference

I attended the fall User Services Conference (later known as the Services & Support Conference) several times, starting in 1988. In 2005, I presented my first paper and did so each time I attended the conference after that. In 2007, I volunteered for the first time to read submitted papers as part of the program committee. In 2010, I served as track chair for the Instructional Support track in addition to presenting a paper and participating on a panel discussion.

The work I do on my own conference papers frequently involves research or mastering a new skill. Editing others' papers requires me to read at a deeper level than I normally do. The conference participation also provided opportunities for networking where I have made professional contacts that have lasted over the years.

### 3.2.2 Other International Conferences

At one time, my job involved providing support on Microsoft Word and Adobe Acrobat along with advice on formatting guidelines for graduate students as they prepared to create and submit an electronic thesis or dissertation. I had the opportunity to attend two international symposia and a national conference, presenting on the challenges of providing technical support.

Since my degrees are in statistics, I formerly provided a lot of statistical software support; one year, I attended the SAS Users Group International (SUGI) conference. I attended the Society for Technical Communication (STC) annual conference when it was held in a nearby city. Attending these two extremely large conferences at my own expense provided unique learning and networking opportunities—plus I gained confidence from attending alone.

### 3.2.3 Local and Regional Conferences

When I worked for the former Academic Computing department, we would host an annual Computing and Technology Symposium. I would present at least once at each of these events, along with working on the planning of the event. I have also presented at an annual statewide higher education technology conference on numerous occasions. Presenting at local conferences helped me gain confidence in public speaking and provided networking opportunities with colleagues at other colleges in the state.

## 3.3 Join Groups

In addition to over 25 years of Association for Computing Machinery membership where I achieved ACM Senior Member status in 2011, I have joined additional professional organizations and paid any required dues or costs out of my own pocket. I also served on a few university committees. In some of these groups, I served in a leadership role for a year or two, giving me an opportunity to improve my non-technical skills.

### 3.3.1 Professional Organizations

Professional organizations that I have belonged to in the past or currently include the Association for Women in Science (AWIS), the Society for Technical Communication (STC), and the American Society for Training and Development (ASTD). During the years that we maintained a local STC chapter, I served terms as newsletter editor, secretary/treasurer, vice-president, and president (sometimes taking on two roles in the same year).

*3.3.2 University Committees*

University-wide committees I served on include a Library Oversight Committee for a specific short-term project, the ETD Task Force for during implementation of our ETD program, a search committee for a new Registrar, and the WVU Council for Women's Concerns (CWC) for six years. These groups gave me opportunities to work with faculty and staff across campus and to hone my skills in delegation, event planning, and meeting management, especially the year I spent as chair of the CWC.

## 3.4 Other Professional Development

I decided to participate in a relatively new initiative sponsored by WVU Human Resources Training and Development (T&D), the Professional Development Institute (PDI) as part of their Mountaineer Leadership Academy [7]. The PDI sponsors workshops on topics such trust in the workplace, accountability, and work/life balance during the year and provides a method for me to document all of my professional development activities, including webinars and books, for formal acknowledgement.

Over the years, I have attended other WVU T&D workshops and vendor-provided presentations on topics such as customer service, time management, coaching and supervision, project management, working with difficult people, and improving presentation skills. Although these professional development activities do not enhance my technical skills, I have used what I learned to improve as a trainer and technical support provider.

## 4. MANAGEMENT PERSPECTIVE

As part of my research for this paper, I decided to ask a variety of IT managers who work in higher education about how they handle any plateaued employees on their teams. I did not conduct a scientific survey; I invited a group of managers that I know personally to report their experiences. I did allow the managers to pass the survey form on to another manager if they wished. I allowed the managers to provide responses anonymously via an online form since in some cases, I know who their employees are and I wanted the managers to be able to speak freely. I set the form up to not collect IP addresses or other identifying information and asked a co-worker to rearrange the rows of data before I reviewed the results since some managers had let me know when they had completed the form. However, the anonymity of the responses means I cannot give credit for the content I am quoting below.

### 4.1 Strategies

Interview question: *"What strategies have you employed to maintain a plateaued employee as a productive member of your team? Do you employ different strategies for those on a plateau by choice? What has worked best so far?"*

Many of the respondents included assigning new challenging tasks or projects that would take the plateaued employee out of their comfort zone while staying within the confines of the job description. Other tips included allowing that employee more autonomy, to provide mentoring and motivation as needed, and to keep the employee plateaued by choice involved in new projects.

One of the responses: "Even though their career may have plateaued, by virtue of working in the ever changing field of technology, they need training. Sometimes this goes hand in hand with professional development (think conferences like SIGUCCS). I also like to give these employees options to be part of committees outside their comfort zones as well as opportunities to be on decision-making teams. Sometimes this works, sometimes it doesn't. Complacency is only a dirty word if they are not performing effectively."

Another response: "I evaluate their work performance and like to have frequent discussions with regard to their desires and the needs of the department. Productive employees are happy to engage and appreciate being able to participate in discussions that impact the unit. Although an employee may have plateaued, I think to provide learning opportunities for them to expand on their working knowledge and also give them opportunities to lead smaller projects. It's important to recognize that many employees who have plateaued are very productive employees who have chosen this path and they shouldn't be taken for granted just because they don't choose to advance their position."

### 4.2 Morale and Attitude

Interview question: *"Do you encounter any issues with the morale of a plateaued employee? Does this employee's attitude have any effect on the other team members? Any tips of dealing with morale or attitude issues due to undesired career plateaus?"*

The majority of the responses indicated that there was greater risk of morale issues with those employees who were not plateaued by choice and that a negative attitude could infect other team members and could prove to be a real barrier to advancement for that employee. One respondent advised managers to "…address the attitude issue as soon as possible before it affects the morale of the unit."

### 4.3 Additional Comments

I asked the respondents to feel free to add additional comments to the end of their form submission. I have included three of those comments here, choosing the ones that resonated most with me:

"I believe that a lot of plateaued employees can be very valuable to the organization, but it's about finding a good fit for them and what they may still be passionate about within their skill set or knowledge base. However, I caution there is a difference between a plateaued employee and a difficult employee who is not willing to participate or engage in becoming a productive member of the team. Those need to be handled differently."

"I find that honesty is best. When I could not create an opportunity for an employee or find funding for him or her to attend professional development events, I was very honest and did not make empty promises. When I was able to help people to grow professionally and acquire skills and abilities to add to their resume, I was very honest in letting them know that these skills and abilities would not help them in their current unit but they would probably help if they wanted to seek employment elsewhere. No manager wants to lose a good employee, but my goal is to help people to grow and achieve their career goals even though it may be detrimental to the unit for which I am responsible."

"Don't fall into the trap that any one group of employees is better or worse than the other. Employees who choose to stay in a position can make that choice for good or bad reasons, just as employees who want to progress may do so with good or bad intentions to others. The manager must take an active stance with all of the employees to keep them engaged, productive, meeting the unit's mission and informed. If you can follow these steps, you'll probably have satisfied, if not happy, employees."

## 5. CONCLUSION

What I learned from my reading and from the small group of information technology managers that I queried is that due to the evolving nature of information technology, you need to keep learning new skills even if you wish to stay in the same job and that you need to stay engaged and productive in your work. I was gratified to learn that some of the actions I had taken on my own over the years to increase my job satisfaction were also used by the IT managers with their employees. Reading the managers' comments helped me feel less unique in my decision to not seek a higher position and motivates me to continue to perform as an active member of my team, whatever that team turns out to be after the reorganization is complete.

I have learned that those who choose to remain on career plateaus are not necessarily less talented or less desirable employees than those who wish to pursue positions with more responsibility or management roles.

## 6. Future Steps

By the time I present this paper, I will have a new niche in the Information Technology Services organization chart and a modified job description—not because I have sought a new job but as the result of a major restructuring of our main IT units on campus. My goal is to remain committed to providing excellent customer service to WVU faculty, staff, and students in whatever that new role will be.

I plan to start a work gratitude journal as described by Mo Nishiyama in the *SIGUCCS Plugged In* newsletter [3] to help me focus on the positive aspects of my job. I will register again for the WVU MLA Professional Development Institute if it will be available again.

I plan to complete the SIGUCCS mentoring program that will end at the annual conference in November 2014 and to continue developing my technical and non-technical skills through a variety of activities.

## 7. ACKNOWLEDGMENTS

I'd like to express many thanks to Amy Baker and previous supervisors for supporting my professional development efforts over the years. I'd like to thank the members of the WVU ITS Assistant Directors' Group (2013-2014), who reviewed my interview questions and discussed this topic with me informally in addition to responding. I'd also like to thank Gail Rankin, my ACM SIGUCCS mentor for 2014, for her advice on this paper.

## 8. REFERENCES

[1] Lee, Patrick Chang Boon. 1999. Career strategies, job plateau, career plateau, and job satisfaction among information technology professionals. *SIGCPR '99: Proceedings of the 1999 ACM SIGCPR Conference on Computer Personnel Research*. (New Orleans, LA, USA). SIGCPR '99. ACM, New York, NY, 125-127. DOI=http://doi.acm.org/10.1145/299513.299632

[2] Lee, Patrick Chang Boon. 2003. Going beyond career plateau: Using professional plateau to account for work outcomes. *Journal of Management Development*, Volume 22 Issue 6, 538-551.

[3] Nishiyama, Mo. 2014. A gratitude journal: The first 60 days. *SIGUCCS Plugged In*. Volume 2 Issue 3, page 5.

[4] Rozny, Noël. 2012. How a career plateau can help you get to the next level. myPathfinder Career Blog. http://myfootpath.com/mypathfinder/career-plateau-level/

[5] Sharma, Surajit Sen. Stuck on a career plateau. http://www.hrcrossing.com/article/270059/Stuck-on-a-Career-Plateau/

[6] WVU Information Technology Services. http://it.wvu.edu/

[7] WVU Professional Development Institute http://mla.hr.wvu.edu/pdi

# Status Updates: Keeping the Campus Community Informed

Shawn Plummer
SUNY Geneseo
1 College Circle
Geneseo, NY 14454
(585) 245-5577
plummer@geneseo.edu

Laurie Fox
SUNY Geneseo
1 College Circle
Geneseo, NY 14454
(585) 245-5577
fox@geneseo.edu

## ABSTRACT

To keep the campus informed about scheduled maintenance and unscheduled outages, Geneseo uses a status system built on WordPress and a monitoring server running Opsview. We will show how we use the two of these systems to provide information to the college community and provide ways for users to check the status themselves. We will also talk about best practices for communication during emergencies and the use of social media to inform the community.

## Categories and Subject Descriptors

K.6.4 [**Management of Computing and Information Systems**]: System Management – *Quality assurance.*

## General Terms

Management, Performance, Reliability, Human Factors.

## Keywords

SUNY Geneseo; Status; Monitoring; Communication; Social Media.

## 1. INTRODUCTION

Over the past few years, Geneseo has reworked and revised our notification and communication methods. We have installed new monitoring and status servers, and improved our communication methods to the campus.

Communication during technical upgrades, outages, and other emergencies is important to our customers. It must be informative, accurate, and timely, and delivered using methods that customers are comfortable using.

## 2. SYSTEM MONITORING

How do we know when something is not working? Our previous monitoring system was built on Big Brother[1], and our services and systems were grouped by broad categories that were mostly

meaningless to our customers. This tool was primarily used by our systems and networking staff.

These Big Brother examples show that the top-level groupings (see Figure 1) were meaningless to our customers. Most of the campus did not know which category the service they were using fell into. We could fix some of this opaqueness by having better category names, but we also needed the ability to include dependencies. Dependency was one of the major features we were interested in when we searched for a new monitoring solution.

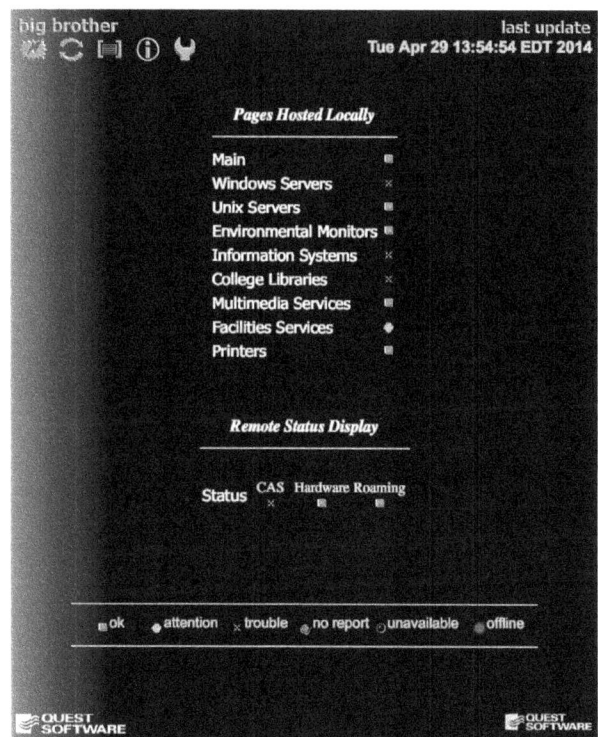

**Figure 1. Big Brother Top Level Groupings.**

The second level information available on Big Brother (see Figure 2) was also worthless to our customers. These servers have names that rarely match up with the services they provide to the campus.

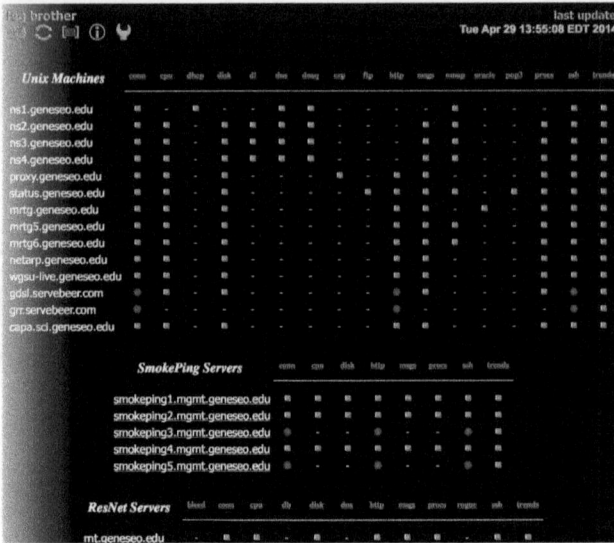

**Figure 2. Big Brother Second Level Information.**

Our new Opsview monitoring system is affectionately called "Monitaur". The main page (see Figure 3) keywords show the status of services customers actually know and care about. Information about the servers that run our services is mostly hidden from the user. We have worked hard to make sure that the tests that control whether a service is shown as up or down are meaningful tests. Errors that do not impact the service (such as log entry warnings) are not reflected in the status of the server.

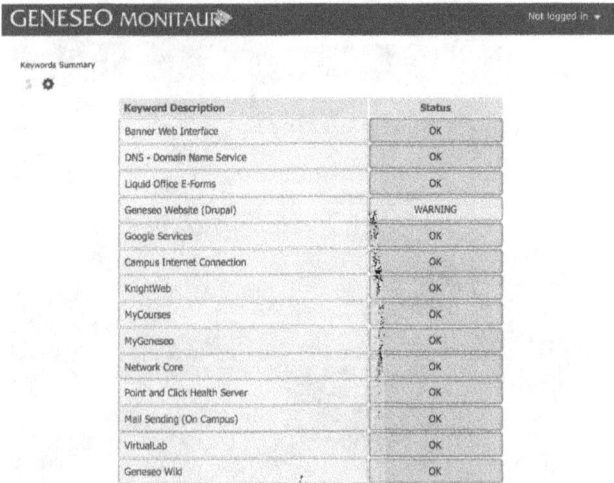

**Figure 3. Opsview Main Page.**

Opsview second level pages include dependencies. For example, our portal service "myGeneseo" relies on services such as DNS, Active Directory, the web servers, and the database server. Monitaur can display the status of each service test (see Figure 4.)

**Figure 4. Opsview Second Level Service Page.**

While customers can visit our monitoring system and see the current status of services, most never will. The next step in our project was to examine how we notify our customers of planned upgrades, outages, and emergencies.

## 3. STATUS SYSTEM

Our department utilized a homegrown web application for posting status messages to the campus. This basic system was functional but not able to be upgraded or expanded to include alternate methods of communication to the campus.

Our status notifications were displayed on the stand-alone status page, posted to the department webpage, and sent to an email mailing list. The mailing list consisted of primarily our department professional staff, our student employees, and a handful of customers who self-subscribed to the list.

After looking at many options for a status reporting system, we eventually settled on a stand-alone WordPress installation. Some of the major things we got in our status system upgrade were:

- The ability for users to self-subscribe to notices via email or SMS messaging

- Users could select just certain tags they were interested in (examples include Banner, Web, or the learning management system)

- Automatic Twitter posting of all status updates

Our WordPress installation utilizes plugins to increase the functionality of the status system. The Custom Field plugin allowed us to add additional fields included in each status. The WP to Twitter plugin posts each of our statuses to the department Twitter feed. Our user subscriptions are managed by the Subscribe2 plugin.

Since its installation in early 2012, we have posted over 1160 status messages. There are 100 users subscribed to the site, and our Twitter feed has 550 followers. These numbers represent about 8% of our user base.

## 4. POSTING STATUS MESSAGES (WHAT MAKES A GOOD STATUS POST)

It is the goal of our department to post status message for planned and unplanned outages. We also send notices of upcoming changes that may impact our customers.

It is often challenging to create a status message that is informative enough for our technical staff and clear to our non-technical users. We have identified several guidelines for creating a status post:

1. Posts should mention impacted services in the message, using names customers are familiar with. They may also include server names for our technical staff.
2. Scheduled outages should include the word "scheduled" or "planned" and a date in the title. (see Figure 5)
3. Statuses must be posted at the beginning and end of planned maintenance.
4. Post titles should be 100 characters or less to ensure Twitter notices are clear. (Twitter posts also include a link to the full status information.)
5. Custom fields should be completed. Our custom fields include notification type (outage, problem, maintenance, upgrade, new service), date (for scheduled events), and type of status (upcoming, ongoing, resolved)
6. A summarizing status post should be made at the conclusion of all outages and emergencies.

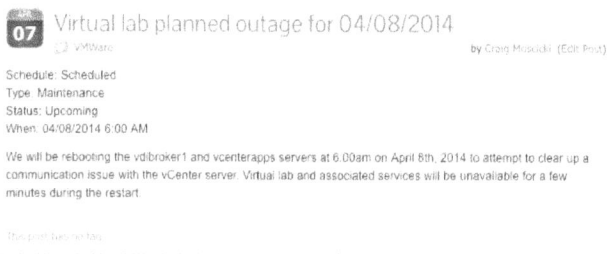

**Figure 5. Scheduled Outage Status Post.**

## 5. COMMUNICATION DURING OUTAGES

Good communication during an outage or emergency is critical. Customers rely on our notifications when there are problems. Often times their opinion of our department is shaped by how that outage or problem is handled.

During an emergency, those fixing it are often extremely stressed and working as hard as they can to fix the problem. Communication to our customers is often viewed as secondary to fixing the problem and can be a distraction from resolving the issue at hand. Fielding questions about why the service is down, what is being and done, and how much longer it will be down from many different people slows down resolution of the problem and increases stress on the people restoring service for the campus. In these situations, we designate someone not directly responsible for fixing the problem as the Incident Communications Liaison. When an outage initially occurs (or for short outages), the Incident Communications Liaison is usually the same person that initially notices the outage. For longer outages we will designate someone, usually our Support Services Director, as the communication liaison.

This Communications Liaison fields all customer questions and provides status messages to the campus. They also have the critical responsibility of asking the person fixing the problem for updates on the status of the problem at regular intervals.

During major system outages, we take the time to fully describe the outage and its impact to our customers. We also determine internally what our status-posting plan will be.

It is also extremely important during an outage that the entire team is kept up to date about the status of the outage, what tasks are being taken to resolve it, and how things are progressing. We have good success with two tools for this process. The first tool is our ticketing system. During outages we will create a ticket for the outage, and add as subscribers to the ticket all parties that need to be informed (usually the CIO and directors of several of our internal groups in CIT). Then all activities performed during the outage can be recorded to the ticket so that everyone is kept up to date. The ticket then also serves as an excellent post mortem to the outage as it includes what occurred, how the issue progressed, and the resolution. This allows us to review the ticket and make any necessary changes to our process and systems in the future. Using a ticket in our ticket system does have the downside of being fairly on sided communication and works best when just one person is updating the ticket communicating information to several people.

To facilitate more interactive communication we now have created an Incident Response room in our department wide Chat program (HipChat). It serves much the same purpose as the ticket above but is far more useful when multiple people are working on a problem together and allows for much more rapid collaboration. All of our directors and interested parties in the department can follow along and be kept instantly up to date on the status of the issue. The chat program also allows our support personnel to update our system admins about new problems or provide more information that can be critical in diagnosing the problem. Since the chat is persistent and logged, people connecting late to the chat can read the past posts and get updated quickly and it serves as an excellent post mortem of the outage much like the ticket.

Regular communication with customers during an outage is important, especially the longer the outage lasts. During extended outages, customers start to wonder if the problem is still being worked on, or if it is resolved but just not working for them. Establishing a "next communication time" lets customer know when to expect the next notification about the status of the service. (see Figure 6) Even if the status simply states that things continue to be down the customer knows that they are not forgotten.

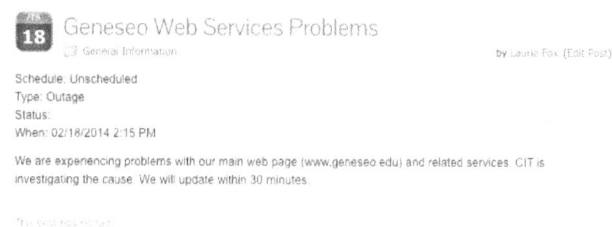

**Figure 6. Status Post with Future Update Time.**

Other tips for communicating to your users during an outage:

1. Engage customers via Twitter and email when there are problems and link to status posts. This increases the awareness of your status system and Twitter feed. (see Figure 7)

2. Encourage all department chairs and secretaries to subscribe to the status system to receive updates during outages.

3. Search for mentions of the services that are impacted during the emergency to respond to random mentions on social media.

4. Automatically subscribe select users to the status system, including all technical staff and student employees of the department.

5. Have a plan for if your electronic communication systems are not working. These could include:
   a. Off site hosted status systems
   b. Off site hosted documentation
   c. A phone tree for calling all campus departments to let them know of the outage status

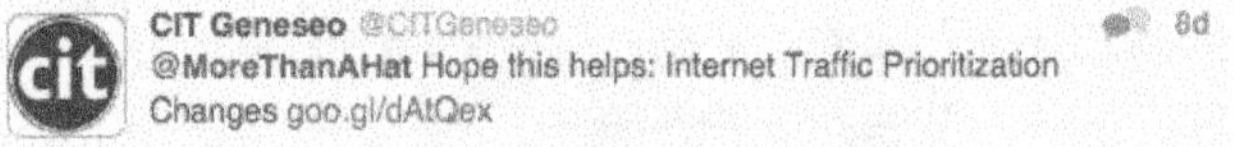

**CIT Geneseo** @CITGeneseo                    8d
@MoreThanAHat Hope this helps: Internet Traffic Prioritization Changes goo.gl/dAtQex

**Figure 7. Twitter reply with link to previous status post.**

While we hope to avoid outages, they do happen. Proper communication can go a long way to removing the sting of an outage, and in some cases it can actually increase satisfaction of your customers.

# 6. REFERENCES

[1] WordPress *http://wordpress.org*

[2] WordPress Plugins *http://wordpress.org/plugins/*

[3] Opsview *http://www.opsview.com*

[4] HipChat *https://www.hipchat.com*

# Intrusion Detection: Tools, Techniques and Strategies

Vijay Anand
Industrial Engineering and technology
Southeast Missouri State University
Cape Girardeau, USA 63701
vanand@semo.edu

## ABSTRACT

Intrusion detection is an important aspect of modern cyber-enabled infrastructure in identifying threats to digital assets. Intrusion detection encompasses tools, techniques and strategies to recognize evolving threats thereby contributing to a secure and trustworthy computing framework. There are two primary intrusion detection paradigms, signature pattern matching and anomaly detection. The paradigm of signature pattern matching encompasses the identification of known threat sequences of causal events and matching it to incoming events. If the pattern of incoming events matches the signature of an attack there is a positive match which can be labeled for further processing of countermeasures. The paradigm of anomaly detection is based on the premise that an attack signature is unknown. Events can deviate from normal digital behavior or can inadvertently give out information in normal event processing. These stochastic events have to be evaluated by variety of techniques such as artificial intelligence, prediction models etc. before identifying potential threats to the digital assets in a cyber-enabled system. Once a pattern is identified in the evaluation process after excluding false positives and negative this pattern can be classified as a signature pattern. This paper highlights a setup in an educational environment to effectively flag threats to the digital assets in the system using an intrusion detection framework. Intrusion detection framework comes in two primary formats a network intrusion detection system and a host intrusion detection system. In this paper we identify different publicly available tools of intrusion detection and their effectiveness in a test environment. This paper also looks at the mix of tools that can be deployed to effectively flag threats as they evolve. The effect of encryption in such setup and threat identification with encryption is also studied.

## Categories and Subject Descriptors

K.6.5 [**Management of Computing and Information Systems**]: Security and Protection – Access controls, Authentication, Cryptographic controls, Information flow controls, Verification.

## General Terms

Management, Performance, Reliability, Security, Verification.

## Keywords

Attacks; Virtualized; Intrusion; Pattern; Anomaly; Honeypot; Honeynet; Sanitization

## 1. INTRODUCTION

The reference to cyber enabled infrastructure implies an infrastructure whose access and control is enabled by computing hardware and software at minimum and may additionally have networking components for remote access and control. As cyber-enabled infrastructure has become ubiquitous, interest in this infrastructure has also increased. Some of this interest is maleficent which has a lot of potential to damage. There is a need to identify such attacks on to system. Attacks that can be staged on a cyber-enabled infrastructure needs to be detected for any corrective solutions. Hence the requirement for intrusion detection is very important. The detection aspect does not necessarily mean prevention, but it triggers countermeasures which may or may not always result in prevention. Attacks are of two kinds, passive and active. A passive attack is one in which the attacker is not controlling the attack outcomes in real time where as an active attack is one in which an attacker is basing actions on the feedback received on outcome of an attack. In this paper we highlight the different types of attacks and their classification, the available techniques to detect these attacks, with an emphasis on the cryptographic aspect of a cyber-enabled infrastructure, available tools for detecting attacks, setup and insight about outcomes.

## 2. ATTACK CLASSIFICATION

An attack into a cyber-enabled system broadly categorizes the disruption of confidentiality, integrity, authenticity, availability, privacy and value of a digital asset. Digital Assets in this context refers to:

- Digital personal data (Email, Facebook content etc.),
- Computing Systems(Server, PC, Tablets, Smartphones),
- Networking Infrastructure(Wireless(802.11, 3G, LTE), Wired)

Attack types on a cyber-enabled system can be broadly classified into active and passive attacks [1]. This method of classification is chosen based on the adversary type over the details of the attack. Detection systems need to adapt on the type of adversary and detection engines need to quantify behavior for effective attack identifications. Active attacks are attacks where the attacker is molding attacks based on the system response [2]. A cyber enabled system is an automaton whose responses are predetermined by the system designer. An active attacker can look at the system response and intelligently stage attacks to gain access to a digital asset. Detection of such attacks can be difficult. Passive attacks [1][3] on the other hand have no real time intelligence associated with it. The attack can be classified as automaton attacking another automaton. The attack automaton does have some intelligence but it is predetermined by the automaton creator which can be simple or sophisticated. The exploits these attacks leverage can be quantified on software and system vulnerabilities. The exploit classification can be broadly put into:

- Input Based Exploits: these types of exploits includes the set of threats which take advantage of vulnerabilities in input handing and input events of a computing service. The different vulnerabilities are Boundary Condition Error, Input Validation Error, Failure to Handle Exceptional Conditions, Origin Validation Error. These exploits can be controlled through indirectly or directly derived from inputs.
- Environment Based Exploits: This category of exploits are based on threats emanating from vulnerabilities that change the constructs upon which a cyber-enabled system is designed upon. An exploits are based on either changing the configuration or the environment for which the system was designed.
- Design Errors Exploits: This category of attacks is based on threats in multi-process systems where components of a system are designed without proper interaction to avoid exploitation (i.e., design error attacks)...
- Ciphering System Exploits: This type of exploits represents the threats on the Access Validation Errors, which are encountered within a ciphering system framework due to faulty design or implementation.
- Unknown Exploits: This category of exploit, does not fall under any of the broadly recognized exploit types, and requires individual analysis and treatments to understand the exploits.

There have been few studies in categorization [1] [4] [5] of attacks. In this paper we categorize the attacks based on the subversion of the underlying principle of secure design and architecture. These exploits comprise an attack which can be broadly classified as:

Privilege Escalation attacks: This category of attack tries to subvert the principle of least privilege [6] in secure system design. The objective of the privilege escalation is the ability to get access to digital assets beyond the boundaries of a given privilege.

Access Disruption attacks: These attacks are the most common ones manifesting more broadly as Denial of Service [7] attacks.

Depth of Defense [8] attacks: These attacks are based on the premise that a pivot which does not belong to important services in a cyber-infrastructure is used to gain access to important services.

Confidentiality attacks: These attacks are based on weak ciphers or vulnerable crypto systems that are used in a cyber-infrastructure.

Integrity Attacks: This is similar to confidentiality attacks in the sense that vulnerable algorithms are used in cyber infrastructure.

## 3. The Setup

A typical laboratory environment for computing studies has a set of licensed computers and some servers that are accessed through the equipment. A high level overview of a laboratory setup is shown below. An important thing to note that with the advent of Bring Your Own Device (BYOD) policy the laboratory environment is much more diverse. The only similarity that is expected from all the devices is that of software running in the systems that is used to access licensed software in the servers in the laboratory framework. In an old configuration the problem lies how many intrusion detection systems need to be put. A laboratory with "X" number of computers which are homogenous in their build would potentially require a single intrusion detection system. The other intrusion detection systems have to match the server abilities. Depending on the types of the software the server or a collection of servers have the number of Intrusion Detection System (IDS) each fine-tuned for a specific datatype has to be chosen. This kind of network intrusion detection if there is no end to end encryption. That does not solve issues if the attack happens after the decryption of data. In such a case there is a need for Host Intrusion Detection System (HIDS) [9] to effectively identify the types of intrusions that are encountered in a laboratory setup. The issue after this is that of storing the logging information and such logging typically should be on a Network Area Storage (NAS), away from the devices to collect and analyses. Different tools can be used for post analysis of this data like Suricata.

As shown in the diagram below there is a firewall associated with this network along with the Intrusion Detection System. The firewall is a layer 2/3 device on the network which can discriminate traffic between endpoints and apply some policy based rules within end points. The firewall does not have the capability to inspect the content of a network connection though where the challenge lies in attempt to identify an intrusion.

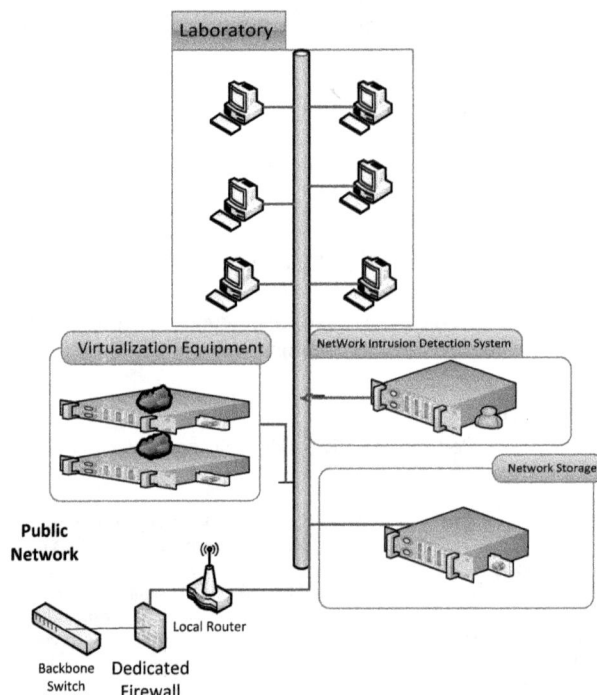

**Figure 1: A laboratory setup with Intrusion Detection System**

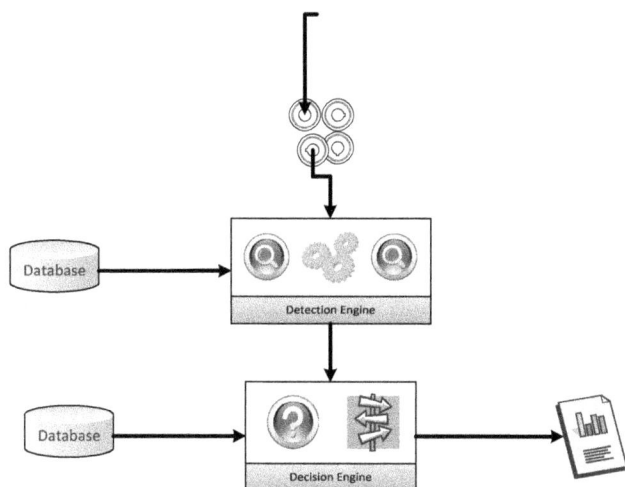

**Figure 2: Components of an Intrusion Detection System**

## 4. Intrusion Detection System

There are a few different entities in a cyber-infrastructure that are installed to protect digital assets. The first one is firewall at the network perimeter. As highlighted in Figure 1 a firewall is layer2/3 device [10] that only look at network end points to make decisions. The firewall has no visibility into the data in network. A firewall always sits on the path of the traffic and can potentially be a bottleneck in case the firewall cannot take decisions in real time. Another important element in digital asset protection is that of an anti-malware [11] software which looks at applications and flags applications with known patterns of malware signatures. The anti-malware software is very operating system specific [12][13] and typically looks at stored procedures in an application to make a decision. It is pretty effective on non-active attacks where the malware is resident on a system and the system then analyzes the application to sort a legitimate application from malware. The anti-malware software typically operates at an application layer and hence has visibility to content of network endpoint. But an anti-malware software is not capable of analyzing or detective an active attack. This is where an Intrusion Detection System [14] plays a major role in identifying an attack at the application level. A typical Intrusion Detection System has the components as shown in figure 2. All application data from the content of the end point of networked element is passed through a detection engine. The detection engine then looks at stored patterns of intrusion signatures for live and non-active attacks and then logs the information. A thing to be noted is that the intrusion detection system does not have an actionable outcome [14]. The actionable outcome is left to the system operator to look at log files for analysis and then modify operating system constructs' and firewall policies accordingly. If an intrusion detection system actively modifies the operating system constructs or the firewall constructs such a system is referred to as an intrusion prevention system (IPS) [16]. Intrusion Detection Systems are broadly classified with respect to placement within a cyber-infrastructure as Host based or Network based [13][14][15]. A network based intrusion detection system is an independent installation of other elements of a cyber-infrastructure that passively monitors the network behavior [16]. IDS can be an active device but since it does not have any preventive role it is typically installed as a passive device. As a passive device the IDS profiles all the traffic

entering within the perimeter of a network and logs interesting traffic that has a match within its signature database. A Host based IDS[17] on the other hand is an application software that is installed on an operating system which profiles traffic at the host level and logs interesting traffic. Host based traffic typically would execute as an independent process within a system. Some IDS could be executed in both Network and Host mode and these are generally referred to as a Hybrid IDS [18]. The core of IDS as shown in the diagram is that of the detection engine. An important categorization of IDS based on detection engine provides another nuance for choosing IDS for an appropriate application. The detection engine if is based on pattern detection of known attacks signatures then the IDS is referred to as a signature based IDS system. Signature based IDS [19] are based on matching "pattern" for "known patterns" [20] of activity detrimental to elements in the infrastructure. The Benefits of a signature based IDS are:

- Low alarm rates: Effectively the IDS detection engine has to look up a list of known signatures of attacks and log it or report into the monitoring system if a match is identified.
- Signature based IDS are very accurate.
- Speed: Signature based IDS can be relatively fast since the pattern match is based on what traffic is observed and what signature is stored as an attack signature. Based on the percent match attack quantification is done.

A few pitfalls of a signature based IDS system are:

- Signature of an attack is causal to knowledge of an attack. Hence if new attacks are formulated signature based IDS have no measureable benefit. The quality of IDS is as strong as the signatures from which pattern matching can be done. It therefore requires constant updating of signatures to account for new signatures.
- One of the biggest drawbacks of a signature based IDS on the network are by fragmenting of a packet. If an attack deliberately fragments it packets to deliver an attack attacks can be masked.
- Update of a signature is required on a constant basis and the signature dataset has to update before assuring security within a network.

The most common open source IDS Snort [16] primarily uses the signature based detection and the financial structure of Snort type IDS is based on subscription to getting the latters patterns of attack signature.

Another kind of IDS is based on the premise of anomaly detection [21] wherein the IDS looks for traffics patterns and tries to profile traffic based on mathematical or intelligence based computations. The idea is identify anomalies in traffic patterns and if there is an anomaly detected that traffic set can thereafter be analyzed further to identify further issues. Anomalies in time series data are data points that significantly deviate from the normal pattern of the data sequence. Time series is a sequence of data points, measured typically at successive times, spaced at (often uniform) time intervals. A typical way of using anomaly detection is to learn a model of normal behavior

- Using supervised(**e.g., classification**) or unsupervised method(e.g. Clustering, probabilistic models with latent variables such as Hidden Markovian Models)

Based on this model learnt from a suspicion score is constructed

- function of observed data (e.g., likelihood ratio/ Bayes factor)

- captures the deviation of observed data from normal model
- raise flag if the score exceeds a threshold

This kind of attack detection engine [22] is pretty good to identify new attacks into a system. As a side effect of this technique of intrusion detection the IDS does a thorough screening of all traffic. The downside of this detection engine is that of false positives and false negative in the detection mechanism. It can be very resource exhaustive for capturing all traffic for analysis and performance may not be real time. Of the open source IDS systems "Bro" [23] is the one that is known to an anomaly engine extensively. Once a pattern has been recognizes from anomaly detection that particular pattern can then become a signature.

An intrusion detection engine cannot detect all the attacks that are encounter in a cyber-infrastructure. To maximize the number of intrusions detected in a cyber-infrastructure it is important to having multiple IDS with competing technologies executing simultaneously thereby improving the probability of intrusion detection.

The next aspect for IDS is to creating a testing framework [24] so as to identify that a particular IDS is properly setup. One of the ways to do it is having an attack framework for testing purposes. An important aspect of commissioning and IDS is to test it thoroughly and this attack framework becomes an integral part. It is also recommended that the testing is done periodically after commissioning. This attack framework is based on penetration testing tools known. Since penetration testing tool's attack set changes with time the testing periodically aspect of the IDS installation is a part of due diligence effort on part of security practitioners. An important aspect in the testing time is to have the testing framework be isolated from the real network. Isolation is important since some of the attack vectors have a potential to cross the plane of test systems.

The final aspect of the IDS setup is to identify attackers by some network identifiable features. One way to attract attacks onto a cyber-infrastructure is to have potentially vulnerable software which can be monitored. This can be created by creation of honey nets and honeypots

- Honeypot [25] is a computing construct made up of special software applications that can be easily compromised by a cyber-attack.
- Honeynet [26] is a networking construct whose purpose is to attack attackers and can be easily compromised.

Any traffic that enters and exits through the honeynet/honeypot constructs is deemed as suspicious and needs to be carefully monitored. If a successful attack is constructed further attacks on the computing resources can be launched.

The monitoring server in this setup formulates the instantiation of honeypots and intrusion detection system [27] [28] which allows behavior monitoring for risk analysis. The question which arises in this situation is what types of honeypots need to be setup. Most of the classroom operating system is standard so at least one honeypot with a classroom image has to be setup. One important thing in this setup is that connectivity from this honeypot to any other system is restricted though the firewall. The only element this honeypot can access is the firewall in a cyber-infrastructure. There are certain services that need to be enabled in for students to complete their assignments. The other honeypots should be decided based on the software services that are expected to turn on to complete assignments for a given class. This can vary depending on the scope of the class. Any service that is turned on

the network requires a honeypot service equivalent on an operating system. If services are hosted on a Linux machine then a Linux honeypot needs to be established and if services are hosted on a Windows device then a Windows honeypot needs to be established.

Another important aspect of this design is that of cryptographic data that is encountered by endpoints crossing the network. Most installations are networking based IDS. As discussed earlier most NIDS don't have visibility to encrypted traffic hence the challenge to incorporate encrypted traffic is critical in understanding of an intrusion. One of the mechanisms of identifying intrusions in end systems is utilizing host intrusion detection (HIDS) systems. Since the traffic is already decrypted on the host machine the host IDS can detect encrypted data that is missed by the network IDS. This implies that all images that are installed in the school devices require installing a host IDS whole logs are collected for analysis and detection.

The setup that was used in this exercise was having an anomaly detection engine IDS, having a pattern detection IDS, a commercial IDS, a honeypot setup, a testing framework with attack systems.

## 5. CONCLUSIONS

In this paper the need for IDS and the different kinds of IDS are highlighted. A setup is shown in allowing detection of variety of intrusions into a system including cryptographic type intrusions.

## 6. REFERENCES

[1] Amiel, Frederic, et al. "Passive and active combined attacks: Combining fault attacks and side channel analysis." Fault Diagnosis and Tolerance in Cryptography, 2007. FDTC 2007. Workshop on. IEEE, 2007.

[2] Serjantov, Andrei, Roger Dingledine, and Paul Syverson. "From a trickle to a flood: Active attacks on several mix types." Information Hiding. Springer Berlin Heidelberg, 2003.

[3] Stefano Zanero. 2009. Wireless Malware Propagation: A Reality Check. IEEE Security and Privacy 7, 5 (September 2009), 70-74. DOI=10.1109/MSP.2009.142 http://dx.doi.org/10.1109/MSP.2009.142

[4] Gao, Zhiqiang, and Nirwan Ansari. "Tracing cyber attacks from the practical perspective." Communications Magazine, IEEE 43.5 (2005): 123-131.

[5] Bass, Tim. "Intrusion detection systems and multisensor data fusion." Communications of the ACM 43.4 (2000): 99-105.

[6] Schneider, Fred B. "Least privilege and more." Computer Systems. Springer New York, 2004. 253-258.

[7] Zargar, Saman Taghavi, James Joshi, and David Tipper. "A survey of defense mechanisms against distributed denial of service (DDoS) flooding attacks." Communications Surveys & Tutorials, IEEE 15.4 (2013): 2046-2069.

[8] Rocha, Francisco, Thomas Gross, and Aad van Moorsel. "Defense-in-depth against malicious insiders in the cloud." Cloud Engineering (IC2E), 2013 IEEE International Conference on. IEEE, 2013.

[9] Jacob Zimmerman, Ludovic M, Christophe Bidan, "Experimenting with a Policy-Based HIDS Based on an Information Flow Control Model," Computer Security Applications Conference, Annual, p. 364, 19th Annual Computer Security Applications Conference (ACSAC '03), 2003

[10] Achi, H., A. Hellany, and M. Nagrial. "Network security approach for digital forensics analysis." Computer Engineering & Systems, 2008. ICCES 2008. International Conference on. IEEE, 2008.

[11] Sikorski, Michael, and Andrew Honig. Practical Malware Analysis: The Hands-On Guide to Dissecting Malicious Software. No Starch Press, 2012.

[12] Shari Lawrence Pfleeger "Anatomy of an Intrusion" IT Pro, 2010

[13] Raheem A. Beyah, *Michael C. Holloway, and John A. Copeland "Invisible Trojan: An Architecture, Implementation and Detection Method"

[14] Mell, R. B. A. P. "Intrusion detection systems." National Institute of Standards and Technology (NIST), Special Publication 51 (2001).

[15] Zhang, Xinyou, Chengzhong Li, and Wenbin Zheng. "Intrusion prevention system design." Computer and Information Technology, International Conference on. IEEE Computer Society, 2004.

[16] Roesch, Martin. "Snort: Lightweight Intrusion Detection for Networks." LISA. Vol. 99. 1999.

[17] Wagner, David, and Paolo Soto. "Mimicry attacks on host-based intrusion detection systems." Proceedings of the 9th ACM Conference on Computer and Communications Security. ACM, 2002.

[18] Aydın, M. Ali, A. Halim Zaim, and K. Gökhan Ceylan. "A hybrid intrusion detection system design for computer network security." Computers & Electrical Engineering 35.3 (2009): 517-526.

[19] Kumar, Sandeep, and Eugene H. Spafford. "A pattern matching model for misuse intrusion detection." (1994).

[20] Lee, Sin Yeung, Wai Lup Low, and Pei Yuen Wong. "Learning fingerprints for a database intrusion detection system." Computer Security—ESORICS 2002. Springer Berlin Heidelberg, 2002. 264-279.

[21] Lazarevic, Aleksandar, et al. "A Comparative Study of Anomaly Detection Schemes in Network Intrusion Detection." SDM. 2003.

[22] Depren, Ozgur, et al. "An intelligent intrusion detection system (IDS) for anomaly and misuse detection in computer networks." Expert systems with Applications 29.4 (2005): 713-722.

[23] The Bro Network Security Monitor http://www.bro.org/

[24] McHugh, John. "Testing intrusion detection systems: a critique of the 1998 and 1999 DARPA intrusion detection system evaluations as performed by Lincoln Laboratory." ACM transactions on Information and system Security 3.4 (2000): 262-294.

[25] Provos, Niels. "A Virtual Honeypot Framework." USENIX Security Symposium. Vol. 173. 2004.

[26] McCarty, Bill. "The honeynet arms race." Security & Privacy, IEEE 1.6 (2003): 79-82.

[27] Thonnard, Olivier, and Marc Dacier. "A framework for attack patterns' discovery in honeynet data." digital investigation 5 (2008): S128-S139.

[28] Lee, Wenke, and Salvatore J. Stolfo. "A framework for constructing features and models for intrusion detection systems." ACM transactions on Information and system security (TiSSEC) 3.4 (2000): 227-261.

# Organizing Chaos: Student Workforce Management Tools

Andrew Lyons
University at Albany ITS-CSS
1400 Washington Avenue
Albany, NY 12222
011-518-442-2636
alyons@albany.edu

## ABSTRACT

To successfully manage a student workforce, one must make sense of all of the interconnected elements involved, including hiring, scheduling (both initially and for changes), monitoring attendance, timesheets and payroll, and more. There are many tools available to address these needs, some specialized and some Swiss Army knives. I will discuss common managerial needs and how specific tools meet those needs, giving summaries of the tools and needs as implemented at a few institutions. There will be a specific focus on the tools we use at the University at Albany, what works well, and where there are opportunities for growth and adjustment.

## Categories and Subject Descriptors

H.4.1 [Office Automation]: Office Automation – *time management (e.g., calendars, schedules).*

## General Terms: Management

## Keywords

Scheduling tools, Student workforce, Time tracking

## 1. INTRODUCTION

This paper discusses the functions of a manager of a student workforce and the variety of tools that a manager might use to facilitate performing those functions. While many of the concepts may apply to a variety of work situations and environments, discussion will focus on higher education technical support environments. I hope to address the difficulty of choosing a tool or method without knowing the landscape of available features. Even without selecting one solution as "the best," this discussion should inform managers as they work to manage their employees most effectively.

## 1.1 THE AUTHOR

My direct experience in the area of student workforce management comes from three portions of my career:

- Over two years with ITS at Hamilton College as part of the Student Technology Consultant workforce of about 25

- Over three years with IT Services at Hobart and William Smith Colleges as a Senior Technical Support Specialist, working closely with the student workforce of about 10

- Over four years with ITS at the University at Albany as an IT Support Specialist and the manager of the student Tech Consultant workforce of about 25

## 1.2 UNIVERSITY AT ALBANY AND INFORMATION TECHNOLOGY SERVICES

The University at Albany is one of the State University of New York research centers and is located in New York's Capital District. It hosts over 17,000 undergraduate and graduate students and 6,000 employees. The Information Technology Services division has about 130 staff supporting and maintaining the many enterprise operations at the University. The ITS-Client Support Services HelpDesk, with four professional employees, employs 20 to 25 Tech Consultants to work the walk-up counter in front of our office as well as the satellite support desks in the Information Commons areas of the University Libraries. The Tech Consultants handle approximately 2,500 support interactions per year, plus unrecorded customer service functions, such as providing directions to printers and other resources.

## 2. MANAGERIAL FUNCTIONS

Student workforce managers need to perform several key functions to assure appropriate support is available when needed. These functions include

- Recruitment and onboarding

- Creation and population of the coverage schedule

- Changing the schedule as needed

- Monitoring attendance and punctuality for scheduled shifts

- Collecting and verifying time sheets for payroll

## 3. COMMON SOLUTIONS

The solutions by which managers fulfill the need for the above functions fall into three main groups: manual, packaged, and homegrown tools.

## 3.1 MANUAL TOOLS

In the short term, the simplest solution for performing the managerial duties is using existing non-automated and non-integrated tools for each functional need. This often involves three main elements:

- Spreadsheet(s)
- E-mail
- Time sheets

At first, spreadsheets seem great for scheduling, given their easy conversion of calendars, flexible filling, and varied color-coding. A work schedule built in a spreadsheet will clearly communicate the who-works-when information necessary. However, when managing multiple locations with many people who need to make occasional minor changes, using these tools can be cumbersome when only one manager has update functionality. The issue can be somewhat alleviated by using a shared and editable spreadsheet in a network- or Internet-accessible location, but there are always risks of accidental or intentional changes interfering with its use.

**Figure 1. Manually-managed schedule in a worksheet document. [1]**

Using e-mail or other electronic messaging for shift change arrangements (drops, takes, and trades) is useful, given the inherent linkage of name, time and date, and request or notice information. It is an improvement on just updating the schedule document, as employees and managers might not know to look for changes or might not notice them sufficiently far in advance. E-mail becomes cumbersome when employees, eager to cover vacancies, might read their oldest e-mail first and reply to a request for help without seeing a message already covering it. This is not necessarily functionally prohibitive, but it can be confusing and frustrating.

Many departments use written time sheets for recording what hours employees actually work for payroll purposes and for verification against the planned schedule. Written time sheets have two main flaws: they are easily inflated or falsified and they

are inefficient to validate. The manual entry of hours, while arithmetically simple, tends to reward people who are tardy or leave early while providing no incentive to arrive early or stay to the end of a shift, visual attendance verification by a manager notwithstanding.

All three of these tools also run into the problem of scale. For a single location with few employees, it is simple keep track of all the elements, but as the numbers of locations and employees increase, the complexity grows dramatically. Scale issues demonstrate the need to automate some or all of the functions.

## 3.2 PACKAGED TOOLS

### 3.2.1 Whentowork (whentowork.com) and Whentohelp (whentohelp.com)

When to Work is a popular solution for scheduling and payroll activities. It is web-based, hosted, and low-cost. When to Help is a related tool for approved entities, like volunteer charity groups.

It includes a flexible schedule view for both employees and managers, allowing varying time frames with one click or filtering based on such criteria as name, location, coverage, or date. For scheduling, employees may be authorized to work at certain locations based on their abilities/roles.

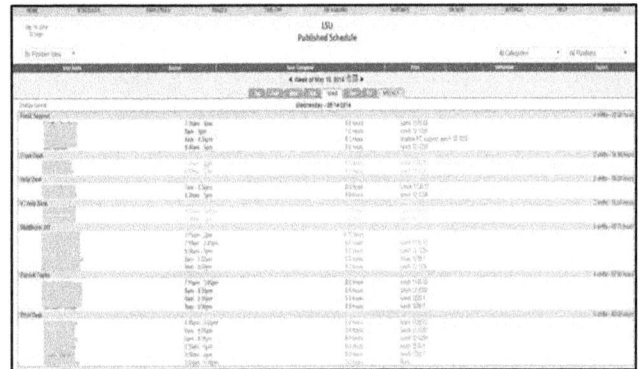

**Figure 2. Schedule list view with multiple locations separated in When to Work. [2]**

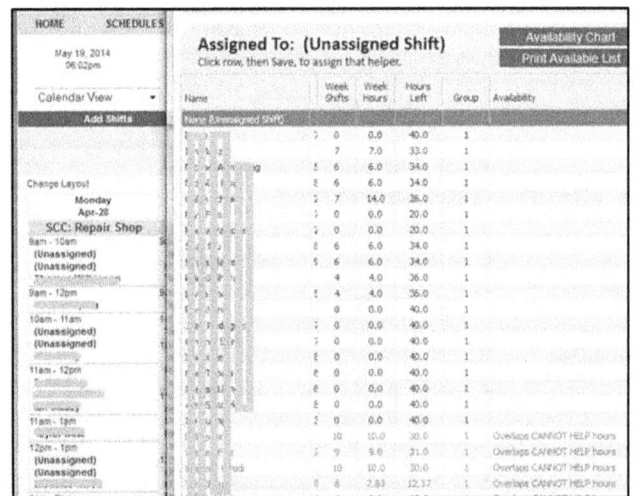

**Figure 3. Shift filling view, including unassigned hours (left, yellow) and eligible employees (right, black) in When to Help. [3]**

Employees can also select ranges of time for which they are available to work and indicate preferred hours within the available ranges.

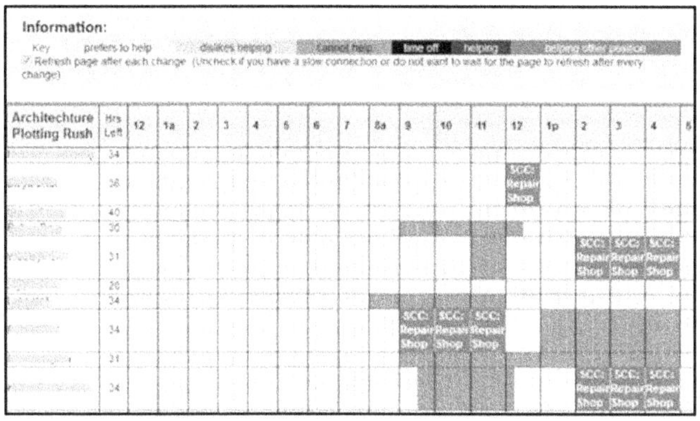

**Figure 4. Availability settings for employees in When to Help.** [3]

The shift trading and posting board makes modifications simple, so that employees can attempt to swap or give up hours when other obligations arise. To facilitate reliability, the schedule can be exported to some external calendar formats. [7]

### 3.2.2 ConPortal (conportal.sourceforge.net)

ConPortal, the tool that we use at UAlbany, is a free, open-source solution developed at Pomona College and Bucknell University. It is a s on PHP and MySQL. While it is not widely used and has no official support, it includes many features and allows for significant customization.

Scheduling, time tracking, and monitoring current coverage are the most valuable features for student scheduling at our institution. Shifts can be assigned by a manager or opened to employees to take, with options to schedule and phase the beginning of shift taking. Shift taking may be further customized by limiting maximum hours per week, limiting to certain seniority, or just open to all employees. Once shifts are in place, they may be temporarily or permanently dropped and picked up easily.

Time tracking is based on punch in and punch out times through the web interface. The ability to punch in or out is restricted to authorized workstations by an IP address table, so it automatically corroborates employee location. The employees can then view and print time sheets each for pay period.

There is a monitoring feature to notify a designated e-mail address whenever there is a coverage anomaly, either a dropped shift not picked up or a scheduled shift where the person is not punched in by ten minutes after the hour, allowing a manager to more reliably make changes to cover priority locations and take corrective action with employees.

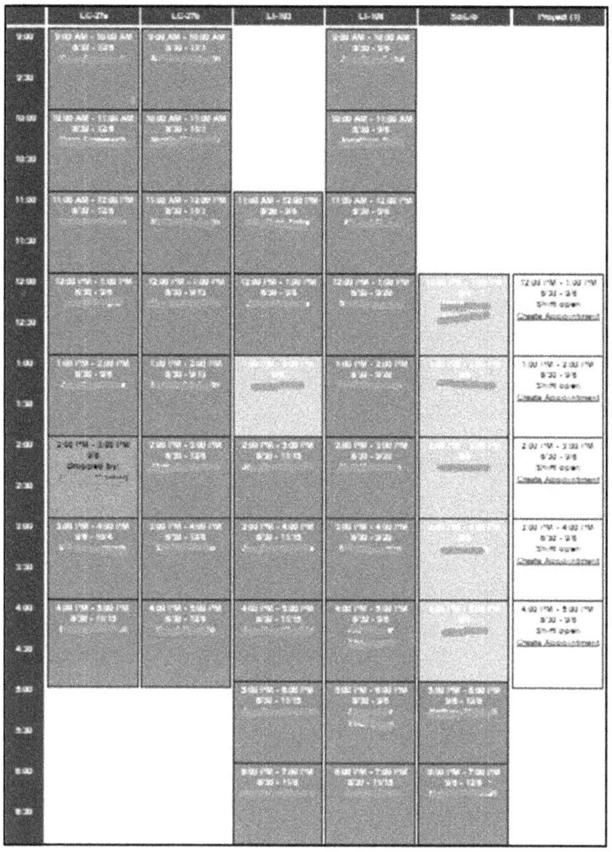

**Figure 5. Daily schedule of all shifts in ConPortal.**

### 3.2.3 ScheduleSource TeamWork (ScheduleSource.com)

TeamWork is a suite of scalable applications that can provide a large- or small-workforce management solution. While it has many more features than are likely relevant for our concerns, its Employee scheduling module should cover most requirements. Its highlights include robust scheduling capabilities, such as assigning limits per day or week and self-service sign-up and shift trading.

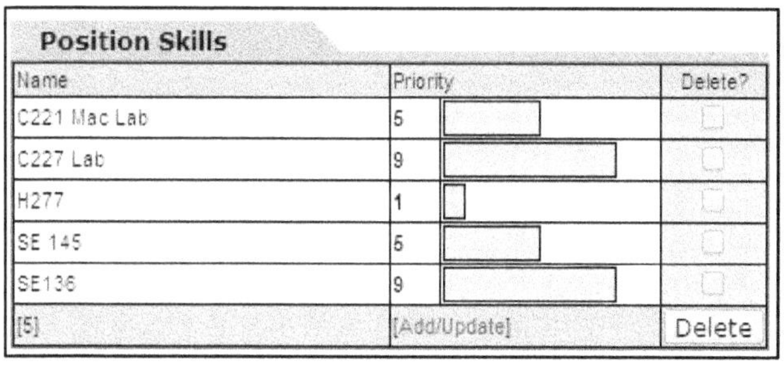

**Figure 6. Employee role and location settings in ScheduleSource TeamWork.** [4]

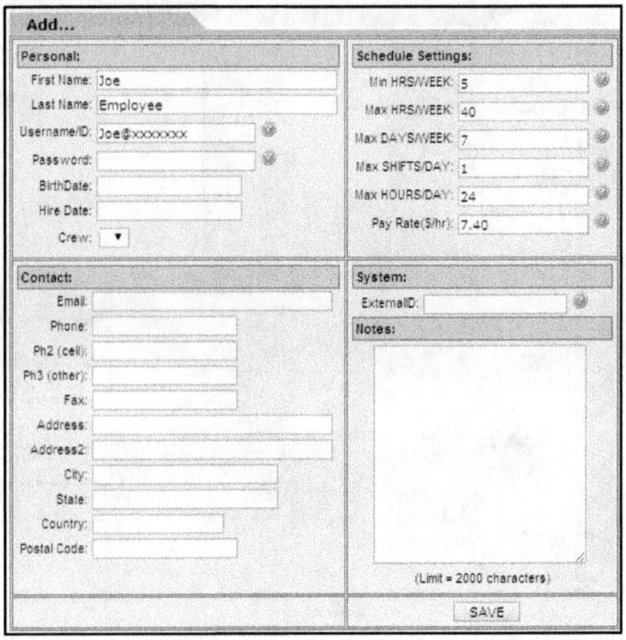

Figure 7. Employee profile settings, including hour requirements in ScheduleSource TeamWork. [4]

TeamWork also has a well-developed schedule view, allowing filtering based on a host of variables, including location, day, or employee. It can display in a list or grid format.

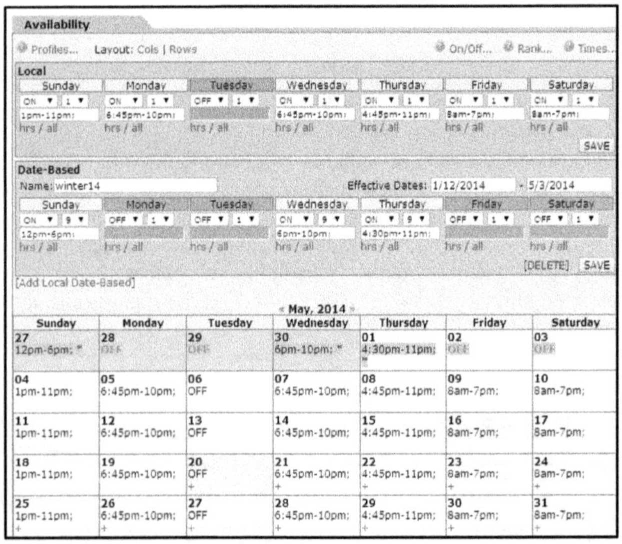

Figure 8. Employee schedule availability settings in ScheduleSource TeamWork. [4]

There is no current status alert built into the Scheduling module, but Time & Attendance has this, as an add-on with their time-tracking equipment.

### 3.2.4 ShiftPlanning (shiftplanning.com)
ShiftPlanning is a scalable, hosted suite of tools that provides many features for managing a workforce. The market for this tool appears to be mainly corporate, but there is no reason to explicitly segregate along this division.

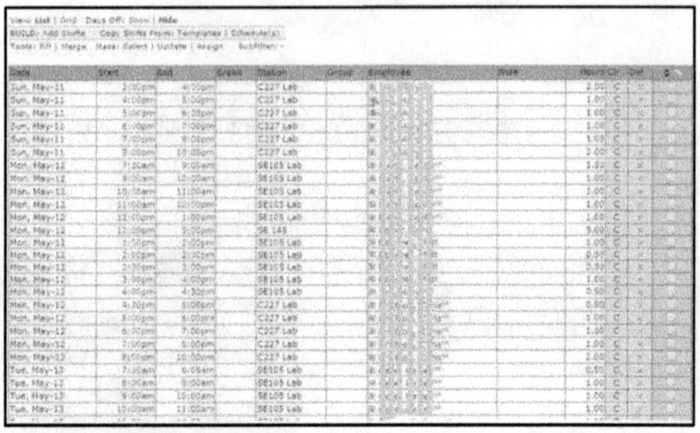

Figure 9. Schedule list view in ScheduleSource Teamwork. [4]

Automation, integration, and validation are the key features of ShiftPlanning. The schedule may be easily filled using pre-set availability and shift periods, then managers or employees can trade as needed and view it in a variety of ways.

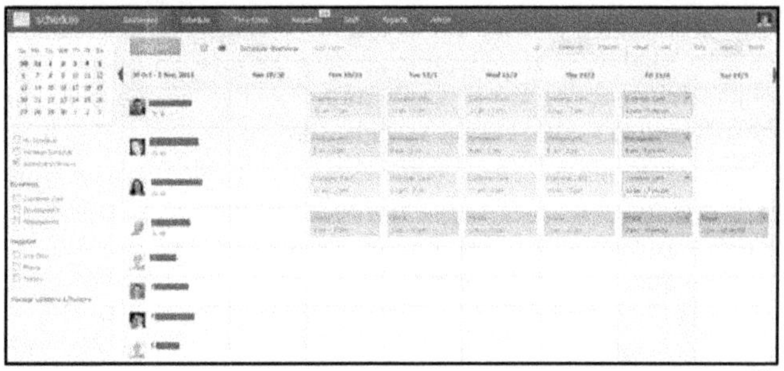

Figure 10. All employees schedule by week in ShiftPlanning. [6]

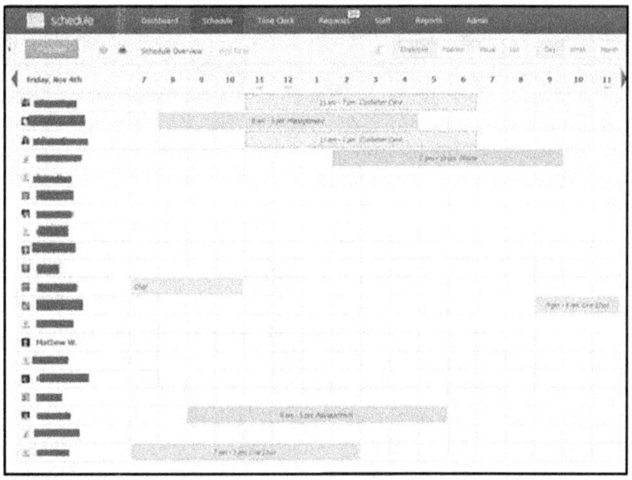

Figure 11. All employees schedule by day in ShiftPlanning. [6]

There are interfaces for using single-sign-on tools, which facilitates login by not requiring separate credentials; payroll tools to import and export shift data; and social and other media platforms for contacting people through popular means beyond just e-mail and the dashboard.

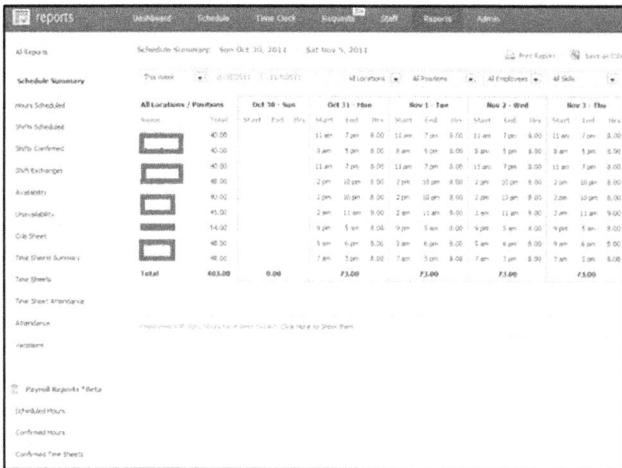

**Figure 12. Payroll summary for exporting from ShiftPlanning.** [6]

The time clock feature can be secured to specific IP addresses or dedicated terminals, can track GPS information for a mobile workforce, and can capture camera images of the employee, to verify honesty and presence.[6]

## 3.3 HOMEGROWN TOOLS

Homegrown tools likely include the most important features to the institution that develops them and significant customization for the local environment. They tend to be targeted to a few specific needs, growing (some might say "bloating") only when necessary. The benefit of a homegrown solution, unlike many packaged tools, is that there are no inherent restrictions to what may be modified, customized, or enhanced.

However, being homegrown, there would be no support outside of the developing team, so changes and fixes might be slow and longer-term maintenance may be unavailable if, say, the industrious student or employee who created the tool graduates or leaves the job. This would be a problem if platform changes, like updates to operating systems for desktop applications or browser or plugins for web applications, lead to compatibility issues. One example of this is with deprecated HTML code falling out of support with major browser makers, forcing the occasional use of a reliably-outdated browser, like Netscape, for certain management functions.

## 3.4 TOOL-AGNOSTIC FEATURES

In many cases, there are features that any successful tool would include. These go beyond management functions to be general application functionality. These features include

- Access control: Restricted and authenticated login for users and administrators perhaps linked to other campus authentication systems, like Active Directory or LDAP. Allow only intended users access.

- Multiple platform access: Availability on common browsers or desktop and mobile operating systems. Allow access from any location to facilitate ease of making changes.

- Support and costs: Ongoing accessibility of and cost for licensing and support can vary dramatically. Some organizations prefer certain kinds, such as open-source or fully-supported, from prior experiences

| | WhentoWork/ WhentoHelp | ConPortal | ScheduleSource TeamWork | ShiftPlanning |
|---|---|---|---|---|
| **Access control** | | | | |
| Authenticated login | Y | Y | Y | Y |
| Login via LDAP/AD/SSO | | Y | | Y |
| Login via OpenID or other third-party federation | Y | | | Y |
| Permission levels (e.g. student, staff, administrator) | Y | Y | Y | Y |
| **Scheduling** | | | | |
| Flexible shift creation (e.g. arbitrary length, varying times) | Y | Y | Y | Y |
| Staff can assign hours | Y | Y | Y | Y |
| Students can request hours or ranges | Y | | Y | Y |
| Students can pick hours | | Y | Y | Y |
| Easy changes to shift schedule | Y | Y | Y | Y |
| Trade requests | Y | | Y | Y |
| Multiple employee roles for duties/locations | Y | | Y | Y |
| Integrate or export schedule to common calendar tools | Y | | | Y |
| **Monitoring** | | | | |
| Time punch in/out | | Y | Y | Y |
| Current coverage dashboard | | Y | Y | Y |
| Coverage anomaly notifications (e.g. late, no-show) | | Y | | Y |
| **Support** | | | | |
| Price/month | $30 | $0 | Low | $44 |
| Professional/contract | Y | | Y | Y |
| Community or none | | Y | | |
| **Accessibility** | | | | |
| Web app accessible via common browsers/plugins | Y | Y | Y | Y |
| Mobile version or app | Y | | | Y |
| **Payroll** | | | | |
| Self-service print of time sheet | | Y | Y | Y |
| Integrate with payroll services | Y | | Y | Y |
| Manager view and verify time sheets | | Y | Y | Y |
| Time clock for detailed timing | | Y | Y | Y |
| Correction of errors on time sheets | | Y | | |

**Figure 13. Comparison of features among employee scheduling and time tracking tools discussed.**

## 4. EVALUATING AND COMPARING TOOLS

When determining if a tool meets a manager's needs, the above functions and features are at the core of the decision. Some may be more or less important in a given environment, thus deserving different weight in consideration. There is also the consideration of overall interface, feel, and function for each product, which each manager may find different.

## 5. CONCLUSIONS

After considering the tools and methods above in some details and others in summary, a few points have become clear about selecting a solution for scheduling and tracking student employees. Firstly, any of these solutions could technically work in almost any environment, so the scale and complexity of the workforce and available budget will likely determine if manual, homegrown, open source, or hosted solutions are most appropriate. Secondly, as with any purchase or implementation, test-driving before purchasing is essential to making an informed decision, thus setting up the process for success. Lastly, while there are many good tools available for communication and verifying legitimacy, there is no substitute for active relationships, defined and efficient processes, and a motivated workforce in providing successful customer service.

## 6. ACKNOWLEDGMENTS

I offer thanks to my SIGUCCS colleagues who provided their experiences and other details on processes and products; my reviewers, Jenna Pitera and Lauren Adams, for valuable feedback on my drafts; and my supervisor and teammates at UAlbany for supporting the time commitment to develop this paper and the accompanying presentation.

## 7. REFERENCES

[1]  Maxam, Gretchen, Hamilton College (Personal communication, May 16, 2014)

[2]  Koerber, Jeff, Towson University (Personal communication, May 14, 2014)

[3]  Yee, Diane, Rice University (Personal communication, May 19, 2014)

[4]  Pletscher, Hank, Saginaw Valley State University (Personal communication, May 14, 2014)

[5]  Mares, Inge, Portland State University (Personal communication, May 28, 2014)

[6]  "Online Employee Scheduling Software | Workforce Management." *ShiftPlanning* N.p., n.d. Web.  June 2014. <http://www.shiftplanning.com/>

[7]  "Employee Scheduling." *Software*. N.p., n.d. Web. June 2014. <http://whentowork.com/>.

# Polishing a Dirty Rock:
# Rebranding a Product with an Existing Negative Impression

Allan Chen
Menlo College
1000 El Camino Real
Atherton, CA 94027
+1-650-543-3889
achen@menlo.edu

## ABSTRACT

We all have implemented projects and/or services that haven't gone quite as well as we had hoped. In some cases, they have gone completely sideways, and the community of users have a bad taste left in their mouths.

How might one "restart" such a service and gain a new foothold with users? What rebranding methods should be considered? How much effort is required?

In Fall 2014, Menlo College rebranded and re-launched its virtual desktop implementation (VDI) offering. Historically, this service has suffered an unfavorable perception by the community through misinformation, little to no cultural education, and performance problems.

We will discuss what we've done, the challenges we faced, the process we used and lessons learned. Please note that, due to the publishing deadline for this paper, full implementation has not yet been completed.

## Categories and Subject Descriptors

H.3.4 [**Information Systems**]: Systems and Software – *Distributed systems*

## General Terms

Documentation, Human Factors, Performance, Standardization

## Keywords

Virtual Desktop; Virtual Desktop Infrastructure; VMWare; Unidesk

## 1. INTRODUCTION

Menlo College is a small, private undergraduate institution located in Atherton, CA, about 30 miles south of San Francisco. Roughly 700 students matriculate annually at Menlo. Curriculum is focused on business, with degrees in fields such as Accounting, Finance, and Management. A Psychology degree is also offered.

Menlo employs 30 full-time faculty and an average of 50 adjunct faculty. The full-time faculty are all PhD or otherwise hold "academically-qualified" degrees. Many of the adjuncts are "professionally-qualified" with extensive experience in industry.

Between 80-90 professional staff (not counting athletic coaches, whose numbers fluctuate quite a bit) handle operations and administration. Our largest departments are Enrollment Management (which encompasses Admissions, Financial Aid, and the Registrar), Advancement/Alumni & Development, and Student Affairs.

## 2. VIRTUAL DESKTOP INFRASTRUCTURE (VDI)

A virtual desktop infrastructure, or VDI, offers a computing experience similar to what most users are accustomed, but via a very different method.

Most users' perception of a desktop is of a physical computing chassis that sits either under or on a desk, directly connected to a monitor, keyboard, mouse and other peripherals. While the computer is usually connected to the network and some files might reside on network-based resources, all the computational work is done by that local machine.

In comparison, a virtual desktop runs on a centralized system. A single cluster of servers runs a large number of virtual desktops. Any one user connects to just one of these desktops. All computational work is done by the servers. Resources such as memory and processing power are shared across all the virtual desktops housed on that cluster.

The user is still typing on a local keyboard and looking at a monitor, but what he or she is actually seeing is the video feed of what is happening on the central system. Many users connect via "thin clients" that have little to no operating system of their own. Their entire purpose is to server as an interface between the user and the central system.

# 3. VDI AT MENLO COLLEGE

## 3.1 Background

Different vendors exist in the VDI market.[1] Prominent ones include Citrix, which does both desktop and application virtualization, and VMWare, which is oriented more towards delivery of entire desktops as a whole. Microsoft has a solution as well, and hosted solutions from Amazon and other companies have also entered the market recently.

Menlo College uses VMWare Horizon View[2] as its platform. Desktops are "delivered" to the end user via this platform. View is the "broker" that handles this communication.

We use a product from Unidesk[3] to actually manage our desktops. While VMWare could deliver desktops directly, Unidesk provides us with greater control of desktop configuration and better management of resources, especially memory and storage. With Unidesk, we are able to create applications as "layers" that can be applied in any number of combinations. The operating system itself is a separate package as well. This means that we can update any one application at a time, rather than having to build an entire new desktop each time.

## 3.2 Implementation

In late 2010, Menlo College entered into an agreement with Unidesk as one of its initial partners. The first virtual desktops were deployed in Spring of 2011. Unidesk version 1.0 was used (2.6 is the current version).

The majority of thin clients used were from industry-leader Wyse or 10Zig, a brand that essentially repackaged Wyse products. The solution from Panologic[4] was also adopted. The main difference with the Panologic devices was that they required an additional management interface.

### 3.2.1 Technical Challenges

A number of technical issues arose as the virtual desktops came online. The infrastructure (servers, networking, etc.) components predate the current bank of institutional knowledge. User support issues included the lack of support for many USB devices (the Wyse-based clients supported only the USB 1.1 protocol, meaning that devices ranging from printers to flash drives sometimes did not work). Panologic devices worked better with peripherals but were not universally deployed. Of course, since VDI relies so heavily on the network, even minor obstacles or surprises had widespread impact on reliability. In general, users had less flexibility in how they worked due to the technical limitations of VDI.

### 3.2.2 Education and Cultural Efforts

A key part of launching any new service is education and cultural adjustments. While the goal of a virtual desktop solution is to mimic a physical desktop experience as closely as possible, there will always be differences. For the most part, VDI at Menlo College was deployed without a significant training program nor was the cultural impact addressed. Even though virtual desktops were often replacing what were actually slower, out-of-date physical desktops, users expected a "new desktop" experience from day one. The inherent inability to meet this expectation had a dramatic effect on the overall program.

The benefits of VDI were not effectively explained to the community. With Unidesk, applications could be updated as needed, meaning that security and consistency could be assured. Furthermore, new applications could be added in less than half an hour, from layer creation to deployment. With centralized processing on robust servers, a virtual desktop was technically more powerful than a physical one in many ways.

## 3.3 State of VDI, Prior to Re-Launch

In Spring 2014, prior to our rebrand and re-launch, virtual desktops had a bad reputation on campus. It was seen as unreliable and a detriment to one's ability to get work done. Efforts had been made in the previous year to improve public understanding of the system. What it was and was not, what it could do and could not, and how it could in fact be a better fit for many users than physical computers. Most importantly, the benefits to the college as a whole from a financial and operating perspective had been touted repeatedly. At our small institution, many offices of influence have traditionally appreciated analysis from these perspectives.

These efforts did little to change opinions, however. As a result, users continued to point only towards how virtual desktops were inferior to physical computers, and ignored the benefits. Lack of video streaming (multimedia has traditionally not been viable on virtual desktops), dependence on a network that was not seen as reliable, and an apparent decrease in performance compared to a physical machine were cited repeatedly.

Where "VDI" stopped and other services began was also murky to users. If a user accessed a VDI for a specific service – to use our ERP, for instance – we would receive support requests for the ERP that were actually VDI-related, or vice-versa. Users could not conceptualize the difference between the products since the basic premise of a virtual desktop was not sufficiently explained.

It had become clear that incremental fixes and an "underground" education and training effort would not suffice. The damage had been done. We needed to take a more drastic approach.

## 3.4 Timing Factor - Network Upgrade

The re-launch was timed to coincide with the completion of a major network upgrade on campus. The entire infrastructure – from wired to wireless, from network design to software configuration and management – was being replaced or rebuilt from scratch. This was a very high profile project supported by the Board of Trustees. Not surprisingly, the Office of IT decided to time the announcement of the new VDI platform and product with the completion of this major project. Even if performance did not dramatically improve, we would be able to point towards increased stability and new features to drive positive impressions.

The network had to be completed before school started in August. Our target date for completion was July. This gave us a window of opportunity for rebranding, marketing, and re-launching our virtual desktop product in early Fall of 2014.[1]

---

[1] Because virtual desktops were not offered to students, re-launching prior to the start of the school year was not necessary. In fact, because of the busy schedule at the start of the year, we strongly considered waiting for mid-September to early October.

# 4. REBRANDING

## 4.1 My Menlo Desktop

Our first priority was coming up with a new brand. We focused on the following paradigm – VMWare View was a platform, just like Windows on computers or Android on phones. A virtual desktop, or VDI as we traditionally called it, was akin to a generic name for an application, such as a word processor. The specific product had a memorable name, such as Word.

Using this approach, our missing component was the product name.

We eventually settled on "My Menlo Desktop." This evoked an institution-specific connotation that also strongly implied the sense of personal ownership and customization that we could provide.

A brand needs a strong slogan. We decided to emphasize the fact that My Menlo Desktop offered a full desktop experience with access to all of one's applications and files (including those for "on campus" use only, such as our ERP client) that could be accessed from anywhere.

As a slogan, we chose "BYOD: Bring Your Own Desktop" to capitalize on the mobile device movement with the same acronym. It also continued the emphasis on personal ownership.

The final component of the brand was a logo. Figure 1 illustrates the image we chose. We originally wanted a logo that emphasized the personal ownership, but found most options too complicated or obtuse. We settled on one that emphasized a modern and hopefully dynamic look, that reinforced the name of the project.

**Figure 1. My Menlo Desktop logo.**

## 4.2 User Audience

We decided to offer My Menlo Desktop only to faculty and staff. There were a number of reasons for this.

- Our Microsoft licensing already covered these users, but not student use on student-owned computers

- We felt that student use, even if offered, would not be very high

- Restricting to 150 faculty and staff plus labs would be an easier load on our servers, with still room for growth.

## 4.3 Features

We chose the features of My Menlo Desktop carefully. We needed to provide a high quality experience with compelling features to engage users to give us a second chance. We made the following decisions as a result:

- "Persistent" desktops
  Each desktop would truly be unique to each user. Every time that user connected, it would be to the same desktop. Users could make configuration changes (e.g. desktop background) and those personalizations would remain in place. VDI, as a technology, is commonly deployed in a "nonpersistent" state, whereby the desktop is reset each time a user disconnects.

- Comprehensive suite of applications
  In addition to traditional productivity applications such as Microsoft Office, we included clients for instant messaging and chat (Pidgin), social media (Tweetdeck for Twitter), and entertainment (Spotify).

- Web access
  The most important feature we implemented was the ability to access My Menlo Desktop from a standard web browser. This enabled a true "connect from anywhere" capability.

- Performance enhancements
  On the technical side, we upgrade to dual-core desktops. We also installed special cards in our servers that dramatically improved graphics and overall "sense of responsiveness" performance.

- Default printer settings
  It was important that a user see that his or her local printer was listed and set as default. We developed a complex but effective script, applied by Active Directory, to achieve this.

## 4.4 Marketing

It was important that we build a cohesive and comprehensive marketing campaign to promote the new offering. As mentioned before, we timed the announcement to coincide with the completion of the network upgrade. In theory, the upgrade alone should give the impression that our desktops ran faster. In addition, we implemented a number of key marketing elements.

### 4.4.1 Web and Social Media

We placed both marketing and a general increase in access via the web in several locations. Several pages were added specifically for the My Menlo Desktop product, explaining what it was and what it could do.

We also placed direct links from the faculty/staff quicklinks page as well as on the general OIT page. We wanted to provide as few clicks as possible to the service.

Finally, we advertised the launch extensively via Twitter. We decided to avoid the Facebook page since many students read that.

### 4.4.2 Video

To parallel some of the marketing elements from the networking project, we recorded several videos that discussed the product. We acquired testimonials from several users on how My Menlo Desktops were of benefit to their productivity.

### 4.4.3 Posters and Brochure

A small number of posters and flyers will be utilized to make the launch more visible. Our goal is to get the logo and message out to the public consciousness as broadly as possible.

We printed a tri-fold brochure that quickly described My Menlo Desktop, and placed one on every faculty and staff physical workstation on campus

### 4.4.4 Articles and Formal Releases

We wrote several "formal" announcements of the service. These were turned into online articles for our website, items for the OIT Newsletter (Hangin' with IT), and other channels. As needed, we could create a document.

### 4.4.5 Use Cases

We developed several use cases that we could point to as examples of how My Menlo Desktop was a powerful tool.

#### 4.4.5.1 Example Use Cases

- You're an admissions counselor on the road. You need access to your files back at Menlo College. Get to the hotel business center, connect via the web and you're there. Log out and it's all secure.

- You're on vacation and a colleague writes asking for some obscure file you left on your computer. You connect to My Menlo Desktop and actually print the file to your office printer. The document is waiting for your colleague when he or she arrives in the morning.

- You need a specific application to complete a task, or to access some other service. You call up OIT and make a request and 20 minutes later it's not only on your desktop but available for anyone else that uses My Menlo Desktop. On demand.

### 4.4.6 Consistent language

We felt that it was critical that we use consistent language across the entire department and all advertisements about the product. We developed an "elevator pitch" so we could explain the product to a non-technical person within 30 seconds, for example.

#### 4.4.6.1 Elevator pitch

"My Menlo Desktop is your desktop, with your files and your applications, that you can access anywhere. It's kind of like how companies offer services "in the cloud." The cloud lets you get to specific things, like your files or passwords wherever you are. With My Menlo Desktop, you get your entire desktop, from Menlo College's own special cloud."

#### 4.4.6.2 Examples of language

"A desktop for you, wherever you want it"

"A desktop we provide to you, for you to use whenever you need it, from the cloud"

"Just like your physical desktop, except you can access it anywhere"

"Customized to Menlo's and yours needs"

### 4.4.7 Training

While our hope was that users would understand "connect and use" fairly well, we did offer a series of training sessions to emphasize the significance of the program.

### 4.4.8 Miscellaneous marketing elements

We also utilized a few other elements

- Email signatures with logo

- Stickers and postcards placed around campus

## 5. STATUS AS OF SUMMER 2014

At the time of this paper's submission for publication, we have not yet launched My Menlo Desktop. We have made a great deal of progress in planning, branding and testing, but a number of items still remain.

Our tentative go-live date is mid-September 2014. We have chosen this timeframe because it will be after the excitement of the start of the school year, yet still early in the overall fall term. We intend to do two weeks of promotion and marketing prior to the launch.

Thus far, we have begun to use the new name when delivering desktops. This has led to fruitful discussions about changes, goals, and the overall plan that will hopefully lead to support from early adopters.

We have been testing the configuration that we have chosen for the desktops, and are currently upgrading our servers to improve performance. We are still seeing some issues, such as print processing, that need to be worked out. Overall, though, we are seeing dramatic improvements in media streaming, launching of key applications, and ability to handle heavy workloads.

We remain optimistic about launch, and hope to present our findings at a later time.

## 6. REFERENCES

[1] See http://en.wikipedia.org/wiki/Desktop_virtualization for a general discussion on virtual desktops.

[2] VMWare Horizon View web page http://www.vmware.com/products/horizon-view/

[3] Unidesk home page http://www.unidesk.com/

[4] See http://en.wikipedia.org/wiki/Pano_Logic for information on Panologic. The company has since gone out of business.

# Portable Cloud Computing System - A System which Makes Everywhere an ICT Enhanced Classroom

Takashi Yamanoue
yamanoue@cc.kagoshima-u.ac.jp

Soshi Tetaka
k2158486@kadai.jp

Kentaro Oda
odaken@cc.kagoshima-u.ac.jp

Koichi Shimozono
simozono@cc.kagoshima-u.ac.jp

Kagoshima University
Korimoto, Kagoshima
890-0065, Japan
+81-99-285-7187

## ABSTRACT

A "Portable Cloud Computing System (Portable Cloud)" is discussed. This system is a portable system that can turn any room into an ICT-enhanced classroom or an ICT-enhanced meeting-room. The Portable Cloud is a carrying case, which contains Wi-Fi access points, a network switch, and a server cluster. The server cluster includes a NAPT (Network Address Port Translation) router, a DHCP server, a captive portal, and application servers. The Wi-Fi access points, the NAPT router, the captive portal and the DHCP server make the space where the Portable Cloud is located, Internet accessible. The application servers contains applications such like "Distributed Web Screen Share (DWSS)", "Slide Plus", and "OwnCloud". The DWSS is a web application which transmits a live screen image of a PC to a large number of Web clients. Slide Plus is an interactive live slide presentation tool for a large audience with Web clients. OwnCloud is open source software by owncloud.com. This software enables file sharing among students and teachers similar to that found in Dropbox. We are using the Portable Cloud for our seminar class, meetings of grass-root groups, and academic conferences. We can't imagine holding our seminar class without the Portable Cloud.

## Categories and Subject Descriptors

K.3.1 [Computer uses in Education ]: Collaborative learning, Computer-assisted instruction

## General Terms

Design, Performance.

## Keywords

Cloud; Network; Wi-Fi; BYOD

## 1. INTRODUCTION

Today, almost every student and every teacher in universities and colleges carries a their mobile phone or laptop PC. If we can use these devices for classes, then we don't need permanent computers in computer laboratories. Also, any classroom can be a computer laboratory. If there are no permanent computers in every

*SIGUCCS'14*, November 2–7, 2014, Salt Lake City, UT, USA.
ACM 978-1-4503-2780-0/14/11.
http://dx.doi.org/10.1145/2661172.2661198

computer laboratory, IT administrators of universities and colleges no longer need to maintain those PCs. Some universities, such like Kyushu University in Japan [2], are moving towards such a campus without permanent computers in computer laboratories.

In order to make a normal classroom a computer laboratory without permanent computers, the room should have high performance Wi-Fi access points and a high performance up-link network. It would take a long time and be expensive to make every classroom in our campus an IT enhanced classroom.

To quickly an inexpensively make normal classrooms IT enhanced classrooms, we are developing a "Portable Cloud Computing System (Portable Cloud)". The Portable Cloud is a portable system that can turn any room into an ICT-enhanced classroom or an ICT-enhanced meeting room. The Portable Cloud is a carrying case, which contains Wi-Fi access points, a network switch, and a server cluster. The server cluster includes a NAPT (Network Address Port Translation) router, a DHCP server, a captive portal, and application servers. The Wi-Fi access points, the NAPT router, the captive portal and the DHCP server make the space where the Portable Cloud is located Internet accessible. The application servers contains applications such like "Distributed Web Screen Share (DWSS)", "Slide Plus", and "OwnCloud". The DWSS is a web application which transmits a live screen image of a PC to a large number of Web clients. For example, students can see the display of the teacher's PC without using a projector and screen. Every student can see small text displayed on the teacher's PC, even if they are seated far away from the teacher. Slide Plus is an interactive live slide presentation tool for a large audience with Web clients. The DWSS and Slide Plus are developed by our laboratory. OwnCloud is an open source software by owncloud.com. This software enables file shraing among students and teachers similar to Dropbox. Having servers located at the classroom or the meeting room may improve the bandwidth between clients and the servers because the bandwidth of TCP is heavily depend on delay. We are using the Portable Cloud for our seminar class, meetings of grass-root groups, and academic conferences. We can't imagine holding our seminar class without the Portable Cloud.

## 2. OUTLINE OF THE SYSTEM

Figure 1 shows an outline of the portable cloud. The carrying case contains high performance Wi-Fi access points, a PC cluster with software, a network switch. The system may have a power system with a battery for places without power. The system can be connected with the Internet or a campus LAN. Figure 2 shows the structure of the portable cloud. "LAN IF" is a LAN interface which connects the portable cloud and the Internet or a campus LAN. "Wi-Fi AP" is a Wi-Fi access point or a set of Wi-Fi access points. Servers of "Server-1" .. "Server-4" are the servers in the PC cluster. These servers contain the software such as DWSS which add functions to the Portable Cloud.

## 3. FUNCTIONS
The portable cloud has following functions.

### 3.1 DHCP, DNS SERVER, GATEWAY
In order to provide the Internet accessiblility to users' mobile phones and laptop PCs, one server of the Portable Cloud contains a DHCP server, a DNS server and a Gateway. The gateway has a "network address port translation (NAPT)" function.

### 3.2 WI-FI ACCESS POINT
The Wi-Fi access point or the set of Wi-Fi access points is the key equipment in the Portable Cloud. In order to provide a comfortable Wi-Fi environment for dense mobile clients, the Wi-Fi access point should have very high performance. There are high performance Wi-Fi access points such like [12] and access points with latest technology such like IEEE 802.11ac. We are using IEEE 802.11ac Wi-Fi access points with beam forming function.

### 3.3 CAPTIVE PORTAL
An unmanaged Wi-Fi environment can be campus network vulnerability. So the Portable Cloud is equipped with a simple management tool. To connect, a user will open a web browser and selects the SSID of the Portable Cloud's Wi-Fi access point. Once they input the correct pass-phrase, a web page like Figure 3 will be shown. The page displays the terms of use of the Portable Cloud. The page can be an authentication page in addition to the terms of use.

Users of the Portable Cloud can not use its functions without an appropriate guide. So, after the user clicks the accept button on the terms of use page, a menu page (Figure 4) with links to the functions of the Portable Cloud will be shown. This web page re-direction function is realized by pfSense [8], a captive portal software.

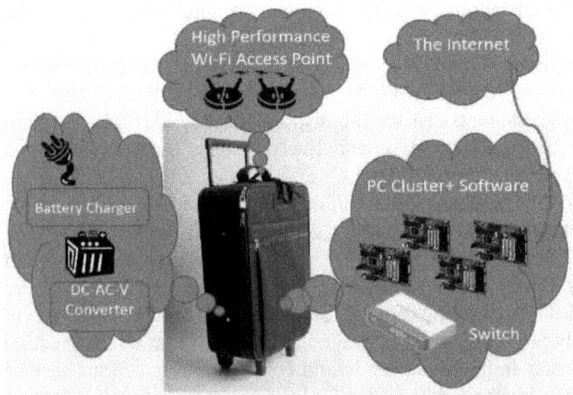

**Figure 1. Outline of the Portable Cloud**

### 3.4 SCREEN SHARE
If the desktop image of the meeting presenter can be viewed by an audience using devices like the user's smart phone or PC, without the need to install software, the meeting can be more productive. We are investigating live desktop image sharing systems for such situations. Fortunately, a modern smartphone or a modern laptop PC usually has the capability of running an HTML5 browser. We first developed a live PC desktop image sharing system, called Web Screen Share, which uses HTML5 and WebSocket

technology. We have improved Web Screen Share by introducing *inter server connection nodes* (*ISC nodes*) to the system.

The presenter's desktop image is multi-casted to all web servers of a group using ISC nodes. To minimize the delay between when the presenter's desktop image is changed and when the change is shown at the last web client, this system adopts a balanced binary tree connection of ISC nodes. To assign web clients evenly to web servers, this system uses a tournament based load balancing algorithm. We call our improved system *Distributed Web Screen Share* (*DWSS*) (Figure 5.) .

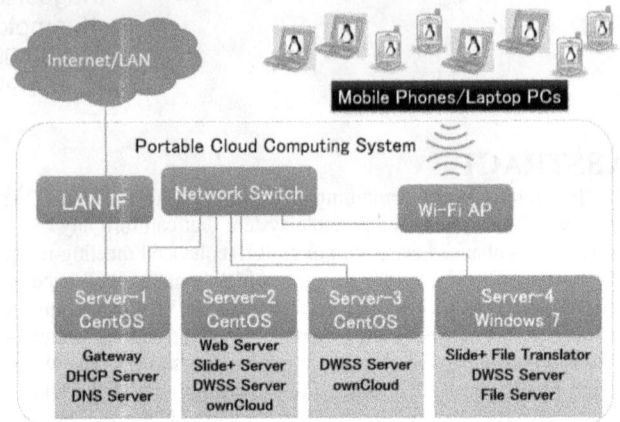

**Figure 2. Structure of the Portable Cloud.**

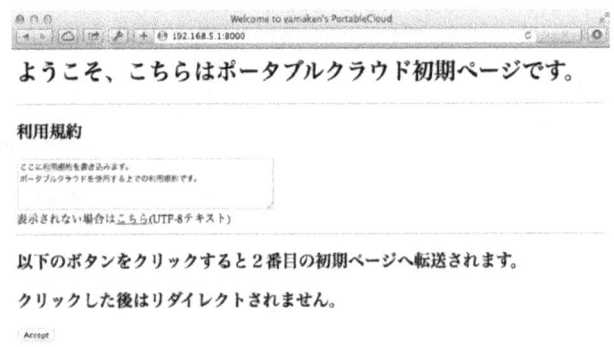

**Figure 3. The terms of use page.**

**Figure 4. Portable Cloud functions menu.**

## 3.5 SLIDE SHARE

We often use presentation software, such as PowerPoint in classes and meetings. Audiences would like to see the presenter's slides on their own smartphone or PC. The teacher and audience would also like to interact. *Slide Plus*, a slide sharing system among web clients, is a tool which does both [5]. Slide Plus not only provides real-time broadcasting of the presenter's slide image to connected devices, but also supports real-time chatting among participants. Participants can also see a previously presented slide or advance at will with Slide Plus.

## 3.6 FILE SHARE

The teacher of a class sometimes distributes printed teaching materials to students in the class. When the number of students is large, distributing materials can be time consuming and can interfere with the class. Also, printing a large number of teaching materials can waste paper and is not green. The file sharing system of the Portable Cloud solves these problems when equipped with OwnCloud, an open source file sharing software [7]. The teacher can upload material by dragging and dropping using a Web brower. Students can download the material themselves by dragging and dropping from their web browser when the teacher directs them to do so.

## 3.7 URL RELAY POINT

The teacher of a class sometimes shows a URL of a web page and lets students browse the web page in class. However, it is not always easy for students to correctly browse to a precise and long URL. The Portable Cloud provides a URL relay point which generates a short URL from a given URL, such as the service provided by bit.ly, and redirect the web client to the original URL when the short URL is given to the web client.

## 4. EXPERIENCES

In order to confirm the effect of the Portable Cloud, we have compared the performance of two Web Screen Shares. One uses the server of the Portable Cloud and another uses the server on the Internet (in Japan). Both of them use the Portable Cloud. For each server, two PCs are connected to the portable cloud using its Wi-Fi access point. One PC sends motion pictures to the server and another PC receives the motion pictures from the server (Figure 6). Table 1 shows the results of the comparison. It is clear that the web screen share, which uses the server of the portable cloud, is much better than the web screen share, which uses the server on the Internet. We have been using this portable cloud about one year for our seminar class (Figure 7). We also have used the portable cloud for academic meetings.

## 5. RELATED WORK

### 5.1 Portable multi purpose LAN socket server

Masuda et. al. has developed the portable multi-purpose information outlet server [4]. This server provides the Internet connectivity to participants of meetings. The Portable Cloud detailed in this paper provides various functions which support classes and meetings in addition to the Internet connectivity.

### 5.2 ε-ARK

ε- ARK is an information device for self help and cooperation help during a disaster [6]. This can be used as a usual information terminal when not needed during a disaster. During a disaster, this device provides a database, a router, an application gateway, a server and other functions. Functions of e-ARK are similar to the Portable Cloud, however, the purpose is different. Higher performance is required for satisfying the purpose of the Portable Cloud.

### 5.3 Portable Super Computer

The portable super computer was developed for a programming contest [1]. This is a computer cluster equipped with GPUs and battery. GPUs are used for high performance computing. The battery is used for satisfying the regulation of power comsumption of the contest. The hardware structure of the portable super computer is similar to the Portable Cloud. However, the software included is different.

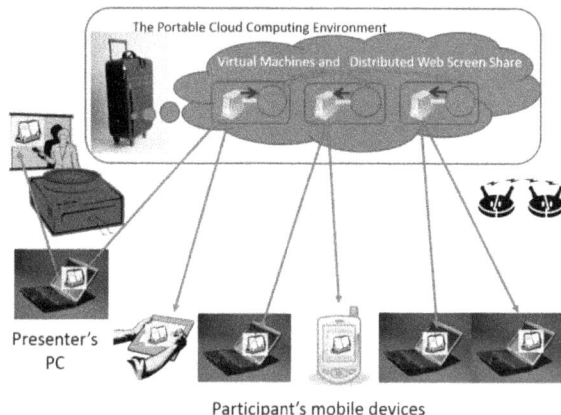

**Figure 5. Distributed Web Screen Share.**

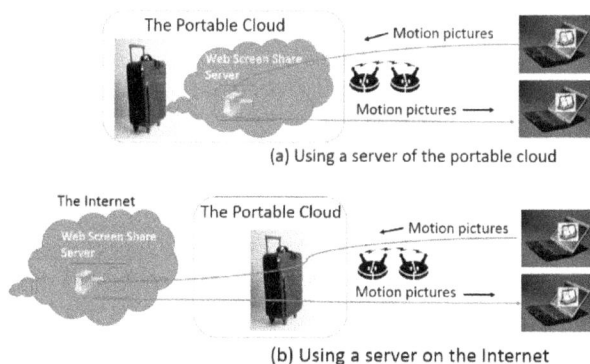

**Figure 6. Comparing performance of Web Screen Share servers.**

**Table 1. Results of the comparison.**

|  | (a) Portable Cloud | (b) The Internet |
|---|---|---|
| Received Pictures Rate (%) | 100 | 50.8 |
| Average Frame Rate (fps) | 6.17 | 3.01 |
| Average Delay (ms) | 108 | 598 |
| Standard Deviation of Delay (ms) | 41.1 | 113.9 |

**Figure 7. A seminar using the portable cloud.**

## 5.4 Moodle Lite

Moodle Lite is a Moodle[11] system for mobile phones and other mobile devices [13]. This can be used in regular classrooms without computers. This enables ubiquitous e-learning without PCs. More than that, students can access Moodle outside of the campus during fieldwork projects or while commuting between their home and campus. It can also be used as a clicker[4] or audience response system in the classroom. Moodle Lite and the Portable Cloud both make anywhere an IT enhanced classrooms using users' mobile devices. Moodle Lite does this by extending Moodle, but relies on the communication environment of the place. On the other hand, the Portable Cloud creates an IT enhanced classroms by providing both the hardware and software. The Portable Cloud does not need to rely on the existing communication environment because it also provides Wi-Fi access points.

## 5.5 ACM SIGUCCS Conferences

ACM SIGUCCS conferences provide various IT tools such as Wi-Fi access points, the Internet reachability, smartphone applications such like Event Board, and so on, in order to support the conference [9]. The portable cloud provides functions of such IT tools.

## 6. CONCLUSIONS

We have shown the portable cloud, its structure, its functions and its performance. We have confirmed its usufulness by using it in our seminar classes and accademic meetings. We are improving the portable cloud. In order to enhance the security of the portable cloud, we are considering implementing a system such as [14][15] in the portable cloud.

## 7. ACKNOWLEDGMENTS

We thank Mr. Matsushita who developed Slide Plus which is a function of the portable cloud.

## 8. REFERENCES

[1] Atsumi, K. 2014. Development of a portable super computer, http://www.slideshare.net/kalab1998/20130601gpgpu. (In Japanese).

[2] Fujimura, N. 2013. Bring your own computers project in Kyushu university. In *Proceedings of the SIGUCCS 2013* (Chicago, IL, November 3 - 8, 2013). ACM, New York, NY, 43-50. DOI=10.1145/2504776.2504789

[3] Masuda, H., Saitoh, A., Masuzawa, T. 2003. Implementation of portable, easy-to-setup, and multi purpose LAN socket server, *IPSJ Symposium Series*, vol. 2003, 49-54. (In Japanese).

[4] Murphy, T, Fletcher, K., Haston, A. 2010. Supporting clickers on campus and the faculty who use them. In *Proceedings of the SIGUCCS 2010* (Nofolk,VA, October 24-27). ACM, New York, NY, 79-84. DOI=10.1145/1878335.1878356

[5] Matsushita, S., Oda, K., Shimozono K, Yamanoue, T. 2012.. Audience Centric Slideshow Sharing System, Summer Symposium in Shizuoka 2012, *IPSJ Symposium Series* Vol.2012-No.4 (20-22 Jul. 2012), Shizuoka Japan, 201-205. (In Japanese).

[6] Ohno, H. Inomata, A. 2008. A Technical, Systematic and Operational Consideration for Realizing ε-ARK device using Apple iPhone, *IPSJ Technical Report*, IOT, Vol. 2008(87), 13-18. (In Japanese).

[7] ownCloud. http://owncloud.org/.

[8] pfSense. http://www.pfsense.org/.

[9] SIGUCCS Conferences. http://siguccs.org/conferences/.

[10] Takeoka S. My Raspberry Pi. http://www.slideshare.net/takeoka1/raspi32.

[11] Wainwright, K. 2009. The care and feeding of a Moodle campus. In *Proceedings of the SIGUCCS 2009* (St. Louis, October 11-14). ACM, New York, NY, PAGENUMBERS. DOI= 10.1145/1629501.1629551

[12] XIRRUS: http://www.xirrus.com/.

[13] Yamanoue, T., Fouser, R. J., Wada, T., Hidaka, M., Suzuki, Y., Terada, M., Takenoshita, A., Beppu, Y., Nedachi, Y., Yukawa, K., Rodriguez, H., Suenaga, K., Yamanaka, Y., Okamura, T., Brasier, A. E., Seto, H., Dogome, K., Yamada, T., Oto, N., Ito, M., Nedachi, M. 2011. Information and Communication Technology Infrastructure and Management for Collaboration with Regional Universities and Colleges, In *Proceedings of the SIGUCCS 2011* (San Diego, CA., November 12 – 17, 2011). ACM, New York, NY, 25-30. DOI= 10.1145/2070364.2070372

[14] Yamanoue, T., Oda, K., Shimozono K. 2012. Capturing Malicious Bots using a Beneficial Bot and Wiki. In *Proceedings of the SIGUCCS 2012* (Memphis, TN., October 15-19). ACM, New York, NY, 91-96. DOI=10.1145/2382456.2382477

[15] Yamanoue, T., Oda, K., Shimozono, K. 2013. A Malicious Bot Capturing System using a Beneficial Bot and Wiki. *Journal of Information Processing (JIP)*, vol.21, No.2, 237-245.

[16] Yamanoue, T., Koarata, Y., Oda, K., Shimozono, K. 2014. A Technique to Assign an Appropriate Server to a Client, for a CDN Consists of Servers at the Global Internet and Hierarchical Private Networks, In *proceedings of the 2014 IEEE 38th Annual Computer Software and Applications Conference Workshops (COMPSACW)*, (Västerås, Sweden, July 21-25) , IEEE, 90-95.

# Towards Requirements for Supporting Course Redesign with Learning Analytics

Robert K. Morse
Indiana University, School of Informatics & Computing at IUPUI,
535 West Michigan Street, Indianapolis, Indiana 46202
(317) 916-7865
rkmorse@iupui.edu

## ABSTRACT
With increased focus on quality, many Colleges and Universities run large enrollment online courses by maintaining course masters or *frameworks*. A framework enables curriculum managers to instantiate hundreds of course sections by keeping under control the quality of common elements of instruction. Current research in learning analytics tools suggests their applicability for the purposes of course design however, the current set of tools were built to support either course or student interventions. Little work has been done to examine the challenges of developing tools for the purpose of supporting the course redesign process. This research is the first phase of a larger project aimed at developing a "Best Practice Finder" which would aggregate section level data to help curriculum managers improve the design of their frameworks. This phase of the research seeks to investigate key requirements for the support of the use of learning analytic systems for the purpose of course redesign. Responses from 71 program chairs of Ivy Tech Community College of Indiana were collected to gauge the relative importance of curricular, institutional, and statistical knowledge they would need to make sense of learning analytics. Three main approaches to sense making emerged: a course centered, an institution centered, and an information centered approach. This work paves the way for an articulation of a full set of requirements for supporting course design focused learning analytics.

## Categories and Subject Descriptors
J.1 [**Administrative Data Processing**] Education; K.3.1 [**Computer Uses in Education**] Collaborative learning, Computer-assisted instruction (CAI), Computer-managed instruction (CMI), Distance learning.

## General Terms
User Support, Management, Measurement, Documentation, Performance, Design, Standardization, Theory.

## Keywords
Learning analytics; analytics; distance education; online course development; education administration.

Permission to make digital or hard copies of part or all of this work for personal or classroom use is granted without fee provided that copies are not made or distributed for profit or commercial advantage, and that copies bear this notice and the full citation on the first page. Copyrights for third-party components of this work must be honored. For all other uses, contact the owner/author(s). Copyright is held by the author/owner(s).
*SIGUCCS'14*, November 2–7, 2014, Salt Lake City, UT, USA.
ACM 978-1-4503-2780-0/14/11.
http://dx.doi.org/10.1145/2661172.2661199

## 1. INTRODUCTION
This research attempts to establish a solid foundation for applying learning analytics to the task of course redesign. Instead of focusing exclusively on the presentation of the analytic data, this research will first identify the knowledge demands for making design decisions based on learning analytic data.

Imagine for a moment a design scenario where a course is designed according to the Quality Matters(QM) design standards. A major concept presented by QM literature is the principle of alignment where by course materials, activities, and assessments align to session level objectives which in turn align to course level objectives. [6] For precision in referencing this mapping later, Ivy Tech has called it the Session Alignment Matrix (SAM). In this scenario alignment which is captured in the SAM is evaluated across two conditions. Horizontal alignment is achieved when the material, activities and assessment align within a session. Vertical alignment is achieved when there is progression in the elements of instruction from one session to the next session. For instance, if the student is asked to write a culminating assignment like a presentation of a final project to class mates have they learned all the skills needed to be successful? Do students have the resources they need or know how to access the resources (in this scenario they might need guidance on PowerPoint or where they can get help with academic presentations)?

This research is a case study on the design and support of a learning analytic system for Ivy Tech Community College of Indiana. Ivy Tech is the largest singly accredited Community College system in the United States. It covers the entire state of Indiana. It is the largest college in the state and has an annual enrollment of 125,000 students. One in four enrollments is for online courses. The college is creating a large data warehouse which pulls together institutional data from the student information and the learning management system. In 2006 the college adopted Blackboard as its learning management system. This research aims at designing and supporting a learning analytics front-end for the data warehouse which can be used by curriculum owners to make improvements to courses semester to semester.

Furthermore the decision making process of curriculum owners when reacting to learning analytic systems to improve course designs from semester to semester is not well understood.

## 2. BLACKBOARD DATA REPORTING OPTIONS
Reporting from the Blackboard System is currently handled through one of several mechanisms. Blackboard can be extended by developing java based packages known as building blocks. Kunnen & Nucifora [3] were awarded a grant through the Blackboard Greenhouse Initiative for their building block called ASTRO, Advanced System Tracking and Reporting. The tool

Table 1: Categorization of the Contextual Knowledge Needs for Sensemaking

| Domain Knowledge | | System Knowledge | | Statistical Knowledge (Stats) |
|---|---|---|---|---|
| Curriculum Knowledge (Content) | Pedagogical Knowledge(Design) | Technical Knowledge(Tools) | Institutional Knowledge (Institution) | |
| Course Objectives | Teaching Methods | System Definition of a Click | Data Refresh Rate | Meaning of Statistics Vocabulary Meaning of Graphs |
| Course Content | Point Distribution Instructional Modality | Categories of Tools, ie. Content Files, Communication Tools, Assessments | Default Tools Schools/Departments Term Structure Class Size | |

allows the system administrator to easily run reports on system usage across groups, schools, divisions, or other categories supported by course identifier naming conventions. From a technical perspective the tool was a massive step forward from the direct querying that was required of system administrators to get information out of the advanced system reporting (ASR) tool.

Although ASTRO makes the data of the ASR more accessible by summarizing key patterns of activity, the results are still only accessible to a system administrator role.

John Fritz [1] of University of Maryland-Baltimore County (UMBC) has developed a building block called Check My Activity. This allows students to compare their activity in the course against other students in the same class. It categorizes the grade book to allow students to check their activity against an anonymous set of their peers so students can self-regulate their learning behavior. There are a large number of tools that make the learning data more visible for the purposes of monitoring and changing behaviors.

Until recently only the ASR schema has been documented well for product developers. Starting with release 9.1 Blackboard announced an effort they are making to document the full learning system schema through a project known as Open Database.

In 2011 Blackboard acquired an analytics company, iStrategy, and began developing its own data warehouse product. By partnering with schools already invested in learning analytics like UMBC, Blackboard continued to develop its reports in the Analytics for Learn product.[5] Analytics for Learn provides limited support for the contextual knowledge needed to make sense of learning analytic data which this research attempts to define more fully.

## 3. METHOD

Program chairs at Ivy Tech Community College of Indiana who have decision making responsibilities for courses or course content were surveyed to identify the sources of knowledge that support their use of eLearning analytics. All chairs of programs with statewide online course were surveyed. It was expected the categorization of the responses would match to proposed knowledge sources groupings, which includes knowledge of the statistics, knowledge of the domain, and knowledge of the institution.

A web based survey was created presenting real data but for a hypothetical course. The hypothetical course was IVYC 301

Designing an Online Course. The IVYC prefix is used for a certification track at Ivy Tech so, the scenario although made up for the sake of this study was still plausible. At the top of survey was a short video walkthrough of a new analytic tool which guides the program chair through available learning analytics to identify the "best practice" in implementing the course.

Therefore this draws on three available data sets that are regularly reported to program chairs. Each semester since Fall 2008 the end of term grade data from our student information system has been prepared in an Excel Pivot Table and distributed on CD college-wide. The second area of data presented in the survey was a bar graph of tool use collected from the ASTRO building block. The third source of data for the survey was a chart of summary statistics based on the Student Evaluation of Instruction. This presented the question number and the responses for one section of the contrived IVYC 301 course.

The survey consisted of two parts. First, three samples of data as described above from an actual course, but presented as the IVYC301 course, were presented along with the prompt to rank the importance of the five sources of knowledge. Refer to Table 1 for more information on the five sources of knowledge. For each of the sets of rankings participants were asked to provide a rationale for their ranking. The second part of the survey asked participants for additional demographic information including years teaching, years teaching online, years teaching at Ivy Tech, and the certifications they had completed

A list of 350 program chairs from across Ivy Tech Community College who are responsible for the 150 online statewide course frameworks that are distributed each semester was generated from the Outlook email lists for each program. An initial survey invitation was sent to the combined list of 350 program chairs. Two weeks following the initial email one reminder email was sent to all participants who had not submitted a survey.

## 4. SURVEY RESULTS

71 responses or about a 20% response rate to the survey was collected. There was representation from across the college. In fact the representation of those responding follows the same pattern as the school representation in the statewide library of courses.

The main content of the survey asked respondents to rank order the importance of the five sources of knowledge already proposed

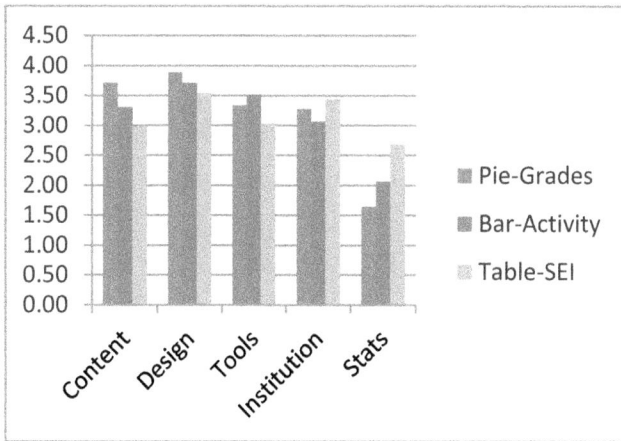

**Figure 1: Means by Contextual Knowledge Type**

to support their making sense of the data presented in the graphs. The mean of the ranking was calculated. For all cases, additional knowledge of the course design was the most important source of additional knowledge and statistical knowledge was the lowest.

For the grade data, the second most important knowledge source was knowledge of the content and objectives. The *Content* category had a mean score of 3.71. For the learning management system activity data, the second most important knowledge source was the knowledge of the tools used in the course. The *Tools* category had a mean score of 3.52.

Beyond the simple calculation of means a correlation coefficient was calculated within the knowledge types showing the strength of correlation between an application of the knowledge type to another application.

There were only two knowledge types that showed significant correlations, $r > .5$. For the Content and Objectives knowledge type, there was a significant correlation between Grades and Activity data. ($r = .72$)

For the Institutional knowledge type, there was a significant correlation between the Grades data and the Activity data. This represents a moderate positive correlation showing that for those that ranked institution data high for making sense of grade data also rated it high for the making sense of the Activity data. ($r = .53$)

Each of the demographic factors was examined systematically for its effect on the rankings. There were only two conditions that seem affected at all by demographic factors. *Years at Ivy Tech* appeared to affect the need for additional content knowledge. This might be due to the role that program chairs play in developing curriculum at Ivy Tech. The program chairs are responsible for writing the course objectives in a document known as the course outline of record. The other demographic factor that affects the rankings of knowledge types was a significant difference between groups with Quality Matters (QM) Training and without QM Training. Quality Matters is an internationally recognized quality course improvement program whose main instrument is rubric of design standards for online courses. [6] Given QM's strong focus on course design, it is not surprising that those who participated in training expressed a much stronger need for knowledge about the course design than was expressed by those without training. What is surprising is that this effect seems to be concentrated around the course design knowledge for the Activity data only.

As far as the survey is concerned the remaining area of analysis was to explore the themes that emerged from the rationale of the rankings. The emergent themes were coded, grouped, and recoded so that a full set of requirements could be connected back to the feedback collected from actual users.

## 4.1 Emergent Requirements for Analytic Tools Supporting Course Redesign

**1. Knowledge Support Requirements**
1.1 Suggest support with course design for those seeking support with content and objectives.
1.2 Suggest support with content and objectives for those seeking support with course design
1.3 Suggest support with institutional definitions for those seeking support with statistics.
1.4 Suggest support with statistics for those seeking support with institutional definitions.

**2. Data Requirements**
2.1 Broad access to data
    2.1.1 Visibility of aggregate information to a broad audience
    2.1.2 Visibility of course specific data to appropriate instructors or chairs only
2.2 Integration with data from external tools
2.3 Connection to research literature for external validation
2.4 Availability to query historical data
2.5 Availability to query multiple ratings by multiple instructors

**3. Interface Requirements**
3.1 Provide clear graphs
3.2 Provide clear and related descriptions
3.3 Include chart legends
3.4 Allow for a variety of support paths.
3.5 Allow for a variety of data display options.

**4. Functional Requirements**
4.1 Ability to Display Historical Trends
4.2 Ability to Calculate Interater Reliability
4.3 Ability to Conduct an Item Analysis of any Assessment
4.4 Ability to Make Comparisons at Multiple Levels

## 5. DISCUSSION

Emerging out of the rankings and rationales were three groups of sensemakers. These groups were best defined by the area of knowledge that they felt was most important. The largest group was course centered. They indicated that the course design, course objectives and course content was the most important. A secondary group was a group that wanted to make sure that we did not lose sight of the general contextual knowledge of the Ivy Tech environment. Several folks pointed to the overall importance of a statistical foundation to understand what was being presented. These tended to be the veteran members of the program committee who were indicating what they felt their colleagues needed. The final group was much smaller but still worthy of mention. This group could not decide on the relative importance of all the knowledge sources and therefore indicated in their rationale that all the information they could get about a course was important.

In addition to the groupings of sensemaking, the largest contribution of this study is the validation of the proposed knowledge support typology. Emerging out of the data was one additional knowledge source. Program Chairs indicated that they want to know demographic information about the instructors and students from each section. How many of the sections are taught by adjuncts? How long has the instructor taught the course both at Ivy Tech and elsewhere? What is the male/female ratio in the section? What is the academic background for students taking the course?

In 2012, at the Educause Spring Focus session on Learning Analytics, John Fritz said that the main task of learning analytics right now is comparison. [1] Students want to compare their behavior to their classmates. Instructors want to compare their section's performance to the performance of the statewide average. Several program chairs specifically mentioned the need for comparing their sections to the other sections in their region. So, it should remain as a key requirement for applying learning analytics to course redesign that comparisons between sections or groups of sections should be supported. The section to section, section to campus average, campus average to campus average, campus average to statewide average as well as other organic groupings like instructor average to campus average are all needed in a tool that aims at the improvement of the design of course frameworks.

In order to fully support the comparisons described above the presentation of the data in both tabular and visual representations must have clear contexts which are both evident and decipherable without a lot of cognitive effort. It must be clear if a graph represents data from a single section, or if it is an aggregation of data at the campus or statewide level. Although this has already been mentioned in the section of emergent requirements the importance of context was raised by several program chairs. As a rationale for the additional context they wanted for the Student Evaluation of Instruction one respondent said, "Absent this additional contextual information counting responses or assessing percentages is meaningless." (Respondent 32)

Beyond a clear articulation of context it is further evident from the data that program chairs must be able to clearly see the difference between sections of the course. There are two primary areas of difference in course sections that will need to be highlighted by a tool built to improve course frameworks. First, the course settings such as extra credit or feedback options for assessments will need to be highlighted to help explain some of the variance between sections. Second, the instructor behaviors such as speed of returning assignments or the nature of the announcements that they post are indicators of differences in communication styles between instructors. For multiple section courses this will be a unique design challenge as it may not be possible to show the settings of hundreds of sections.

## 6. CONCLUSION

The results of this research are expected to contribute significantly both to the local decision making process of supporting course design frameworks at Ivy Tech Community College of Indiana as well as contributing to the theory of sensemaking and the design of visual analytic systems. The results of the survey produced the requirements for an analytic system from the perspective of user knowledge types. The identification of a user knowledge typology

to categorize the knowledge sources will serve the college well in conceptualizing the types of users to support with this and other information technology system. Other colleges and universities with similar structure for academic leadership may find the typology useful for describing their users' needs. It is an attempt to provide evidence for which sources of knowledge are the most important when exploring eLearning data for the purpose of course redesign.

## 7. ACKNOWLEDGEMENTS
The author would like to acknowledge Dr. Nathaniel Samba and Dr. Davide Bolchini for their careful review of this manuscript.

## 8. REFERENCES
[1] Diaz, V. and Brown, M. 2012. Learning Analytics: A Report on the ELI Focus Session (ELI Paper 2: 2012) [White Paper]. Louisville, CO: EDUCAUSE Learning Initiative. Retrieved from http://net.educause.edu/ir/library/PDF/ELI3027.pdf

[2] Dyckhoff, A. L., Lukarov, V. , Muslim, A., Chatti, M.A. and Schroeder, U. 2013. Supporting action research with learning analytics. In *Proceedings of the Third International Conference on Learning Analytics and Knowledge* (Leuven, Belgium, April 8-12, 2013). LAK '13. ACM, New York, NY, USA, 220-229. DOI=http://doi.acm.org/10.1145/2460296.2460340.

[3] Fritz, J. 2010. Classroom walls that talk: Using online course activity data of successful students to raise self-awareness of underperforming peers. *The Internet and Higher Education. 14*,2 (Mar. 2010), 89-97. DOI: 10.1016/j.iheduc.2010.07.00

[4] Kunnen, E. and Nucifora, S. 2007. Advanced system reporting & tracking: building block development project and open source initiative. Unpublished grant proposal.

[5] Lori Lockyer and Shane Dawson. 2011. Learning designs and learning analytics. In *Proceedings of the 1st International Conference on Learning Analytics and Knowledge* (Banff, Alberta, Feb. 27 – Mar. 1, 2011). LAK '11. ACM, New York, NY, USA, 153-156. DOI=10.1145/2090116.2090140 http://doi.acm.org/10.1145/2090116.2090140

[6] Norris, D. M. and Baer, L. L. 2013. Building Organizational Capacity for Analytics. Louisville, CO: EDUCAUSE. http://net.educause.edu/ir/library/pdf/PUB9012.pdf

[7] Shattuck, K. 2007. Quality Matters: Collaborative Program Planning at a State Level. *Online Journal of Distance Learning Administration*, 10, 3 (Fall 2007). Retrieved from http://www.westga.edu/~distance/ojdla/fall103/shattuck103.htm

# Distributed Campus Computer Infrastructure – Integrate Education, Research, Library and Office Activities

Hideo Masuda
Kyoto Institute of Technology
Matsugasaki, Sakyo
Kyoto, Japan 606-8585
+81 75 724 7956
h-masuda@kit.ac.jp

Kazuyoshi Murata
Kyoto Institute of Technology
Matsugasaki, Sakyo
Kyoto, Japan 606-8585

kmurata@kit.ac.jp

Yu Shibuya
Kyoto Institute of Technology
Matsugasaki, Sakyo
Kyoto, Japan 606-8585

shibuya@kit.ac.jp

Yasuaki Kuroe
Kyoto Institute of Technology
Matsugasaki, Sakyo
Kyoto, Japan 606-8585
kuroe@kit.ac.jp

## ABSTRACT

We have replaced our Campus Computer Infrastructure (that we call "System9") in March. This system integrated education and research activities, library and office activities. Our new system has the following major features: (1) Servers of this system are distributed into three buildings and connected with a 10-giga Ethernet based network (that we call "KITnet5" introduced in SIGUCCS 2013). All service processes are running on Virtual Machines (VMware Infrastructure) and can be migrated from each location to another without stopping the service. (2) The backup system is also distributed into two campuses (Matsugasaki and Saga) and is synchronized in real-time. Moreover this system can be a very stable archiving system because it has the capability of acquiring more than 10,000 snapshots, which can support a better BCP (Business Continuous Plan) in the data availability point of view. (3) All of the University members' electric identification data are provided from our system. In our University, there are several management bodies, such as Educational Affairs, Human Resources Department, International Affairs and Research Department. The system has a function of semi-automatically synchronizing the user's data from the database of each management section. (4) The new identification service provides a feature so that each user can have multiple authorization tokens for each service, protected by a master password. It enables users to store the individual authorization tokens into devices such as BYOD which is considered to be more secure than a single unified password all over the system.

## Categories and Subject Descriptors

H.4.3 [**Information Systems**]: INFORMATION SYSTEMS APPLICATIONS – *Communications Applications*

## General Terms

Design, Management, Experimentation.

## Keywords

Virtual Machine; Distributed System; Disaster Recovery; Multiple Authentication Data.

## 1. INTRODUCTION

The computer system at the Center for Information Science of Kyoto Institute of Technology is updated once every four years (SIGUCCS2006[1], SIGUCCS2010[2]).

In this paper, the design and architecture of the newly updated system (System9) that started operating from March of 2014 is described. This new system is mainly composed of NEC's Express5800/ECO CENTER servers, NetApp's FAS, Oracle's Storage Appliance and about 300 NEC's Mate Type-ME (MY30A/E-7) computers.

## 2. AIMS OF THE NEW SYSTEM

### 2.1 Integration of the On-campus IT Infrastructures

In this University, the systems that are updated once every four years are the Center for Information Science computer system, the computer system for the Information Science course and major educational affairs, the computer systems for office affairs and the library computer system. Up until now, due to different demands for each system, specification planning and procurements are performed separately. However, with progress and development in the virtualization technology with devices as a commodity grew, there is an increase in the common points shared between these systems.

Here, the differentiated Replace Timing is adjusted and the updates are performed for the systems all at once. By doing this, specification planning for all the systems is unified and thus, centralization of the system with the shared common points is made possible.

## 2.2 Geographically Distributed Deployment

In the event of the Great East Japan Earthquake disaster, it is thought to be a good practice to consider about BCP (Business Continuous Plan) in Universities.

Here, the 10Gbps network interconnection [3] that covers 10km of the distance between the Matsugasaki Campus and the Saga Campus is utilized, and the servers and data are geographically distributed as a DR (Disaster Recovery) resolution.

## 2.3 Integrated User Database in our Campus

In the previous systems [4], a product called SyntheUMS is used as the integrated authorization system. It is a system where a set of user name and passwords for campus members is usable for most systems is adopted. However, enrollment confirmation process for the addition and deletion of members is divided accordingly to several management bodies which are Human Resources Department, Educational Affairs, International Affairs, and the Research Department. Here, data is manually extracted from the databases of each management bodies and the processing of each independent data from different databases is needed. Regarding this, with the centralization of the computer system for the office affairs, access to each database for each department is technically expected to become easier.

Here, with the objective of network architecture with a facilitated data distribution, a semi-automatic linking of authentication information is considered.

## 2.4 Multiple Authentication Phrase for BYOD

Due to the diversification of devices connected to the network recently, devices without the mainstream keyboard such as tablets are becoming more popular. In this University, to use the connection service to the Internet provided through wireless APs placed on various location on campus for mobile devices users, user authentication is needed. Regarding this, due to an integrated system used, the set of user name and password is standardized and thus, creation of multiple new accounts is not needed because of the standardization.

However, the input of passwords with complex characters using devices such as tablets is difficult and also, once a password input is done, such devices tend to register and save it. On the other hand, because the system works by enabling a single unified password to be usable for all systems, information leakage on a single account could risk the entire other systems. With the rationale that the password can only be known to the account's owner, due to the fact that the act of only keying in the password confirms that it is the owner, the act of simply letting devices to register and save the password needs to be avoided.

Here, by assigning dedicated passwords per service, even if the devices remember a password, it is considerable that the risk can be lowered.

## 3. IMPLEMENTATION

In this section, described is the main design issue of the implemented system. The overall structure of the system is as shown in figure 1.

## 3.1 V-Motion and Storage V-Motion

In this system, as continued from the previous system, the structure of the system is where the virtualization platform provided by the VMware vSphere is used to run all the services. All the servers are distributed onto 3 different places which are the Center for Information Science's main machine room, the library's server room and the newly constructed server room located at the Saga Campus of this University. Using the technologies provided by V-Motion in between each server, regardless of the location of the physical machine, service can be provided.

Besides that, the storage that stores vdmk is prepared with NetApp's FAS and by using the Storage V-Motion technology, even if there is an interruption due to occurrences such as power outages at one of the locations, minimal operation can be run by servers from the other locations.

## 3.2 ZFS Snapshot for Backup System

In the previous systems, by using the NEC product of iStorage D8's DDR features, regardless of the virtual servers status, after acquiring the snapshot, data is read from a different FC (Fibre Channel) port and backup is stored in the NewTech's RAID disk. This resulted in a problem where the backup data is retrieved server-freely and therefore, although the services are not affected, due to limitations of the FC connection distance, it is not fit for long distance backups and the restore time is very high.

In this system, Oracle's ZFS Appliance is used as the backup range, and snapshot created at the main storage that is the NetApp's FAS is copied. For the stored backup data, by creating a snapshot with the ZFS Appliance, backup data of the acquired snapshot timing is able to be retrieved. By using ZFS, infinite snapshot can be created and therefore, there is less need to care much about the generation management.

Besides that, because the backup is created by a simple copy without using any proprietary format, the files can be retrieved directly during recovery and thus, restore time can be shortened. Furthermore, this ZFS Appliance is installed at both the Matsugasaki Campus and the Saga Campus, and the Matsugasaki campus side is mirrored differentially towards the Saga Campus side.

## 3.3 Custom APIs for Integrated Authentication System

In this system, following the previous systems, NECST's product of SymtheUMS which is an integrated authentication system is adopted. This system uses PostgreSQL as the master DB, and for authentications such as LDAP, RADIUS and Active Directory, specified attributes are individually pushed. As seen from a user, even by using any service of any authentication, the set of username and password is the same. Regarding this procurement, by disclosure of the referring and update for API use of the master DB, addition, change and deletion of authentication data can be done not only with proprietary API but also with homemade tools. Therefore, manual work by hand can be reduced.

## 3.4 Multiple LDAP/RADIUS Instances

As mentioned in the previous section, the integrated authentication system that is adopted for this system is usually used for a unified username and password for all systems However, in this system, a separate and independent LDAP/RADIUS/Active Directory is configured for each service, and a feature is added where it can be chosen either to input the password for the integrated authentication system or to input another attribute value.

# Computer Infrastructure (System9)
Center for Information Science, Kyoto Institute of Technology

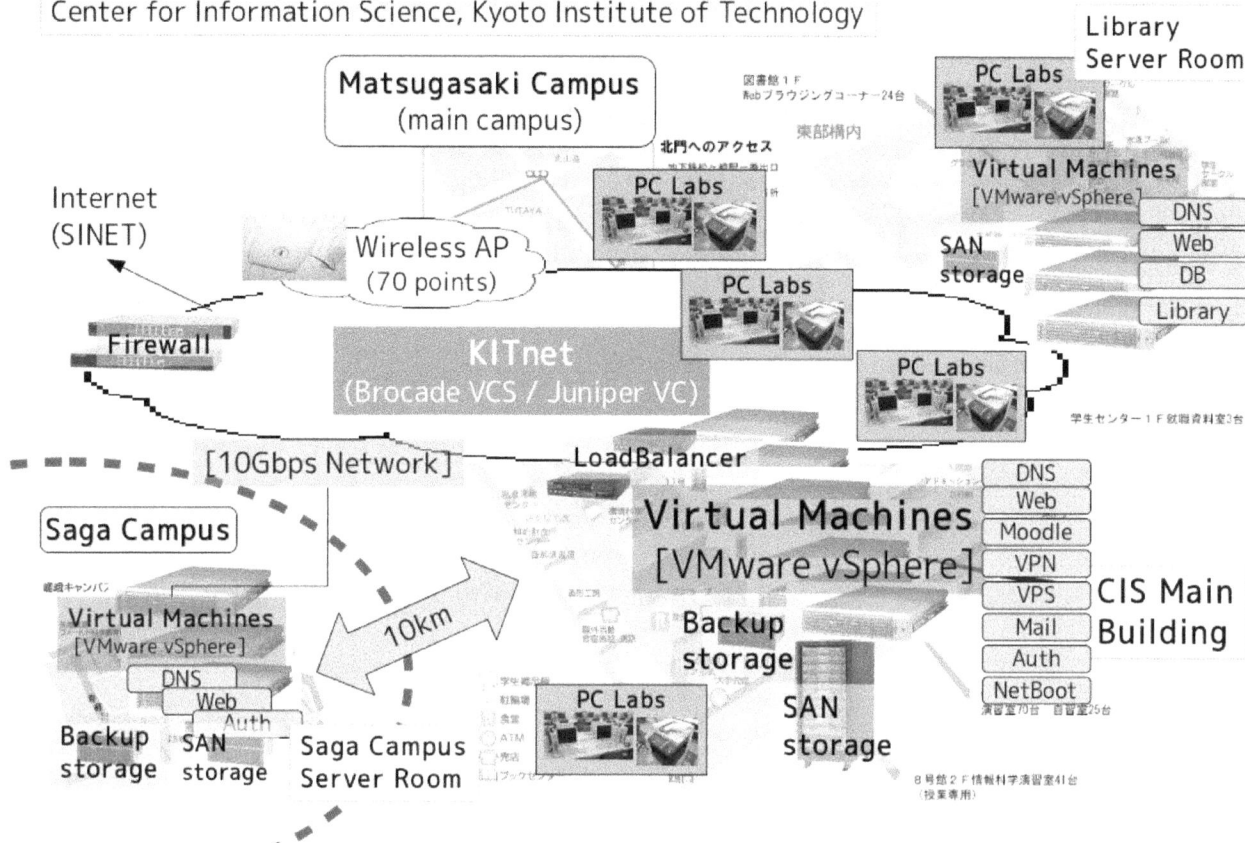

March 2014.

**Figure 1 System Overview of System9**

With this, it makes it possible to implement different authentication passwords for each different service. It is assumed that the system randomly generates the attribute values. In other words, prevention of weak passwords is capable and that the user does not need to remember it as the devices remembers it. By using virtualization technologies, the LDAP/RADIUS/Active Directory server instances can be increased easily.

## 3.5 Dual OS Network Boot System

Before the updated system, as a terminal for exercises, Windows is provided for the entire University while the terminals for the Information Science course, dual boot of Windows and Linux were provided. In the new system, the dual boot of Windows 7 Professional and CentOS 6.5 is provided for all terminals. Besides that, from the viewpoint of the administrators, Netboot is used for any of it. For Windows 7, the combination of Citrix's XenDesktop and CO-CONV's ReadCache is used while for CentOS 6.5, an NFS boot system that uses custom kernel embedded with unionfs.

For printers, FujiXerox's network-supported multifunction devices are placed in each exercise room and each is capable of scanning and printing A4 and A3 sized papers. When printing, there is the feature of user authentication using the multifunction devices' panels, and the calling of own's printing job is implemented. Also, during this time, there is a feature where, by registering the NFC card that each owns; authentication can be done only by simply waving the card.

## 4. CONCLUSIONS

In this paper, the outline of the design plan and structure of the updated computer system of this University is described and its current state is reported. Under a virtualized environment, the server systems that are distributed onto two campus locations are able to operate conjunctively. Besides that, standardization of client PCs and dual netboot of Windows and Linux are implemented. Furthermore, the feature an integrated authentication system that is semi-automatically interlocked with the database of the administrative department and a safer mechanism for usage of devices in the matter of authentication data is also implemented.

In the future, continuous review and resolution of issues is important for a stable system that can operate continuously.

## 5. RESOURCES

VMware Inc.: VMware vSphere,
   http://www.vmware.com/products/vsphere/

Red Hat Inc.: Red Hat Enterprise Linux Server,
   http://www.redhat.com/products/enterprise-linux/server/

Citrix Systems, Inc.: Citrix XenDesktop,
   http://support.citrix.com/products/xendesktop/

CO-CONV: ReadCache System for PVS,
   http://www.co-conv.jp/product/readcache/  (In Japanese)

Shibboleth,
http://shibboleth.internet2.edu/

DEEPSoft Company: DEEPMail
http://www.deepsoft.co.kr:8084/DeepHome_eng/html/

Moodle: open-source community-based tools for learning
http://www.moodle.org/

# 6. REFERENCES

[1] Hideo, M., Seigo, Y., Michio, N. and Akinori, S.: Using coLinux to Provide a Linux Environment on Windows PC in Public Computer Labs, In Proceedings of the 34th annual ACM SIGUCCS fall Conference, 221-224 (2006)

[2] Hideo, M., Kazuyoshi, M., Yu, S., Kouichiro, W. and Yasuaki, K.: KIT's Campus Computer System by Virtual Machine Technology and Integrated Identity Service, In Proceedings of the 38th annual ACM SIGUCCS fall Conference, 251-256 (2010).

[3] Hideo, M., Kazuyoshi, M., Yu, S.: Low TCO and High-Speed Network Infrastructure with Virtual Technology. In *Proceedings of the 37th annual ACM SIGUCCS fall Conference*, 321-324 (2009). DOI= http://dx.doi.org/10.1145/1629501.1629563.

[4] Hideo, M., Kazuyoshi, M., Yu, S. and Yasuaki, K.: High-Speed Network Infrastructure betwwn KIT's Campuses for Computer System Redundancy, In Proceedings of the 40th annual ACM SIGUCCS Service & Support Conference, 109-110 (2013).

[5] Hideo, M., Kazuyoshi, M., Yuki, S., Yu, S. and Yasuaki, K.: Moodle Integration of an Automated Account Enabling System and a User Status Collection System, In Proceedings of the 39th annual ACM SIGUCCS fall Conference, 207-210 (2011).

[6] Kyoto disaster prevention map (In Japanese): http://www.city.kyoto.lg.jp/gyozai/page/0000086399.html.

# The Latest Activity to Realize the Ideal ICT Environment in Kyushu University

Naomi Fujimura
Kyushu University
6-10-1, Hakozaki, Higashi-ku
Fukuoka Japan
+81 92 553 4434
fujimura.naomi.274@m.kyushu-u.ac.jp

## ABSTRACT

In this paper, we describe the latest activities to realize the ideal ICT (Information and Communication Technology) environment in Kyushu University. III (Information Infrastructure Initiative) is responsible for introducing, maintaining, and improving the ICT environment for all students and staff members in Kyushu University. This is the report of our efforts about authentication system, e-mail system, new identification system for students, firewall, wireless LAN for education, BYOPCs, software blanket contract, and so on. As a result, we succeeded in improving the quality of our ICT services dramatically.

## Categories and Subject Descriptors

K.6.1 [**Project and People Management**]: Strategic information systems planning.

## General Terms

Management, Documentation, Performance, Design, Economics, Reliability, Human Factors.

## Keywords

BYOD, BYOPCs, Wireless LAN, Authentication, E-mail, Educational information system, Distance learning system, Blanket software.

## 1. INTRODUCTION

III (Information Infrastructure Initiative) is responsible for introducing, maintaining, and improving the ICT (Information and Communication Technology) for all students and staff members in Kyushu University. We have been striving to realize the ideal ICT environment for research and education in our university.

We upgraded and improved many information systems and introduced some new services recently such as authentication, e-mail, a file sharing system, an educational information system, a distance learning system as well as including an earthquake proof server room.

Kyushu University is the largest general national University in Japan [1]. It consists of five major campuses Hakozaki, Ito, Maidashi,

Ohashi, and Chikushi in Fukuoka city as shown in Figure 1. We have 12,000 undergraduate students, about 4,000 graduate students, and 3,000 doctorate students. The University employs 2,100 professors, 1,200 technical staff, and 850 administrative staff at Kyushu University.

We provide authentication, e-mail, educational information system, wireless LAN, blanket contract software of Office/anti-virus software, server hosting, file sharing system, firewall, and so on for all users. We upgraded and improved almost all of our information systems in March 2014. This paper describes the recent activities around our information systems.

## 2. ESTABLISHING AN EARTHQUAKE-PROOF SERVER ROOM

Our server room is located on the Hakozaki campus near a seashore and is 2 meters above sea level. The threat of earthquakes and Tsunami make it almost impossible to maintain important servers and other equipment. As you may know, we experienced a serious disaster called the Great East Japan Earthquake in March 2011. As a result of that earthquake, we are improving the tolerance against such disasters. We established the earthquake proof server room at the Ito campus to avoid communication interruption even when serious disasters occurs. Ito campus is located on the top of a hill. It stands on hard bedrock and always keeps very stable. In our new server room, we prepared a UPS of 150KVA and our own 300KVA power unit that can operate 5 days without a fuel supply.

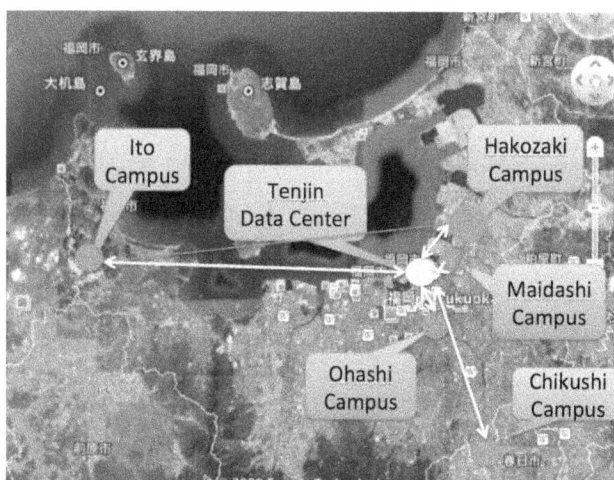

Figure 1. Location of campuses in Kyushu University.

The center of the network topology (star) was in Hakozaki campus. We moved it from the Hakozaki campus to the data center in Tenjin. It is a very safe building and supports high earthquake-resistant by NTT (Nippon Telegraph and Telephone Corporation) the largest communication vendor in Japan. We introduced the new mail servers, as described below, there to keep the high availability. Most important servers are moved there from Hakozaki campus.

## 3. AUTHENTICATION

We had two separate authentication servers before as shown in Figure 2. One was only for staff members and called IDM (IDentification Management system). Another was intended only for students at first and called UMS (User Management System), but it was also used for staff members. The relationship among services and authentication servers was complicated, and we sometimes had difficulty in operating two authentication servers. For example, it is difficult for us to synchronize data between two authentication servers and it failed. We tried to integrate both authentication servers into one server this time [2].

IDM was a server that we purchased. We had been renting the UMS server for the educational information system for four years, and it was time to return it in February 2014. UMS was very flexible and useful. As a result, UMS was used for not only students but also staff members, as shown in Figure 2. However, it was the out of the acceptable policy. We integrated two authentication servers into one in March 2014. Figure 3 shows the new configuration of authentication. The relation among services and authentication servers are straight and simple now.

## 4. SSO-KID FOR STUDENTS

We had been using student ID for authentication for many years. The student IDs are well known in public. It decreased the security in information systems. The services were interrupted as students moved between the undergraduate, graduate, and doctorate schools. For example, the e-mail address depended on student ID, so it changed when a student enter the graduate school (i.e. 1AB10001X@ to 2AB14012Z@). Students are forced to return books borrowed in the undergraduate school, and borrow them again as students of the graduate school in the library. It was difficult for students to receive the continuous service during undergraduate, graduate, and doctorate schools.

Students can receive their own student ID card at the first explanatory meeting for new comers after the entrance ceremony. They have no way to know their own student IDs before that. We had difficulty in managing health care before they received the student ID. We expect to make new comers view lectures, for example, about computer literacy before the beginning of a new semester. However, it was impossible for them to access anything via Web learning system because they have no ID to use it. It is difficult for students to register for lectures that they want to attend early enough. It also makes us difficult to manage some popular and overbooked lectures. We need some other ID mechanisms to use for new comers to access services prior to receiving their ID cards.

We had already introduced SSO-KID (Single Sign On in Kyushu University IDentification) for staff members. We decided to introduce the same ID mechanism for students corresponding to the integration of authentication systems. We arranged the letter of acceptance including the SSO-KID for new comers as shown in Figure 4. We can use the SSO-KID of new comers for health care as early as possible, newcomer seminar for BYOPCs. The bar code is so useful to identify students without fail.

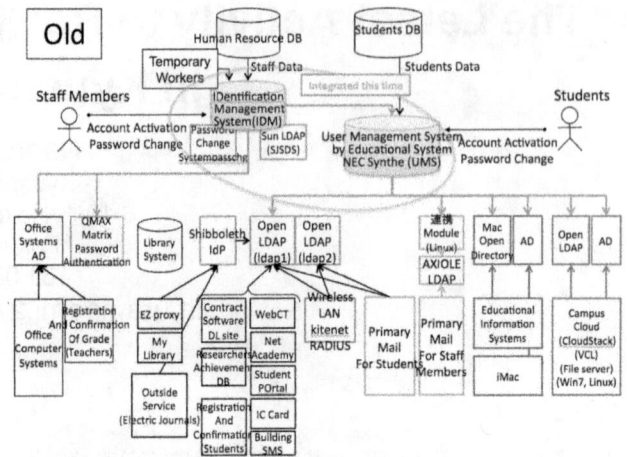

**Figure 2. Old configuration of authentication.**

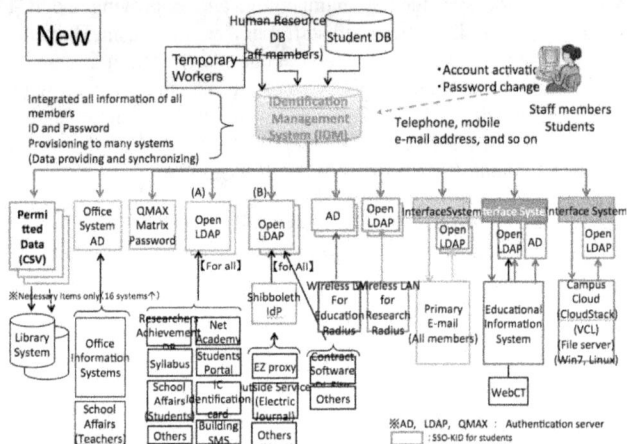

**Figure 3. New configuration of authentication.**

**Figure 4. Letter of acceptance.**

The new ID mechanism is applied for new students in 2014. Students get and know their own SSO-KID year by year. The existing students are supposed to use student ID as usual. It will takes at least 4 years for all students to use their own SSO-KID.

The Bar code in the certificate of acceptance is very helpful for health care and BYOPCs seminars. Students can activate their own ID before the entrance ceremony. It makes it possible to identify students at health diagnostic, reduce of effort to borrow and return books in library, to use the Web learning system before the entrance ceremony and first explanatory meeting, and even register for lectures before classes start.

## 5. MAIL SERVICE

We replaced our mail servers for students and staff members to improve the quality of services [3]. Table 1 shows the parameters for both e-mail systems. We could extend the space for e-mails from 300MB to 1GB for each user without the day limit for free users. We also provide the charge service for users in 1000JPY/month. Users can use 10GB before and 20GB now without days limit as the charge service. We introduced the new alias e-mail address based on their first, middle, and last name.

Figure 5 shows the system configuration. We established the main e-mail servers at the Tenjin data center and backup server at the Ito campus. All users can use e-mail even when a serious disaster happens in Fukuoka area and the network is down on all campuses.

**Table 1. Parameters for previous and current e-mail systems**

| e-mail Parameters | Previous | | Current | |
|---|---|---|---|---|
| | Spool | Days | Spool | Days |
| Students | 300MB | No limit | 1GB | No limit |
| Staff members (Free) | 300MB | 90 days | 1GB | No limit |
| (1000JPY/month) | 10GB | No limit | 20GB | No limit |

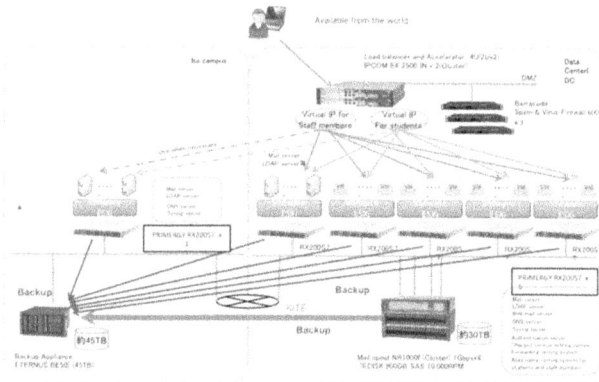

**Figure 5. System configurations for e-mail.**

The primary e-mail address is "student ID@s.kyushu-u.ac.jp" for students. We also provide another e-mail address "john.smith.123 @s.kyushu-u.ac.jp" based on their last and first name. Users can select some variation of first name, last name, middle name, and initial of them. Student can use the name based alias e-mail address for student life long while they are the students in Kyushu University.

We used Mirapoint for mail servers for staff members before. It was a good system, but we found that it was impossible for us to retrieve the message spool and move them to the new mail servers. We

decided to operate both old and new servers in parallel for about three months. After that, all messages would be removed because the day limit was 90 days for free users. We could move only the information about forwarding to the new mail systems.

E-mail address is the same as the old address. E-mail users are expected to set up a new mail account in addition to the old e-mail account. Old messages are kept in the old server, and new messages are delivered to the new server. We adopted free Web mail software (Squirrel Mail) [4] instead of the web mail in Mirapoint. As a result, user interface for Web mail was dramatically changed.

## 6. BYOPCs

We started "Bring Your Own PCs (BYOPCs)" project several years ago. The new students started to use their own PCs in the classroom in April 2013. The following are the activities to realize the project.

### 6.1 Wireless LAN for Education

We introduced the wireless LAN of IEEE 802.11n to realize the BYOPCs in March 2013. We arranged wireless LAN in 366 locations such as lecture rooms, restaurants, library, and so on. One lecture room contains at least one or more access point and the number of access point is 666 in total. The cover ratio is about 72% in March 2013. The number of locations such as lecture rooms increased from 425 to 505 during one year because many faculty members recognized that access points would be established if they insist on it in a lecture room.

### 6.2 Firewall

Many students have file exchange software that is prohibited to use in our university because it violates copyright. We strongly intend to avoid such kind of trouble. We introduced the new firewall in March 2012. We operated it for one year to watch what would happen when we blocked the traffic between inside and outside of the university.

We started to enforce traffic control in March 2013 and could block the traffic of file exchange software against the copyright violation. We introduced the next generation enterprise firewall supported by Paloalto. It can block the P2P traffic of file exchange, but pass the P2P traffic for Skype, Yahoo messenger.

We also blocked the following URL for Web sites to protect our users against menace.

- Mulware
- Phishing site and so on
- Anonymous proxy and so on
- Spyware and Adware

We started to block the HTTP/HTTPS since 18th December 2013 because some serious problems happened in the traffic via HTTP/HTTPS. About 1,000 sites are permitted to pass through the firewall now according to their request. We also blocked the communication against Japanese input assist software such as Baidu IME, Shimezi and so on. Those send all inputted text including login account and password to the outside cloud. Our firewall has been working very well since the real operation started.

### 6.3 Software

We signed the blanket contract for Microsoft Office and anti-virus software supported by Symantec [5]. All students and staff members can install their preferred Office and Symantec End Point Protection on their own personal computers. Students do not have to pay any money for such software as long as they are the members of our University.

## 6.4 Seminar For Newcomers

We present PC seminars for newcomers to avoid confusion in the PC environment in the beginning of lectures [6]. We assigned four days to seminars. Students are expected to attend the seminar according to the schedule assigned to the department. The ratio of attendee is almost 99%. Only 33 of 2,688 students were absent from the seminar. After the seminar, the PCs are set up for wireless LAN, Office, and anti-virus software, and so on. Students can learn at anytime, at any place, without any restriction, and at their own pace with the online educational materials provided by teachers and the Innovation Center for Educational Resource [7] with their own PCs.

## 7. EDUCATIONAL INFORMATION SYSTEM

We first established the educational information system in 1979. We have been trying to increase the number of terminals and PCs for education since then. However, we recognized that it was impossible to prepare enough PCs for all students with the University budget. We decided to adopt the new policy of BYOPCs at last as described above. We replaced the educational information system that consists of 1,087 iMac last February 2014 [8].

We discontinued a part of PC rooms as planned before according to the policy and schedule of BYOPCs in our university. The number of PCs decreased from 1,087 to about 570 in this system replace. Five PC rooms for general education were especially omitted. We also decreased the period for rental from 4 to 3 years. It gives us the flexibility and availability in planning of educational information systems.

## 8. FILE SHARING SYSTEM

We have been operating the file sharing system called Proself [9]. It is so useful and good. The parameters are 1GB and 90 days to keep files. It is intended for users to avoid attached files in e-mail. Staff members want to share files for longer period with large amount of files. We introduced the new servers for a file sharing system that allow users to keep files of 10GB without day limit in addition to the old file sharing servers. Staff members can share files in laboratory, department, and so on with enough security.

## 9. DISTANCE LEARNING SYSTEM

We also replaced and upgraded the distance-learning system. We operated the distance learning system called iClass (Inter Campus Learning Assist and Support System) [10]. We had eight systems in five campuses. The specification was SD (standard definition), and the maximum number of simultaneous connection is three. As a matter of fact, we had some lectures that require the connection for more than three distance learning lecture rooms. The maximum number is about 10 that are connected inside and outside including overseas in those lectures.

We introduced a new distance learning system. The number of equipment is twenty-two for learning and meeting. The screen definition is HD（High Definition). We also introduced the MCU (Multipoint Control Unit). The number of simultaneously connected rooms is improved from 3 to 45 with the MCU. The number of locations increases from 8 to 15 for education including Hakozakix2, Kaiduka×1, Itox5, Maidashix4, Ohashix2, Chikusix1.

The University headquarters moved from Hakozaki campus to the new Ito campus far from the center of the city. People located at other campuses are often forced to go to the new campus if they don't have this equipment for lectures and meetings. New allocation for teleconference is seven including Itox2, hakozakix3, Ohashix1, Chikushix1.

## 10. CONCLUSION

We have the master plan to improve our ICT environment. We replaced almost all information systems, improved the quality of many services, and increased the security and availability of information systems. We are also promoting the BYOPCs project. It is a great success in our University. Many students and professors use the PCs in their lectures such as Computer Science, CALL (Computer Assisted Language Learning), programing languages, and so on. The Innovation Center for Educational Resource is preparing educational online materials and supporting professors. Other information services are also welcomed for all users. We succeeded in improving the quality of information services.

## 11. ACKNOWLEDGMENTS

Many thanks to all the staff members of Information Infrastructure Initiative and users in Kyushu University.

## 12. REFERENCES

[1] Kyushu University. http://www.kyushu-u.ac.jp/english/

[2] Ito, E., Kasahara, Y., and Fujimura, N. 2013. Implementation and operation of the Kyushu university authentication system, In *Proceedings of the SIGUCCS 2013*, (Chicago, IL, November 3 - 8, 2013). ACM, New York, NY, 137-142. DOI=http://dl.acm.org/citation.cfm?id=2504788

[3] Fujimura, N., Togawa, T., Kasahara, Y., and Ito, E. 2012. Introduction and Experience with the Primary Mail Services Based on their Names for Students, In *Proceedings of the SIGUCCS 2012* (Memphis, TN., October 15-19, 2012). ACM, New York, NY, 11-14. DOI= http://dx.doi.org/10. 1145/ 2382456.2382460

[4] SquirreMail. http://squirrelmail.org/

[5] Fujimura, N., Omagari, I., Ueda, M., and Irie, K. 2008. Experience with Software Blanket Contract in Kyushu University, In *Proceedings of the SIGUCCS 2008*, (Portland, OR, October 19-22, 2008), ACM, New York, NY, 307-310. DOI= http://dx.doi.org/10.1145/1449956.1450046

[6] Fujimura, N. 2013. Bring your own computers project in Kyushu university. In *Proceedings of the SIGUCCS 2013* (Chicago, IL, November 3 - 8, 2013). ACM, New York, NY, 43-50. DOI=http://doi.acm.org/10.1145/2504776.2504789

[7] Innovation Center for Educational Resource, Kyushu University. http://www.icer.kyushu-u.ac.jp/en/about

[8] Fujimura, N., Inoue, H., and Hashikura, S. 2009. Experience with the Educational ICT Environment in Kyushu University. In *Proceedings of the SIGUCCS 2009* (St. Louis, MO, October 11-14, 2009). ACM, New York, NY, 167-171. DOI= http://dx.doi.org/10.1145/1629501.1629532

[9] Fujimura, N. and Hirayama, Z. 2011. A Comparison of the Usage and Experience with the File Sharing System with the Different Operation Policies. In *Proceedings of the SIGUCCS 2011* (San Diego, CA., November 12 – 17, 2011). ACM, New York, NY, 131 - 134. DOI= http://dx.doi.org/ 10.1145/2070364.2070397

[10] Takahiro, T, Fujimura, N., Hashikura, S., and Inoue, H. 2009. Introduction and Management of Inter-Campus Learning Assistant System for Distributed Campus, In *Proceedings of the SIGUCCS 2009* (St. Louis, MO, October 11-14, 2009). ACM, New York, NY, 253-256. DOI= http://dx.doi.org/ 10.1145/ 1629501.1629547

# Reach Out and Teach Me!

Mark C. J. Davis, Jr.
Swarthmore College
Swarthmore, PA
610-328-8510
davis@swarthmore.edu

Joel F. W. Price
Swarthmore College
Swarthmore, PA
610-690-1128
jprice1@swarthmore.edu

## ABSTRACT

For a number of years Swarthmore College has offered formal software training sessions in lecture and hands-on formats for faculty and staff. As the technology scene changes, we recognize that each person prefers different learning styles and techniques. Thus, we set out to try to reach faculty and staff by providing a plethora of training options in an effort to meet at least most training needs. In this paper will describe how Swarthmore College's training has evolved to reach people in person, in print, on the web, and on social media. We will also discuss lessons learned as we address the three main problems of offering training via these methods of community outreach.

## Categories and Subject Descriptors

H.5.2 [**User Interfaces**]: Human Factors K.6.1 [**Project & People Management**]: Training

## General Terms

Documentation, Performance, Human Factors

## Keywords

Training; Social Media; Creativity; Outreach; Emerging Technology; Lynda.com; Video; 24/7; Community; User Submissions; Humor

## 1. BACKGROUND

Swarthmore College is a private, nonsectarian, liberal arts institution consisting of over 1600 undergraduate students and employing just over 1100 administration, faculty and staff.

Technology training is offered to a community of end-users through the Information Technology Services Department.

## 2. THE CHALLENGES

There are three main problems with offering training to faculty and staff members. First: lack of attendance. People don't want to sit in a technology training class with other people, even though the information they would obtain would assist them in their daily work. Second: "Get to the point!" Training sessions tend to be too long and too comprehensive. Most people's days are busy and they would prefer brief bursts of training on their own terms. Third: "I didn't know that we had access to training for that!" Most faculty and staff are unaware of the opportunities provided by our Information Technology Services team. All too often, unrealistic goals for training are set, and lackluster promotion of these goals occurs. At Swarthmore College, we have set out to make the process more charming, personal, and engaging.

## 3. TRAINING

### 3.1 Technology Survey

In an effort to understand the kind of technologies being used campus-wide, along with the kind of training preferred, Faculty and Staff were invited to participate in a technology survey.

Faculty for example reported widespread use of many different technologies. For example, nearly all faculty report viewing online training videos, 87 percent reported using online file storage tools like Google Drive, and almost as many reported using Microsoft Office and presentation tools like PowerPoint. Eighty percent of those surveyed have used service like Skype or Google Plus and more than half of those used such services for professional communications. Sixty-six percent reported participating in social networking sites like Facebook, Twitter or LinkedIn.

### 3.2 Our Goals

For years, the goal of the ITS team was to offer trainings with the intent of educating those who showed up, and with the hopes that heads of departments would send their staff. Several things became apparent:

- People were self-selecting to attend based on seeing and responding to email or posted reminders. Some folks who could benefit from training were unable or not selecting to attend.

- Depending on time of semester and day of week and time of offering, people were unable or not selecting to attend.

- People who attended trainings usually found them useful, but seemed unlikely to mention it to coworkers or share information learned there with others.

### 3.3 Outreach

These factors ultimately led to the addition of a team member responsible for outreach to the community in ways that hadn't been explored before. While the goal of offering trainings remains the same, training is now seen as a part of a larger picture incorporating more ways and more convenience to our community.

A particular focus has been on listening and outreach to assess which times are better and worse for community members to attend training through emails, surveys, and in-person meetings. In addition, materials used for outreach, such as the poster in Figure 1, are designed to be more engaging to our community – more interactive, more attractive, and more meaningful to everyday life (both in and out of work).

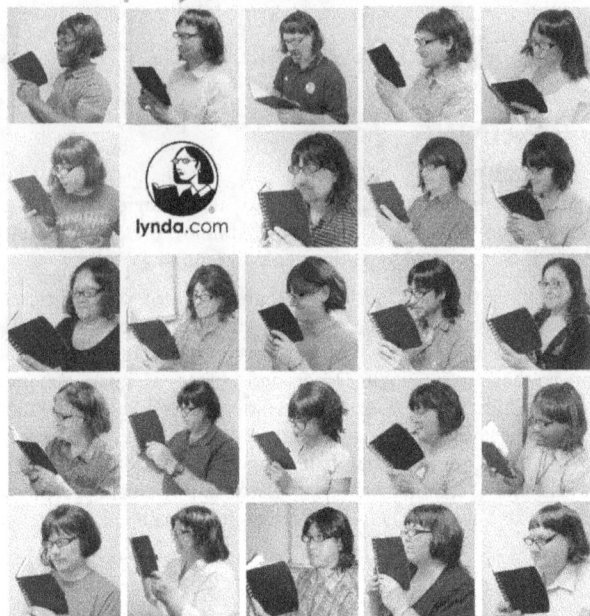

**Figure 1. Promoting Lynda.com [poster].**

### 3.4 In Person

In the 2013-2014 school year, ITS provided 26 sessions of varying types, including computer basics training, Adobe suite training, Bring Your Own Device clinics, a retro arcade game study break, and an annual Tech Fair. These sessions were designed to strike a balance between suggested knowledge, desired knowledge, and exploratory/fun. Although return on investment is very difficult to track for such sessions, our department offered a diverse set of trainings so that people could find ways to collaborate with peers in an interactive setting, letting their interests and needs help shape their learning. A collateral benefit of in-person trainings is hearing struggles one person encounters corroborated by others, which lends direction to future trainings offered by our team.

### 3.5 Online

In 2012 we set out to reevaluate the online training tools we were using. We were previously using Atomic Learning however we found its library to be limited, sometimes out of date, and the videos were too long for people looking for quick bursts of information. Because most people's days are busy and they would prefer brief bursts of training on their own terms, we wanted an online training tool that met those needs. In 2013 we provided all students, faculty, and staff with access to Lynda.com, [1] an online subscription library that teaches the latest software skills through high-quality instructional videos. Lynda.com maintains a very large and up-to-date library of courses taught by prominent technologists and

designers. New titles are added every week. The courses are broken up into bite-size chunks of a few minutes each.

### 3.6 Social Media

Although our ITS department has had a Twitter handle since 2009, the 2013-2014 school year marked the first year in which Twitter became a tool used for outreach, customer support, idea-sharing, and campus amplification of message. We saw this as a great opportunity to meet our goal of incorporating training through social media. Thus careful attention has been paid to establishing a tweeting regimen, with regards to both content and timing. A regular schedule was established in the 2013-2014 school year, with Twitter tips offered on Tuesdays, Lynda.com video tips offered on Wednesdays, and the music picks of members of the department posted each Monday. With the help of an in-house tracking tool (called SwatSocial) and tools such as HootSuite, ITS has been able to use Twitter to reach out to folks who are having trouble and direct them to solutions (e.g. problems with wireless coverage, printing, or Microsoft Office).

On poster advertising, in-person trainings, photos from flickr and Instagram were used to showcase photography from around campus. These posters are hung monthly from October through April each year and are given to each department for posting as well as being posted in several public spaces, including libraries, common spaces, and eateries.

## 4. LESSONS LEARNED & CONCLUSIONS

The advent of handheld devices and flexible work schedules has changed the way we learn and the time we spend learning. Swarthmore College has adapted to this change in a number of different ways. The College has aimed to respond more quickly to changing user needs by offering a wider variety of trainings at different times, fortifying its online learning options, and offering micro-learning opportunities through the use of social media. There has also been an increased focus on increasing the "delight factor" of interactions with the community – design and engagement in a way that is more fun and more personal for those involved. Subjective reports suggest that people have a positive view of the ITS department and its outreach. As a whole, this combination of changes in approach have increased the number of people on campus who attend trainings, and has elevated the awareness of available technologies at Swarthmore as well. ITS team members regularly hear positive feedback about outreach (e.g. Lynda posters, Lynda desktop backgrounds, Drupal posters) and are reporting greater community engagement. In one year, Swarthmore went from zero to 743 users on Lynda.com. Those users watched a total of 14,788 videos totaling 1088 hours, a far higher number than the previous online training had ever yielded. As a result of our change in training methods, the Help Desk has also reported a reduction in the type of requests for help. In the future, the department hopes to continue to meet the current needs of the community, expand the reach of offerings to include more faculty and staff, and to engage students more. An ongoing point of focus will be continuing to address the changing needs of our users.

## 5. ACKNOWLEDGEMENTS

Thank you to everyone at Swarthmore College who contributed to the implementation of various aspects of our training programs. A special thanks goes to Our Entire ITS Staff who helped promote and successfully implement Lynda.com.

Also, a special thank you to our Lynda.com representatives and to ACM SIGUCCS for the opportunity to share how we implemented our Training and Outreach Programs.

## 6. REFERENCES

[1] Lynda.com. http://lynda.com.

# Introduction of New Kyushu University Primary Mail Service for Staff Members and Students

Yoshiaki Kasahara
Kyushu University
6-10-1 Hakozaki, Higashi-ku
Fukuoka 812-8581, Japan
+81 92 642 2297
kasahara.yoshiaki.820@m.kyushu-u.ac.jp

Eisuke Ito
Kyushu University
6-10-1 Hakozaki, Higashi-ku
Fukuoka 812-8581, Japan
+81 92 642 4037
ito.eisuke.523@m.kyushu-u.ac.jp

Naomi Fujimura
Kyushu University
4-9-1 Shiobaru, Minami-ku
Fukuoka, Japan
+81 92 553 4434
fujimura.naomi.274@m.kyushu-u.ac.jp

## ABSTRACT

In the end of fiscal year 2013 (March 2014), Kyushu University Information Infrastructure Initiative introduced new Primary Mail Service for Staff Members and Students. The previous service for staff members had been built using proprietary mail and LDAP appliance, but tight user license and the nature of proprietary system caused several troubles. The previous service for students had been built using open source software (Postfix and Dovecot), but there were some issues with the old implementation of LDAP authentication. With these experiences, we decided to design a new system by merging both system using open source software including Postfix, Dovecot, OpenLDAP, and Squirrelmail. We also extended alias address setting service (previously available for students only) to all the members including staff members. In this paper, we explain the design and implementation, user migration, current status and future works of our new mail service.

## Categories and Subject Descriptors

H.4.3 [**Information Systems Applications**]: Communication Applications – *Electronic mail*

## Keywords

University mail service; On-premises service; Service Migration

## 1. INTRODUCTION

Information and communication service is indispensable for education and research activities in Universities. Among various services, electronic mail is one of the fundamental services even before the Internet had been widely available in the world. Kyushu University has been providing on-premises email services using its own domain name for our University staff members and

SIGUCCS '14, November 2–7, 2014, Salt Lake City, UT, USA.
ACM 978-1-4503-2780-0/14/11.
http://dx.doi.org/10.1145/2661172.2662965

students for several years. Email service for students was started in 1995[1][2], and another service for University staff members started in July 2009 [3].

In the end of fiscal year 2013 (March 2014), Kyushu University Information Infrastructure Initiative introduced new Primary Mail Service for Staff Members and Students. This time, we decided to design a new system by merging two separate mail systems for staff members and students using open source software including Postfix, Dovecot, OpenLDAP, and Squirrelmail. We also extended name-based alias address setting service (previously available for students only) to all the members including staff members.

In this paper, we explain the design and implementation, user migration, current status and future works of our new mail service. The rest of this paper is organized as follows. In Section 2, we discuss the previous mail system. In Section 3, we introduce the overview of our new mail system. In Section 4, we explain about the migration of users from the old system to the new system. In Section 5, we introduce some notable troubles we encountered after migration, current status, and future works. Finally, we conclude the paper in Section 6.

## 2. PREVIOUS SYSTEM

First of all, we will give an overview of Kyushu University and University-wide mail services provided by Information Infrastructure Initiative.

### 2.1 Number of Users

Table 1 shows the approximate number of IDs issued for the University-wide authentication service (also provided by Information Infrastructure Initiative). The main members of our University are students, faculty, and staff. The students consist of

**Table 1. The number of IDs in Kyushu University (Mar 2013)**

| Role | Total No. of IDs (approx..) |
|---|---|
| Curricular students | 19,000 |
| Non-curricular students | 500 |
| Faculty and staff members | 9,000 |
| Temporary staff etc. | 800 |
| Total | 29,300 |

undergraduate and graduate curricular. There are also some non-curricular students such as research students and special register students. In addition to students, faculty, and staff members, there are other members with various roles such as research fellows, temporary staff, visiting researchers, and so on. The number also represents how many people can use "Primary Mail Services".

## 2.2 Previous Mail Service for Staff Members

The previous mail service for staff members (called "Kyushu University Primary Mail Service") was started in July 2009. Before that we didn't have a centralized mail service for staff members. We had established authentication infrastructure and assigned unique SSO-KID to every employee in Kyushu University from Sept. 2007[4], and this enabled us to implement centralized mail service for staff members.

We had to build the entire system within a half a year. Since some of us had some experiences with Mirapoint mail appliance, we decided to purchase some of them and build mail service on top of them. Figure 1 shows the system overview. The number of equipment gradually increased and the final configuration included two message directors, four message servers (for user's mailboxes) and two dedicated LDAP servers.

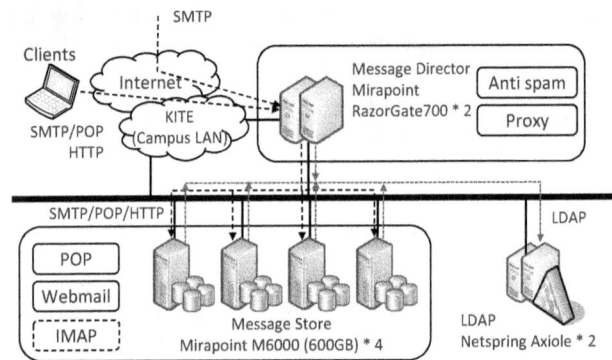

**Figure 1. Overview of Previous Mail System for Staff Members**

Generally speaking, the system offered average functionality for central mail system including standard email protocols (SMTP and POP3) and a decent webmail system. Due to the limited storage capacity, the mailbox quota was 300MB and messages were kept on the system for 90 days. For users who needed more capacity, we provided a premium service ($10/month) with 1GB mailbox quota without message expiration and IMAP support.

One of the largest issues with this mail system was that all the components were proprietary appliance systems with per-user licenses, which caused rather high per-year maintenance cost. Because the total number of employees increased gradually due to reasons such as increase of temporal staff and the need to support more active users temporarily during the beginning of a fiscal year (overlapping newcomers and retired employees), we experienced failure of adding new users due to insufficient user licenses a couple of times in 4 years. The only way to resolve the problem was to pay the additional charge to add more user licenses. License fees also prevented us from enabling full functionality of the system because we couldn't afford purchasing separate license fee for all the users. For example, we only purchased 100 IMAP licenses for premium users.

Another issue was that the appliance systems were black boxes for us. For example, the Mirapoint equipment was developed in

US, so when we had problems, sometimes it took a long time to investigate and fix the source of the problems. We thought many times that if we could have access to the source code of the system, because some of problems seemed quite trivial to fix. We also had a performance issue, which we couldn't resolve during the lifetime of our service. The system could only process and receive about 2 incoming messages per second. We believed it was too slow considering the specification of the system. When we would send a broadcast email messages to all the employees (about 10,000 users), it took almost 1 hour and accumulated more than 2,000 message in the process queue during the broadcast, which caused a disturbing delay to all the message deliveries. We couldn't find a reasonable explanation of the delay, partly because we couldn't obtain enough diagnostic information from appliance equipment to point to the culprit.

## 2.3 Previous Mail System for Students

A centralized mail service for students had been started in 1995 as a part of educational information system. After some system replacements, the service we replaced this time had been started in 2011. At that time the system was (mostly) separated from educational system and became a part of our Primary Mail Service. The system used open source software such as Postfix and Dovecot on top of a virtualized IA server running Red Hat Enterprise Linux. The system offered standard mail protocols such as SMTP, POP3, and IMAP, but no webmail was provided. The mailbox quota was 300MB without expiration. Figure 2 shows the system overview.

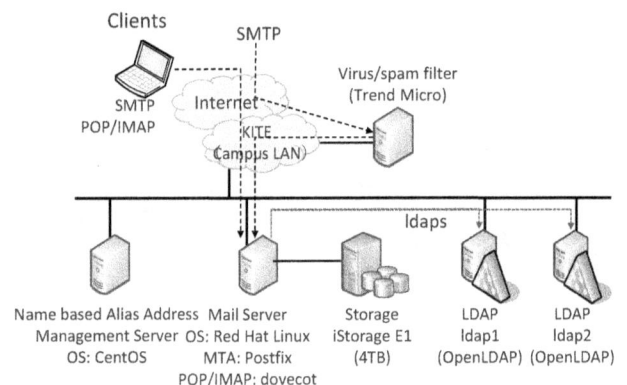

**Figure 2. Overview of Previous Mail System for Students**

Because the system employed standard open source software such as Postfix and Dovecot, it was easier to customize and introduce new services. One such service was name-based alias address setting service we reported in SIGUCCS 2012 [2]. On the other hand, the entire design was inherited from the previous system (as a part of educational system), which was not very efficient for an email-only system. For example, the user authentication and authorization was done via (outdated) pam_ldap and nss_ldap whose LDAP handling was very inefficient (no LDAP connection keep-alive and serialization). Due to this inefficiency we experienced LDAP service overload and other problems [5][6].

## 2.4 SSO-KID

As mentioned in section 2.2, Information Infrastructure Initiative provides unified user IDs called "SSO-KID" to employees. We provide various identity providers (including LDAP servers and Shibboleth IdP) to support using SSO-KID as a user authentication credential for various information services in Kyushu University.

On the other hand, until April 2014 all the students used "Student ID" for user ID of various information services. Also the ID was used as a local-part of their email address. Student ID includes the department code and enrollment year, so it changes when a student proceeds from undergraduate to graduate school or changes departments, which hinders continuity of various information services. To overcome the problem, in April of 2014 we introduced student SSO-KID, which is static throughout the student life in Kyushu University, and started using the ID for our new mail service.

In March 2014, the identity management system would be completely replaced in parallel to mail system replacement. The mail system heavily relied on the proper operation of identity management system, so it was a big concern.

## 3. NEW MAIL SYSTEM

In the middle of 2013, we decided to merge these two mail services and introduce a new "Primary Mail Service for Staff Members and Students". Based on our experience with both systems, we decided to use open source software similar to the student mail system, but employ virtual user with Dovecot's native LDAP support instead of using support provided by the operating system. To have finer control to LDAP attribute, the system also contained dedicated OpenLDAP servers that would receive user information from the central identity management system. We used virtual machines proactively to implement all of them.

Since we would support more than 30,000 users, we decided to incorporate dedicated hardware load balancers with SSL accelerator. Also, we knew it was hard to build a good spam filtering system using only open source software, so we decided to use Barracuda spam firewall, which employed a per-server license policy. We didn't want to be annoyed by a per-user license policy anymore. Figure 3 shows the overview of the entire system.

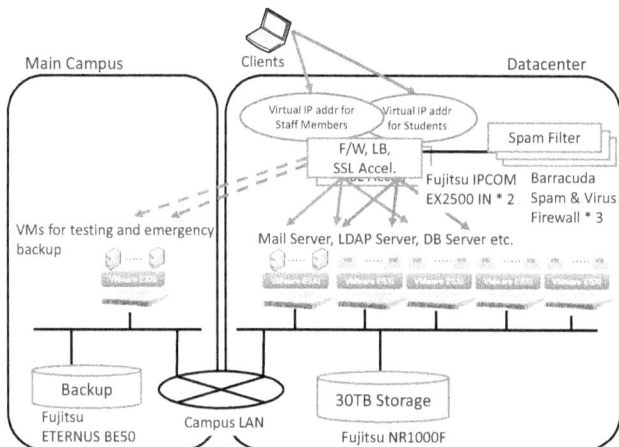

**Figure 3. Overview of New Primary Mail System**

As you see, the main function of the system resides in a datacenter. We had a separate project to borrow a rack in the datacenter and move the inter-campus core switch and border router there for network resiliency, and we also decided to place the new mail system next to the network rack. In case of emergency, we placed a minimum amount of server resource and

a data backup appliance on our own campus. The racks in the datacenter are considered as one of the remote campuses, and these are connected via 10GbE inter-campus LAN.

We tried to provide standard functionalities such as SMTP, POP3, IMAP4, SSL ports for all of these protocols submission port support, and STARTTLS.. The mailbox quota became 1GB without expiration. We also decided to provide webmail, but due to budget constraints, we decided to use free Squirrelmail, a decision which created problems later. While we used the same infrastructure and software to provide services for staff members and students, we used different domain names and separate virtual machines for each service.

For the previous student mail service, the name-based alias address system was developed in-house. This time we wrote detailed specifications and asked the system provider of the new mail system to re-implement it from scratch. The new alias address service supports both students and staff members, to solve our long-standing problem of handling middle names. The default mail address for a staff member was generated mechanically from his/her alphabetical name including first, last, and middle name, but some people didn't want to disclose their middle names for religious reasons.

## 4. MIGRATION

To migrate users to the new system, we needed to move their mailboxes, configurations, and, in some cases, asked them to change the configuration of their mail clients.

### 4.1 Mailbox

We faced a severe problem migrating staff members' email service, because there was no mailbox migration option from Mirapoint to other mail system. The vendor told us that it was impossible to export users' mailboxes from the system. Technically speaking, we could migrate mailboxes using IMAP, but we didn't have enough IMAP licenses to do that. To overcome the problem, we decided to operate both the old and new system simultaneously for about three months (until most messages expired on old system), and asked users to import their messages (retrieved by POP) to the new system via (now freely available) IMAP.

On the other hand, migration of students' email should be no problem, because both the old and new system use the same software. Of course we needed to test it because of differences between versions and a slight change of file hierarchy. We believed any issues would be resolvable, and the migration test finished without problem.

### 4.2 Configuration

For staff members, we could only migrate mail-forwarding settings from the old system to the new system. Mirapoint's enterprise webmail had various useful features such as an address book with many items and message filters, but none of these features were importable to the new service.

For students, we migrated mail forwarding settings and alias address settings. The new system employed LDAP-based virtual users, so we needed to convert ".forward" files to LDAP entries. We didn't provide webmail to students as part of the previous mail service, so we didn't need to worry about migrating webmail settings.

## 4.3 User side settings

As mentioned in section 4.1, we decided to operate the old and the new system for staff members simultaneously, so we had to ask users to change their mail client configuration. There were two options. One was to add a new IMAP user in addition to the previous POP user. By doing this, a user could easily migrate their messages to the new service. Another option was to change the POP server setting of the existing account. By doing this, a user could continue to use the same local mail folders. For the outgoing SMTP server, we kept compatibility with old service and changed the IP address of the server name.

Since we were able to migrate student settings, we announced that students didn't need to change their settings. Actually we overlooked a couple of the old server's configuration settings such as a loose connection security setting from the campus LAN. Some students still relied on such settings, so we had to make the new server a bit less secure than expected. Due to time constraints, we decided to address the issue later.

## 5. OPERATION ISSUES

In this section, we explain some problems we experienced after the system migration, current status and future works.

### 5.1 Troubles after Migration

We tried to test the system migration before the real migration as much as possible, but there was a simultaneous migration of the identity management system so we couldn't test the new ID system prior to the actual migration of our mail system. The mail system was the first and one of the biggest service providers using the new ID system, and there were several login failure complaints due to password migration failures (more than 3,500 users were affected). There were multiple causes of the failure and it took a couple of weeks to fully resolve the problems.

Another issue was forwarding setting migration for students. We believed that interpreting ".forward" file was trivial, so we asked the vendor to do the conversion. Actually they didn't fully understand the syntax of ".forward" and failed to migrate settings of about 100 users. Maybe we should have done the conversion ourselves.

We had few candidates for webmail software other than Squirrelmail due to budget and time constraint, and we didn't realize until the migration that Japanese language support of Squirrelmail was mediocre. There was an unofficial patch to support Japanese language, but it didn't support UTF-8 so it couldn't display some kanji characters (especially for user's real name) properly. Also it didn't work properly when using different UI language other than Japanese.

There were other minor issues such as tweaking the spam filter configuration, SMTP message size limitation, enforcing encryption for LOGIN/PLAIN authentication protocol, failed migration of alphabetical name, and so on.

### 5.2 Current Status and Future Works

Currently most of the severe issues have been resolved, but we still have some outstanding issues to resolve. One of these issues is an account activation timing issue. Due to some miscommunication with the system provider, email accounts become active after each user "activates" their account via the activation web page. This is an issue for new users, especially

students, because as soon as Student IDs are assigned, professors can send email to a Student ID based email address. The delivery fails due to non-existent users if the student hasn't activated his/her account yet. It isn't an ideal situation and we expect the problem will be fixed soon.

Another ongoing issue is webmail. There are still several issues with Squirrelmail (mainly about internationalization). We now realize that users use webmail far more than we expected, so we may need to consider changing webmail software.

Due to budget and time constraint, we deliberately omitted some functionality such as message filters and vacation function. One consideration to solve both issues is adding "sieve" function using Dovecot Pigeonhole plug-in, but again internationalization is a big concern.

## 6. CONCLUSION

In this paper, we explained about our old email service, the design and implementation, user migration, current status and future works of our new mail service. Email service seems one of the mature technologies of the Internet, but we still need much detailed consideration to design and implement "sane" email service. The operation of the new mail system has just started, and we continue to improve the service.

## 7. ACKNOWLEDGMENTS

Our thanks to all the users using our mail service, and staff members of the Primary Mail Service working group and the Authentication Infrastructure working group to develop and maintain these systems in Information Infrastructure Initiative of Kyushu University.

## 8. REFERENCES

[1] Fujimura, N., Togawa, T., Kasahara, Y., and Ito, E. 2011. Primary Mail Service for students based on their names. *IPSJ SIG Technical Report*, Vol. 2011-IOT-14, No. 10, 1-6.

[2] Fujimura, N., Togawa, T., Kasahara, Y., and Ito, E. 2012. Introduction and experience with the Primary Mail Service based on their names for students. In *Proceedings of the SIGUCCS 2012* (Memphis, TN, October 17 - 19, 2012). ACM, New York, NY, 11-14. DOI= http://dx.doi.org/10.1145/2382456.2382460.

[3] Ito, E., Kasahara. Y., and Fujimura, N. 2009. The current status of e-mail services for staff members in Kyushu University. In *Proceedings of ECIP 2009*, D3-4.

[4] Ito, E., Kasahara. Y., and Fujimura, N. 2013. Implementation and operation of the Kyushu university authentication system. In *Proceedings of the SIGUCCS 2013* (Chicago, IL, November 3 - 8, 2013). ACM, New York, NY, 137-142. DOI=http://dx.doi.org/10.1145/2504776.2504788.

[5] Ito, E., Kasahara. Y., and Fujimura, N. 2012. A study of LDAP load balancing for University ICT services. *IPSJ SIG Technical Report*, Vol. 2012-CSEC-57/2012-IOT-17, No. 11, 51-56.

[6] Kasahara, Y., Ito, E., and Fujimura, N. 2013. Gulliver's toss: Google's chronic big load to university mail server and its sudden resolution. In *Proceedings of the SIGUCCS 2013* (Chicago, IL, November 3 - 8, 2013). ACM, New York, NY, 169-174. DOI= http://dx.doi.org/10.1145/2504776.2504815.

# Leveraging Your Local Resources and National Cyberinfrastructure Resources without Tears

Barbara Hallock
Indiana University Pervasive Technology Institute
2709 E 10th Street
Bloomington, IN 47408
bahalloc@iu.edu

Richard Knepper
Indiana University PTI
2709 E 10th Street
Bloomington, IN 47408
rknepper@iu.edu

James Ferguson
National Institute of Computational Sciences
PO Box 2008, Bldg 5100
Oak Ridge, TN 37831-617
jwf@utk.edu

Craig A. Stewart
Indiana University PTI
2709 E 10th Street
Bloomington, IN 47408
stewart@iu.edu

## ABSTRACT

Compute resources for conducting research inhabit a wide range, including researchers' personal computers, servers in labs, campus clusters and condos, regional resource-sharing models, and national cyberinfrastructure. Researchers agree that there are not enough resources available on a broad scale, and significant barriers exist for getting analyses moved from smaller- to larger-scale cyberinfrastructure. The XSEDE Campus Bridging program disseminates several tools that assist researchers and campus IT administrators in reducing barriers to the effective use of national cyberinfrastructure for research. Tools for data management, job submission and steering, best practices for building and administering clusters, and common documentation and training activities all support a flexible environment that allows cyberinfrastructure to be as simple to utilize as a plug-and-play peripheral. In this paper and the accompanying poster we provide an overview of campus bridging, including specific challenges and solutions to the problem of making the computerized parts of research easier. We focus particularly on tools that facilitate management of campus computing clusters and integration of such clusters with the national cyberinfrastructure.

## Categories and Subject Descriptors

C.1.4 [**Parallel Architectures**], C.2.4 [**Distributed Systems**] K.6.3 [**Software Management**]

## General Terms

Clusters, Education, Management, Documentation, Performance, Design, Experimentation, Human Factors, Standardization

## Keywords

Campus Bridging, XSEDE, High-performance Computing, Usability, Supercomputing, Academic Computing, Research Computing, Documentation

## 1. INTRODUCTION

For scientists at the university level in the United States, new avenues of experimentation have meant a constant and ever-growing demand for cyberinfrastructure (CI) resources to complete their experiments. For the purposes of this discussion, these CI resources may range in complexity from something as simple as a plug-and-play external hard drive connected directly with the researcher's personal computer to much more complex supercomputing resources maintained and provided via partnerships between top-tier research institutions in the US, such as the NSF-supported eXtreme Science and Engineering Discovery Environment (XSEDE). XSEDE is "the most advanced, powerful, and robust collection of integrated advanced digital resources and services in the world... a single virtual system that scientists can use to interactively share computing resources, data, and expertise." XSEDE collectively allocates and supports several PetaFLOPS worth of computing resources and has already made great strides in usability and in lowering the barriers of access to major CI resources. Researchers report difficulty obtaining sufficient computing resources to support their research [1], (including allocations of resources through national services such as XSEDE), and using their local resources and national resources, even when they have access to the resources they need. In this paper, we introduce campus bridging as a concept and describe the primary initiatives of the XSEDE Campus Bridging initiative. This paper is intended to inform university and college leadership, CIOs, faculty, campus IT support staff, users, and those who utilize cyberinfrastructure in their scholarship about ways in which they can integrate their local CI resources with national systems such as XSEDE. This can make it easier to use campus-based resources and to leverage national resources such as XSEDE. We focus particularly on tools that make training and information transportable between local campus resources and national resources, and that improve the ability to use local and national resources together to achieve optimal use of both. (In other words, make what you have easier to use and more effective in supporting your research, utilizing federally funded CI resources, all without tears.)

## 2. THE EXTREME SCIENCE AND ENGINEERING DISCOVERY ENVIRONMENT (XSEDE)

XSEDE is a virtual organization funded by a five-year NSF grant award that includes staff from a number of top-tier supercomputing centers across the United States, including (but not limited to) the Texas Advanced Computing Center (TACC), Indiana University (IU), the Pittsburgh Supercomputing Center (PSC), the San Diego Supercomputer Center (SDSC), the National Institute of Computational Sciences (NICS), the National Center for Supercomputing Applications (NCSA), and others. Major CI resources allocated and supported by XSEDE include Stampede (TACC), Blacklight (PSC), Comet (SDSC), and Wrangler (TACC/IU); major affiliated systems such as the Open

*SIGUCCS '14*, November 2-7, 2014, Salt Lake City, Utah, USA.
ACM 978-1-4503-2780-0/14/11.
http://dx.doi.org/10.1145/2661172.2661202

Science Grid and Blue Waters; and local resources such as the IU Mason system and other campus-based CI resources.

# 3. CAMPUS BRIDGING
## 3.1 Defining Campus Bridging

H. Edward Seidel coined the term "campus bridging" in 2009, when as the Director of NSF's Office of Cyberinfrastructure, he charged six task forces of the National Science Foundation (NSF) Advisory Committee for Cyberinfrastructure (ACCI). That task force developed this description of campus bridging:

*"Campus bridging is the seamlessly integrated use of cyberinfrastructure operated by a scientist or engineer with other cyberinfrastructure on the scientist's campus, at other campuses, and at the regional, national, and international levels as if they were proximate to the scientist, and when working within the context of a Virtual Organization (VO) make the 'virtual' aspect of the organization irrelevant (or helpful) to the work of the VO."*
[1]

More colloquially, the goal is to create "virtual proximity"—everything from a modest local campus cluster to the largest systems should feel as easy to use as a peripheral attached directly to the user's computer. The term "campus bridging" reflects the fact that at the time this taskforce was convened, the national, NSF-funded supercomputing resources seemed to the user to be completely isolated from campus resources. One needed a bridge to get from one to the other. (The "virtual proximity" analogy was coined by Von Welch of the IU Center for Applied Cybersecurity Research.)

A number of challenges exist within the discipline of academic CI. Campus Bridging focuses on a select few. In this section, we present the major challenges campus bridging attempts to resolve and mitigate. In the next section we describe the tools and services being deployed by the XSEDE Campus Bridging team to address these challenges.

## 3.2 Where Am I and What Commands Work Here?

Since the time Beowulf computing clusters were introduced in 1995 [2], clusters have become extremely popular as a way to accelerate scientific computing applications. Because such clusters can be built locally and easily, they often are created and set up locally with configurations that are highly variable from one cluster to another. This means that software and libraries available on one cluster may not be available on another, or if they are, the versions might not be the same or they might not be accessible in the same location of the system hierarchy.

Learning to interact with a small number of applications may not be an insurmountable challenge for those with little technical expertise. But the difficulty of effectively leveraging the available CI increases significantly in correlation with the number of resources the researcher has to interact with in order to complete his or her experiment. For those who must operate within multiple systems concurrently to achieve results, this disparity can mean frustration and lost productivity due to the cognitive costs of context switching, especially when not much documentation is available at the researcher's level of technical proficiency.

## 3.3 Documentation

Another significant challenge that campus bridging aims to mitigate is the scarcity of clear, usable documentation available for users who are unfamiliar with the system(s). Where

documentation does exist, it is often incomplete or written for a highly technical audience (e.g. system administrators), making it less useful for researchers without a background in the technical discipline.

## 3.4 Insufficient CI Resources and Allocation "Lag"

A major issue with the research CI ecosystem is the relative scarcity of resources available with which to complete experimental work. XSEDE accepts requests for allocations on a quarterly basis [3]. For researchers on a tight deadline, this allocation timetable can be a challenge. Furthermore, the resources awarded during an allocation process may be as low as half those requested. Information provided by XSEDE [4] makes it clear that preliminary work on XSEDE systems or similar systems in the form of scalability studies provides some performance data that aids the likelihood that a proposal will lead to an allocation of XSEDE resources.

## 3.5 Moving Data and Other Challenges

Most researchers who use national resources such as XSEDE wish to analyze data that is held someplace other than an XSEDE system – either on local storage resources or on some other national repository. Thus means that those who use XSEDE (either in isolation or in concert with collaborators) must move data from one CI system to XSEDE, and then move the resulting output from XSEDE back to local resources.

For a complete examination of the community-driven use cases that defined the XSEDE Campus Bridging program, see [5].

# 4. XSEDE CAMPUS BRIDGING SOLUTIONS

In this section we provide an overview of tools and services (including consulting) that are offered by XSEDE through its Campus Bridging program to aid campus IT organizations, researchers, educators, and those who support researchers and educators.

## 4.1 XSEDE-Compatible Basic Cluster (XCBC) & Documentation Portability

There are tens of thousands of clusters installed on campuses and in research labs in the US. There are a handful of such clusters within XSEDE. In order to increase the compatibility of software between campus resources and XSEDE, the XSEDE Campus Bridging program created the "XSEDE-compatible Basic Cluster" software stack (XCBC). This consists of a definition of a suite of software that represents an open-source subset of the software and tools one can expect to find on any XSEDE cluster, mechanisms for installing that software [6], and tools for installing that software [7, 8, 9,10].

The software definition will evolve over time, and current XSEDE plans call for additions of specific sets of tools (e.g. a set of tools for bioinformatics). Today, one could install the XCBC software stack and have a cluster with an open-source job management system, a standard set of compilers, and basic software and application libraries.

The XCBC can be installed in two ways. If you are building a cluster from scratch, or are so unhappy with your current cluster that you are ready to start over from scratch, you can install XCBC using a cluster installation tool called ROCKS. Instructions are available [9]. Or you might have a cluster that works well and wish to add the ability to run the XCBC software, so that commands that work on an XSEDE cluster also work in the same way on a local cluster. This capability can be implemented by installing sets of packages called RPMs, or Red Hat Package Managers [11], which allow the installation of specific packages or software modules. XSEDE distributes these software modules through a YUM Repository. ("YUM" stems from the Yellowdog Linux distribution, although the current use of YUM repositories goes well beyond the intent of the initial tool that was part of the Yellowdog Linux project [12].) YUM makes it easy to install a particular set of modules from the XSEDE Campus Bridging software repository on a local cluster. You can even sign up for automatic notifications when software in the repository is updated.

This software has a number of benefits. It makes it easier for local IT staff to manage local computing clusters so they can spend more time addressing the specific needs of local researchers and students. It makes it easier for researchers to learn and use computing commands because the same commands work on local clusters and on XSEDE. This approach also means IT staff, researchers, and educators can leverage training resources created by XSEDE and by other educators and staff using the XCBC cluster build. Over time, use of the XCBC can also improve efficiency within a given institution by creating consistency in the setup and management of the disparate clusters that institution operates.

## 4.2 Globus Transfer

Globus Transfer is a fast, reliable, high-performance service that facilitates secure data movement. Designed specifically for researchers, Globus Transfer provides easy, fire-and-forget features. It automates the activity of managing file transfers between any two resources, whether between two XSEDE resources or to/from XSEDE and another machine, such as another supercomputing facility, cloud resource, campus cluster, lab server, desktop, or laptop [13]. The interface is intuitive, providing a drag-and-drop method of file transfer that is similar to graphical FTP software or the interface for user-friendly cloud storage applications such as Dropbox. Globus software has been available on XSEDE resources for some time. During the first three months of 2014, users of XSEDE transferred a collective 1.32 PB to various XSEDE endpoints and an additional 1.30 PB from various XSEDE endpoints [14].

## 4.3 XSEDE Execution Management Service (EMS) – Based on UNICORE 6

XSEDE Execution Management Service (EMS) is a tool for seamless and secure job management, based on an XSEDE-customized implementation of UNICORE 6. With the EMS command-line client tool, users can manage jobs, submissions, and associated data movement tools. Access to resources is provided via shell or scripting environment. Users can run jobs, monitor their status, and retrieve generated output, either in single-job mode or in a powerful and flexible batch mode for multiple jobs. XSEDE EMS services can also be incorporated into a graphical interface using the Eclipse integrated development environment [15]. XSEDE EMS supplies web-accessible architecture that can be incorporated into science portals and gateways. All of the XSEDE EMS architecture utilizes a set of common standards for job creation and control, in a workflow made up of a services layer that handles the job definition and management and a system layer that controls the interface to particular grid resources.

The UNICORE software has been deployed to all XSEDE Service Providers (SPs) as of spring 2014, and is useful in creating automated workflows that require the use of multiple disparate SPs with the XSEDE ecosystem. The benefit is that users trade a significant effort in creating, maintaining, and facilitating those workflows for a smaller effort in learning to interface with UNICORE.

## 4.4 XSEDE Global Federated File System (GFFS)

The XSEDE Global Federated File System (GFFS) is being put into production in 2014. In its initial implementation within XSEDE, GFFS will allow geographically distributed sharing of files independent of physical location. In this regard GFFS has similarities with the well-known Andrew File System (AFS). As XSEDE's implementation of GFFS expands, it will allow file sharing, submitting computing jobs, and sharing computing resources in the form of virtual clusters. The initial deployment of GFFS in 2014 will allow researchers to link, store, and share files on local resources and on XSEDE resources (reducing the need to synchronize multiple copies of an individual file kept in different locations) and to share files with users specified by the file owner [16].

In the XSEDE Global Federated File System, users can use client software to manage files and permissions as they would in a normal file manager. Users can also export local file systems or directories into the GFFS in order to make files at their site available to XSEDE resources, to collaborators at other institutions, or to wherever a client can browse the GFFS. The exported file systems or directories can be used to provide data for analysis, can be shared between collaborators, or can represent job queues via integration with the XSEDE EMS framework. The XSEDE operations team provides the root of the GFFS tree and manages the linking between containers that are exported into GFFS, making them available to be used across XSEDE resources.

## 4.5 Documentation and HPC University

A wide variety of user guides to advanced computing, parallel computing, and using XSEDE are available online. Using the XCBC software build makes it easier to modify these resources for use in local user support documentation and instructional materials. Major sources of documentation available through and affiliated with XSEDE include the XSEDE web site (xsede.org), XSEDE Knowledge Base [17], and HPC University [18].

## 4.6 Consulting Services

Campus bridging is a new area. We hope this paper provides some sense of the opportunities available to campus leaders, campus IT organizations, and research labs. However, there is still a fairly large knowledge gap between "I'd like to make better use of my campus resources by integrating them more effectively with national cyberinfrastructure such as XSEDE" and "I understand how to use YUM to download and install RPMs on my local cluster, and where to look within XSEDE web sites to find documents I can modify easily for local use." XSEDE campus bridging staff are available to help with answers to questions, extended discussions of technical capabilities, instructional sessions by videoconference, and even on-site visits to your location. Contact Campus Bridging staff via email at help@xsede.org, or call the XSEDE Help Desk at 1-866-907-2383 to be transferred to a Campus Bridging consultant (8:00am-5:00pm, M-F, except US federal holidays). A discussion with an expert is often the easiest way to begin using XSEDE Campus

Bridging resources as we are still in the early phase of developing communities of practice.

## 5. CONCLUSIONS

Everyone working in IT in higher education has more than likely experienced a lack of resources related to research computing and research education – not enough computing resources, not enough storage, and not enough time to support researchers and students. This is a matter of US global competitiveness. In this paper, we have explained the concept of campus bridging and described tools that are currently available to the national research and education community. Much as the NSFNET network aligned national efforts in networking during the 1980s, we hope the XSEDE Campus Bridging program will align tools, usage, and documentation of clusters throughout the US. The requirements for alignment differ in their technical particulars, but we believe that aligning disparate campus resources with XSEDE cluster software standards will lead to a more effective national cyberinfrastructure, increase the ease with which researchers can integrate local and federally funded CI resources, and increase the ease with which researchers and educators can find and customize documentation and training materials for local use. Because campus bridging is still in its infancy, XSEDE Campus Bridging personal support and interactions with the national higher education and research communities are particularly important in enabling the community as a whole to work together to achieve the goals of campus bridging and maximize US global research competitiveness.

## 6. ACKNOWLEDGMENTS

This research was supported by the National Science Foundation through funding for the Extreme Science and Engineering Discovery Environment (XSEDE) via award ACI-1053575. This work was also aided by the Indiana University Pervasive Technology Institute, which is supported by a grant from the Lilly Endowment, Inc.

## 7. REFERENCES

[1] ACCI Task Force On Campus Bridging. *National Science Foundation Advisory Committee for Cyberinfrastructure Task Force on Campus Bridging Final Report.* Apr. 2011. doi=http://hdl.handle.net/2022/13210

[2] Becker, D., Sterling, T., Savarese, D., Dorband, J., Ranawak, U., and Packer, C. 1995. BEOWULF: A parallel workstation for scientific computation. In *Proceedings of the International Conference on Parallel Processing* vol. 95. 1995.

http://www.phy.duke.edu/~rgb/brahma/Resources/beowulf/papers/ICPP95/icpp95.html

[3] XSEDE Allocations. https://www.xsede.org/allocations

[4] Hackworth, K. Writing and Submitting a Successful XSEDE Proposal. Apr. 2014. https://meeting.austin.utexas.edu/p4p2yy0hcgg?launcher=false&fcsContent=true&pbMode=normal

[5] What are some examples of Campus Bridging use cases related to XSEDE? https://portal.xsede.org/knowledge-base/-/kb/document/bbsv

[6] http://cb-repo.iu.xsede.org/xsederepo/XSEDE-Campus-Bridging-Cluster-software-strategy-2013.pdf

[7] Brueckner, R. New XSEDE tools to aid campus cluster administrators. Dec. 2013. http://insidehpc.com/2013/12/17/new-xsede-tools-aid-campus-cluster-administrators/

[8] XSEDE Campus Bridging. https://www.xsede.org/campus-bridging

[9] What is the XSEDE Rocks Roll, and how do I use it? https://www.xsede.org/web/xup/knowledge-base/-/kb/document/bdpe

[10] Hallock, B., Knepper, R., Ferguson, J., and Stewart, C. 2014. XSEDE14 Campus Bridging Paper. In *Proceedings of XSEDE 2014 Annual Conference* (Atlanta, Georgia, United States, July 13-18, 2014). XSEDE '14. ACM, New York, NY, in press.

[11] RPM Package Manager. http://en.wikipedia.org/wiki/RPM_Package_Manager

[12] The Yum web site. http://yum.baseurl.org

[13] Globus File Transfer User Guide. https://www.xsede.org/globus/

[14] XSEDE 2014 Q1 Quarterly Report. In Press.

[15] The Eclipse Foundation open source community website. http://eclipse.org

[16] Knepper, R. Campus Bridging Final Report. Sept. 2013. doi=http://hdl.handle.net/2022/17378

[17] XSEDE Knowledge Base. https://www.xsede.org/web/xup/knowledge-base/

[18] HPC University. http://hpcuniversity.org/

# Author Index

www.ingramcontent.com/pod-product-compliance
Lightning Source LLC
Chambersburg PA
CBHW081547220326
41598CB00036B/6595